The Story Of Don Quixote...

Arvid Paulson, Clayton Edwards, Miguel de Cervantes Saavedra

THE STORY OF DON QUIXOTE

"THE GOATHERDS WERE MARVELING AT OUR KNIGHT'S BOMBASTIC SPEECH
AND FLOURISHING MANNERS."

—*Page 38*

THE STORY OF
DON QUIXOTE

BY

ARVID PAULSON
AND
CLAYTON EDWARDS

WITH ILLUSTRATIONS IN COLOR BY
FLORENCE CHOATE
AND
ELIZABETH CURTIS

NEW YORK
FREDERICK·A·STOKES COMPANY
PUBLISHERS

Printed in the United States of America

CONTENTS

VOLUME I

CONTENTS

CONTENTS

CONTENTS

CONTENTS

VOLUME II

CONTENTS

CONTENTS

LIST OF ILLUSTRATIONS

THE STORY OF DON QUIXOTE

VOLUME I

CHAPTER I

WHICH TREATS OF THE CHARACTER AND PURSUITS OF THE FAMOUS GENTLEMAN, DON QUIXOTE OF LA MANCHA

NEARLY four hundred years ago, there lived in the village of La Mancha in Spain an old gentleman of few worldly possessions but many books, who was given to a hardy and adventurous way of life, and who beguiled his spare time by reading the many tales of chivalry and knighthood that were in his possession.

This old gentleman was a tall, gaunt man of about fifty, with a lantern jaw and straggling gray hair, and eyes that had a sparkle of madness in them. His surname was Quixada or Quesada, and though not rich, he was well known to the country folk and had some reputation in the community where he lived.

In his younger days he was a great sportsman and used to get up before the sun to follow his favorite pursuits of hunting and hawking, but as he grew older he spent almost all his time in reading books on chivalry and knighthood with which his library was stocked; and at last he grew so fond of these books that he forgot to follow the hounds or even to look after his property, but spent all his time in his library, mulling over the famous deeds and love affairs of knights who conquered dragons and vanquished wicked enchanters.

THE STORY OF DON QUIXOTE

At the time when Quesada lived, Spain was saturated with this sort of literature, and everybody wasted much time in reading books which had no merit or value of any kind and which were full of the most ridiculous and impossible adventures. On the whole they were the most utter rubbish that it was possible to print. They told about impossible deeds in the most impossible language, and were filled with ambitious sentences that meant nothing under the sun. Señor Quesada spent hours racking his brains to puzzle out the meaning of something like this:

"The reason of the unreason with which my reason is afflicted
so weakens my reason that with reason I murmur at your
beauty."

Or again:

"The high heavens that of your divinity divinely fortify you
with the stars, render you deserving of the desert your
greatness deserves."

Poor Señor Quesada could not understand these sentences. Who could? No man in his right mind certainly, it would have taken a madman to read any real meaning into them. And he wasted so much time in puzzling over them that at last he became quite mad and the words in the books would appear on the walls of his room, written in letters of fire, with so bright a light that they prevented him from sleeping. From trying to read a meaning into things that had no meaning whatever, Señor Quesada was mad—as mad as the books he had been reading.

Señor Quesada lived with his niece and his housekeeper, both sensible women who loved him and who were much

[2]

grieved over the havoc his books of chivalry had worked with his senses. They believed that to talk about these books made the old gentleman worse, so they refused to answer him when he argued about knights and dragons and whether this fair lady was an enchantress in disguise or only a mortal woman, and whether that dragon actually did breathe forth fire from his nostrils, or only sulphur fumes and smoke. His niece and the housekeeper would run away when he started upon one of his favorite subjects; so he turned to the society of the village curate, a learned man for those times, who knew almost as much about books of chivalry as Señor Quesada himself, and to that of Master Nicholas, the village barber. And these three friends would sit up until dawn arguing as to who was the better knight, Sir Lancelot or Amadis of Gaul, and how these both compared with the Knight of the Burning Sword, who with one back stroke cut in half two fierce and monstrous giants.

After he had become thoroughly mad from reading, and more so from such arguments and discussions, Señor Quesada hit upon the strangest notion that ever entered the head of a lunatic. He believed that he and no other was called upon to restore the entire world to the ancient conditions of chivalry, and bring back the tournaments and the courteous knights and fair ladies whose like had existed in the times of the famous King Arthur of Britain. Believing this, it was an easy step for him to think that the world was still full of giants and fierce dragons for him to vanquish, and that as a man of honor and skill at arms he must leave his comfortable home and do battle with them. To his disordered senses things took on a different appearance than was actually the case—inns seemed castles, and towers and hills appeared as giants that moved about in the distance; and Señor Quesada could hardly wait before he could meet them on horseback and overthrow them in battle.

To become a knight and encounter all these strange and visionary dangers it was necessary for him, however, to have a war horse, a stout lance and a suit of armor, and he cast about among his possessions to see what he could find that would answer the purpose—for he had no money to buy them, and no shop could have furnished them for him if he had possessed all the money in Spain. In his attic he found an old suit of armor that had belonged to his great-grandfather and had been lying there for ages, rotting with rust and mildew in company with old chests, bedding and other family treasures. He brought it out and scoured it as best he could and at last made it shine with considerable brightness. But the helmet was only partially complete, for it lacked a beaver and a visor to protect his face, so Señor Quesada constructed these from pasteboard and painted them to resemble the armor as closely as possible. He tried their strength with his rusty sword, and on the first stroke cut them entirely away; so he rebuilt them and forbore to try them again, hoping they would be strong enough, but fearing to make a test that might undo once more all the troublesome work that he had spent upon them.

His armor now complete, he looked in his stables for a

horse to carry him, and found there his old hack, whose every bone was visible and who was more used to carrying sacks of potatoes and onions to market than to bearing the weight of a knight or a man at arms. This horse must have been at least twenty years old into the bargain, but to Quixada's brain it appeared a mettlesome charger and he was quite sure that his new steed would prove equal to any fatigue or danger that might come its way in the course of his adventures. And remembering that all the horses of famous warriors had possessed high-sounding names ne called his horse Rocinante and adopted for himself the title of Don Quixote of La Mancha, under which name he will be known through the rest of the present history.

Another thing, however, remained wanting—a lady-love for whose sake he might do battle and whose affections might inspire him to endure all sorts of dangers and hardships. So Don Quixote straightway searched through his recollection to find one that might answer, and hit at last upon a peasant girl named Aldonza Lorenzo, with whom it is supposed he had been in love when he was a young man. And though Aldonza Lorenzo was more used to winnowing wheat and caring for the live-stock than to fine phrases and courtly manners, and though she was no better than any of the other peasant girls who lived in her locality, Don Quixote believed that she was a lady of high lineage and noble birth and christened her in his mind Dulcinea del Toboso. And he was ready to fight with any man in Spain who would not acknowledge that she was the loveliest and most gifted lady in the world.

[5]

A lance was easily made, and now, possessed of war horse, armor, weapons, and a glorious lady to do battle for, the poor old man was ready, so he believed, to go forth and meet the high adventures that he felt sure were awaiting him.

CHAPTERS II—III

WHICH TREATS OF THE FIRST SALLY DON QUIXOTE MADE FROM HOME

ALL things being ready, Don Quixote wished for no delay, and before sunrise on one of the hottest days of midsummer, he stole from his bed—taking care not to awaken his niece or his housekeeper—put on his ancient armor, saddled Rocinante, and with lance in hand and sword clattering beside him made his way across the fields in the highest state of content and satisfaction at the ease with which his purpose had been accomplished. He could hardly wait for his adventures to begin, or for the chance to try the strength of his mighty arm upon some wicked warrior or, better still, some dragon or giant; but scarcely did he find himself upon the open plain before a terrible thought came to his mind and one that nearly made him abandon his adventure before it was well begun. He reflected that, according to the rules of chivalry, he must be dubbed a knight before he could undertake any battles or engagements, and afterward he must wear white armor without any device upon his shield, until he had proved by bravery and endurance his right to these privileges of knighthood. He consoled himself, however, by resolving to have himself dubbed a knight by the first person who came along; and as for white armor, he determined to make his own rival the brightness of the moon by industrious scouring.

Comforting himself with thoughts such as these, he pursued his way, which he allowed his horse to choose for him, thinking that in so doing he would be guided more surely and more quickly to the adventures that were awaiting him. And as he rode along he amused himself by quoting imaginary passages from the books that he felt sure would be written about his noble deeds—deeds that he would soon accomplish and that would astonish the entire world by their bravery and hardihood. At times he would break into wild speech, calling his lady Dulcinea by name and saying: "O Princess Dulcinea, lady of this captive heart, a grievous wrong hast thou done me to drive me forth with scorn and banish me from the presence of thy beauty!"

And so he went along, stringing such absurd phrases together, while the hot sun rose and grew hotter, until it would have melted his brains in his helmet, if he had any. He traveled nearly all day without seeing anything remarkable, at which he was in despair, for he could hardly wait, as we have said, for his adventures to begin.

Toward evening he came in sight of a common wayside inn, and standing at the door were two peasant girls who looked with astonishment on the strange figure that was approaching them. To the disordered imagination of Don Quixote, this appeared to be a castle with four towers, and the girls who stood in front of the door seemed ladies of noble birth and peerless beauty. He seemed to see behind them a drawbridge and a moat, and waited for some dwarf to appear upon the castle battlements and by sound of a trumpet announce that a knight was approaching the gates.

At this point a swineherd who was gathering his pigs did happen to blow a blast on his horn to scare his charges along the road; and this, appearing to Don Quixote to be the dwarf's signal that he had expected, he drew near in high satisfaction, while Rocinante, scenting stables and hay and water, pricked up his ears and advanced at a brisk trot until the inn door was reached and Don Quixote addressed the astonished girls who were waiting there.

The girls, on seeing an armed man approaching them, had turned to seek safety indoors, when Don Quixote, lifting his pasteboard beaver, said to them in the most courteous manner he could command:

"Ladies, I beseech you, do not fly or fear any manner of rudeness, for it is against the rules of the knighthood, which I profess, to offer harm to high-born ladies such as you appear to be."

The girls, hearing themselves addressed in this strange manner and called ladies, could not refrain from giggling, at which Don Quixote rebuked them, saying:

"Modesty becomes the fair, and laughter without cause is the greatest silliness."

The strange language and dilapidated appearance of the speaker only increased the girls' laughter, and that increased Don Quixote's irritation; and matters might have gone farther if the landlord had not appeared at this moment to see what might be the matter. When he beheld the grotesque figure on horseback whose armor did not match and whose mount was the sorriest one imaginable, it was all he could do to refrain from joining the girls in their hilarity; but being a little in awe of the strange knight, whose lance was pointed and whose sword appeared to have both strength and weight, he spoke courteously to Don Quixote. He told him that if he sought food or lodging he should have the best that the inn could afford for man or beast. And the poor old gentleman, who had been riding in the heat all day without food or drink, climbed stiffly out of the saddle and suffered Rocinante to be led away to the stable, cautioning the landlord to take the utmost care of him, for he was the finest bit of horseflesh in the world. The host, however, looking over the bony carcass of the old farm animal, had more difficulty than before in restraining his laughter.

The girls now perceived that they had a crazy man before them and they entered into the spirit of the occasion.

They helped Don Quixote remove his armor; but the helmet they could do nothing with, for it was tied tightly with green ribbons about his neck and on no pretext whatever would he hear of cutting them.

They laid a table for him at the door of the inn for the sake of the air, and the host brought him a piece of badly soaked and badly cooked fish and a piece of bread as black and moldy as his own armor. And a laughable sight it was to see Don Quixote eat—for, having his helmet on, he could not reach his own mouth, but had to be fed, bit by

[9]

bit, by one of the girls; and for drink he would have gone without altogether if the innkeeper had not brought a hollow reed and putting one end into the knight's mouth, poured wine through the other.

While this was going on Don Quixote heard once more the swineherd's horn and felt entirely happy and satisfied, for he was convinced that he was in some famous castle and that they were regaling him with music; that the fish was trout, the bread of the whitest, the peasant girls beautiful ladies, and the landlord the castle steward. But he still felt distressed because he had not been dubbed a knight, and resolved to remedy this fault as soon as his supper was finished.

As soon as he had eaten his fill, he called the landlord of the inn, and taking him into the stable, knelt on the ground before him, declaring that he would not rise until the landlord should grant his wish and dub him a knight so that he could continue on his adventures according to the laws of chivalry. For Don Quixote, as we have said, looked on the landlord as a person of great authority, with full power to make him a knight if he chose to do so.

The landlord was something of a wag, and well aware that his guest was mad. He therefore decided to fall in with his wishes for the sport of the thing; so he told Don Quixote that he would make him a knight and gladly, that he too had been a knight errant in his time and wandered all over Spain seeking adventures, where he had proved the lightness of his feet in running away and the quickness of his fingers in picking pockets, until he had swindled

[10]

and cheated so many people that he had been forced to retire to this castle of his. Here he lived on his property—and that of other persons—and he accepted money from wandering knights errant in return for the kindness and services he rendered them. And when Don Quixote told him that he never carried money with him in his travels, the landlord assured him he was making the greatest mistake in the world and that he must not suppose that, just because money and clean shirts were not mentioned in the books of chivalry of the time, the knights did without them; that was not the case at all.

At last it was decided that the landlord should dub Don Quixote a knight on the following morning, and that the night should be spent by Don Quixote in watching over his armor in prayer and fasting, as was the custom with knights before they received the title of full knighthood and could go abroad on their adventures with a strong arm and untroubled spirit.

It had been arranged between the landlord and Don Quixote that the watch over the armor should take place in the courtyard of the inn. Don Quixote placed his corselet and helmet by the side of a well from which the carriers drew water, and, grasping his lance, commenced to march up and down before it like a sentinel on duty; and as the hours wore by and the march continued, the landlord called other persons to watch the performance, explaining that the man was mad, and telling of the ceremony that was to take place in the morning. The passers-by, viewing the steadiness with which Don Quixote paced to and fro in the moonlight and the resolute way in which he handled his lance, were struck with wonder both at the peculiarity of the sight and the strange form that Don Quixote's madness had taken.

At last, however, it became necessary for one of the carriers to draw water from the well. He did not observe the madman and he paid no attention to the armor until he stumbled across it, when he picked it up and flung it from him, whereupon Don Quixote raised his lance and struck him such a blow that he fell senseless on the ground and lay there stunned. Soon after this another carrier, who did not know of what had happened to the first one, approached with the same object; and Don Quixote, thinking him an enemy, also struck at him and laid his head open with two cuts from his lance in the form of a cross.

The people of the inn heard the noise of the second encounter and came running to the spot. When they beheld what had happened and saw the battered condition of the carriers they commenced to throw stones at Don Quixote, not daring to approach him; and he, shielding himself as best he could with his buckler, defied them to draw near on pain of their lives, and returned the abuse and hard names they showered upon him. And he shouted at them with such a terrible voice that they became afraid and left him alone, moved not only by his threats but by the entreaties of the landlord, who kept calling out to them that the man was mad and would not be held accountable should he kill them all.

The freaks of Don Quixote were not to the landlord's

liking, and he desired to get rid of the strange knight with as little trouble as possible. He approached the well and told Don Quixote that the time for the ceremony of knighthood had now arrived, and that all the requirements had been met with by the watch that Don Quixote had already performed. He pulled out an account-book in which he kept the record of the straw and grain that he sold and bade Don Quixote kneel down before him. Then he read out the accounts in a solemn voice as though he were repeating some devout prayer, and the stable-boy and the two girls who worked at the inn stood by with a candle, trying to control their laughter. When the reading was finished the landlord took Don Quixote's sword and tapped him sharply on the shoulder, pretending to mutter more prayers while he was doing it, and one of the girls girded the sword about Don Quixote's waist, saying, as she did so:

"May God make your Worship a very fortunate knight, and grant you success in battle!"

Thus the ceremony was ended and Don Quixote was satisfied. And then it came about as the landlord had hoped and expected. The new knight was so eager to set out on his journey that he saddled his horse and rode forth at once, without paying his bill for his supper; and the landlord was so glad to see the last of him that he made no objection to this, thinking himself lucky to have got rid of the knight so cheaply, and he closed the door behind him as quickly as possible, thanking his lucky stars that Don Quixote was gone.

CHAPTER IV

WHICH TREATS OF DON QUIXOTE'S FURTHER ADVENTURES

IT was dawn when Don Quixote quitted the inn. He decided to return home to provide himself with money, shirts, and a squire, as the innkeeper had suggested, and so he turned his horse's head toward his village.

He had not gone far, however, when he heard a feeble cry from the depths of a thicket on the roadside, as of some one in pain. He paused to thank Heaven for having favored him with this opportunity of fulfilling the obligation he had undertaken and gathering the fruit of his ambition; for he was certain that he had been called on from above to give aid and protection to some one in dire need. He quickly turned Rocinante in the direction from which the cries seemed to come; and he had gone but a few paces into the wood when he saw a youth, stripped to the waist and tied to a tree, being flogged in a merciless way by a powerful farmer. All the while the boy was crying out in his agony: "I won't do it again, master! I won't do it again! I promise I'll take better care of the sheep hereafter!"

When Don Quixote saw what was going on he became most indignant.

"Discourteous knight," he commanded in angry tones,

"it ill becomes you to assail one who cannot defend him-self! Mount your steed and take your lance! I will make you know that you are behaving like a coward!"

The farmer looked up and saw Don Quixote in full armor, brandishing a lance over his head. He gave him-self up for dead, then, and answered meekly:

"Sir knight, the youth I am chastising is my servant. I employ him to watch a flock of sheep, and he is so care-less that he loses one for me every day. And when I punish him for being careless, he accuses me of being a miser, saying that I do it that I might escape paying him the wages I owe him. That, I swear, is a sinful lie!"

But the farmer's defense only angered Don Quixote all the more. He threatened to run the man through with his lance if he did not release the boy at once and pay him every penny he owed him in wages. Don Quixote then helped the lad to add up how much nine months' wages at seven reals a month might be, and found that it would make sixty-three reals; and the farmer was given his choice between paying his debt and dying upon the spot. The farmer replied, trembling with fear, that the sum was not so great and asked Don Quixote to take into account and deduct three pairs of shoes he had given the boy and a real for two blood-lettings when he was sick. But Don Quix-ote would not listen to this at all. He declared that the shoes and the blood-lettings had already been paid for by the blows the farmer had given the boy without cause, for, said he, "If he spoiled the leather of the shoes you paid for, you have damaged that of his body; and if the barber took blood from him when he was sick, you have drawn it when he was sound; so on that score he owes you nothing."

When the farmer had heard his final judgment pronounced, he commenced to wail that he had no money about him, and pleaded with Don Quixote to let Andres, the lad, come home with him, when he would pay him real by real. Upon hearing this Andres turned to our knight errant and warned him that once he had departed his master would flay him like a Saint Bartholomew; but Don Quixote reassured him, saying now that his master had sworn to him by the knighthood that he, Don Quixote, had conferred upon him, justice would be done, and he himself would guarantee the payment.

The youth had his doubts, however, and he dared to correct Don Quixote. ·

"Consider what you say, Señor," he said. "This master of mine is not a knight; he is simply Juan Haldudo the Rich, of Quintanar."

To this Don Quixote replied that it mattered little; and the farmer again swore by all the knighthoods in the world to pay the lad as he had promised if he only came home.

"See that you do as you have sworn," said Don Quixote, "for if you do not, by the same oath I swear to come back and hunt you out and punish you; and I shall find you though you should lie closer than a lizard! If you desire to know who it is lays this command upon you, that you may be more firmly bound to obey it, know that I am the valorous Don Quixote of La Mancha, the undoer of wrongs and injustices. And so, God be with you! But keep in mind what you have promised and sworn on pain of those penalties that have been already declared to you!"

With these words he gave his steed the spur and rode away in a triumphant gallop, and was soon out of sight and reach. Now, when the farmer had convinced himself that the undoer of wrongs and injustices had entirely disappeared, he decided to give payment to the lad, Andres, then and there, without waiting till he came home; and so he tied him again to the tree and beat him until he was nearly dead.

"Your valiant knight has made me realize an affection for you hitherto unknown to me. I shall give you added payment for that. Now go and look for him!" he remarked, as he gave him a last blow and untied him. And while the poor boy went off weeping, the lusty farmer stood there and laughed.

Thus it was that our noble knight righted *that* wrong. Don Quixote, however, was thoroughly satisfied with what he had done. He thought himself a most heroic figure and felt that he had made a most auspicious beginning in his knighthood. And as he was taking the road toward his village, utterly content with his own behavior, he said to himself: "Well mayest thou this day call thyself fortunate above all on earth, O Dulcinea del Toboso, fairest of the fair! since it has fallen to thy lot to hold subject and submissive to thy will and pleasure a knight so renowned as Don Quixote of La Mancha, who, as all the world knows, yesterday received the order of knighthood, and hath to-day righted the greatest wrong and grievance that ever injustice conceived and cruelty perpetrated: who hath to-day plucked the rod from the hand of yonder ruthless oppressor so wantonly lashing that tender child."

As he was meditating and speaking in this fashion, he suddenly found himself at four crossroads. Of course, he had to emulate other knights who had gone before him, and follow tradition; so he paused in the manner that all knights do in books, and pondered, and, after much deep concern and consideration, finally decided to leave it to the instinct of his horse. The noble animal, realizing that his master had relinquished his will in his favor, made straight for his own stable, of course.

After he had ridden a few miles, Don Quixote encountered six merchants from Toledo, who were on their way to Murcia to buy silk. They were accompanied by four mounted servants, and three who were on foot. Scarcely had he perceived them when his romantic imagination prompted him to believe that a fresh adventure was intended for him, and he began to prepare for it with great gestures. He fixed himself majestically and safely in the saddle, made ready with his lance, and planted himself firmly in the middle of the road. Here he awaited the arrival of the traders, who appeared to him to be real knights like himself; and as they came close to him, he halted them with a broad sweep of his lance, exclaiming boldly:

"All the world stand, unless all the world confess that in all the world there is no maiden fairer than the Empress of la Mancha, the peerless Dulcinea del Toboso!"

The thirteen men could not help but stand still at the sound of such words; nor did they hesitate about thinking

[18]

that the speaker of them might be lacking in some of his wits. One of the travelers, however, either was curious or had a failing for making fun of people, for he asked Don Quixote to produce the lady before asking him to pay her his respects. Perhaps he was skeptical of his country's harboring such a rare beauty unbeknown to him.

But Don Quixote was not to be fooled. "If I were to show her to you," he replied, "what merit would you have in confessing a truth so manifest? You must believe without seeing her; otherwise you have to do with me in battle. Come on, you rabble! I rely on the justice of the cause I maintain!"

The merchant with a sense of humor tried to plead for consideration. He suggested that a portrait of the fair lady might suffice to bring about a conversion to his conception of her beauty. But Don Quixote was determined that they were intolerant blasphemers who simply had to be thrashed. So he suddenly charged with such vehemence and fury that, if luck had not interfered and made his gentle steed stumble, the trader might have been killed. As Rocinante went down, our gallant hero went over his head, and after he had struck the ground he rolled for some distance. But when he tried to rise he could not: he was so weighted down with armor, helmet, spurs, buckler and lance. To make matters worse, one of the servants, having broken his lance in two, proceeded to batter him with one of the pieces until it seemed as if Don Quixote would be able to stand no more. Finally the man grew tired and went to catch up with his party, which had continued its way.   But Don Quixote still lay on the ground, unable to get up.

CHAPTER V

In Which the Narrative of Our Knight's Mishap is Continued

WHEN Don Quixote began to realize that he was, so to speak, anchored to the ground, he turned his thoughts to his usual remedy, his books on knighthood and chivalry, which, in fact, had been the cause of his downfall.   He decided that the passage to fit his case was the one about Baldwin and the Marquis of Mantua when Carloto left him wounded on the mountainside—for that he had been wounded by brigands he had no doubt.   So he began to feign severe suffering, rolling to and fro on the ground, and repeating words that he had read in his books and ascribed to Baldwin as he lay wounded; until he finally was discovered by a peasant from his own village, a neighbor of his, whom he took for Baldwin's uncle, the Marquis of Mantua.   This good neighbor of Don Quixote's was much concerned over his ravings.   He removed the knight's breastplate, back piece and visor, expecting to see him badly wounded; but he found no trace of blood or marks upon him.   Then he succeeded in hoisting poor Don Quixote up on his donkey, which seemed the easiest mount for him, while he tied the pieces of his arms on Rocinante. And thus they proceeded toward the village.   Because of

[20]

his blows and bruises, Don Quixote had a hard task sitting upright on the ass, and he emphasized the romance of his situation by constantly heaving sighs to heaven. But every time the peasant was driven by these sighs to ask him his trouble, he replied in the language of a different hero from a different book.

It was nightfall when they arrived at Don Quixote's house in the village. His housekeeper, the curate, and the village barber were all in confusion, for it was now six days since the old gentleman had disappeared from La Mancha with his hack and armor. They had just come to the conclusion that his books were to blame for his dilapidated mentality, and agreed that they ought to be condemned to be publicly burned, when the peasant suddenly arrived with Don Quixote himself. They all ran out to greet and embrace him while he was still on the donkey—he had not dismounted because he could not. He insisted that he was severely wounded—through no fault of his own, however, but that of his horse—and asked that they put him to bed and send for the wise Urganda to cure him.

The good people carried him to bed, but still they could find no wounds, although he insisted that he had been wounded in combat with ten giants, the greatest and most bloodthirsty in the world. Then he asked for something to eat; and then fell asleep.

CHAPTER VI

Of the Diverting and Important Scrutiny Which the Curate and the Barber Made in the Library of Our Ingenious Gentleman

EARLY the next morning the curate and his friend Master Nicholas, the barber, went to Don Quixote's house to settle their grievance with the cause of all the mischief—the books of their demented friend. The curate asked the niece for the keys to the library, and she was only too willing to let him have them. They all went in, followed by the housekeeper, who grew faint-hearted as soon as she caught sight of all the beautifully bound books in the room. She ran out as if beset, returning immediately with a bowl of holy water and a sprinkler, with which she implored the curate to sprinkle the room, so that none of the magicians who might come out of the books would be left to bewitch her.

She was afraid that their ghosts might survive and bother her in revenge for having instigated their banishment from this world.

The curate was amused by the housekeeper's fear. He asked the barber to give him the books one by one, as he was afraid that among the many there must be some innocent ones which did not deserve the penalty of death. But both the niece and the housekeeper made emphatic and vociferous remonstrances against such leniency and insisted that a bonfire be made in the courtyard for all of them. Now, the barber had a particular leaning toward poetry, and he thought that *such* volumes ought to escape the stake; but he was promptly overruled by the conclusions of the niece, who reasoned that enough harm had already been done by books. "Your worship," she pleaded with the curate, "had best burn them all; for if my uncle, having been cured of his craze for chivalry, should take to reading these pastoral poems, he might take a fancy to become a shepherd and stroll the woods and pastures, singing and piping. What would be still worse, however, would be his turning poet; for that, they say, is both an incurable and infectious malady."

Against such logic, strongly supported by the housekeeper, the arguments of the two men came to nothing; and the barber saw his favorite form of literature thrust into the heap that was being prepared in the yard for illumination. Only a few books were saved from this fate, and they only through the boldness of the curate and the barber together against the united efforts of the female members of the party. There was one volume in particular, called "The Tears of Angelica," which the curate fought for valiantly. "I should have shed tears myself," he said, "had I seen that book burn."

CHAPTER VII

OF THE SECOND SALLY OF OUR WORTHY KNIGHT, DON
QUIXOTE OF LA MANCHA

WHILE the curate was praising the merits of "The
Tears of Angelica," there was suddenly a tremendous outcry and noise from Don Quixote's bedroom. They
hastened to see what was the matter, and when they reached
his room they found him out of bed, sword in hand, cutting
and slashing all around him, raving and shouting, with perspiration dripping from his body. He imagined that he
was keeping at a distance several bold and daring warriors,
and he kept exclaiming that the envious Don Roland had
battered him with the trunk of an oak-tree because of his
illustrious achievements in chivalry. They finally succeeded in forcibly putting him to bed, having wiped away
the perspiration—which he insisted was blood. He then
asked for something to eat; and when it was brought he
fell asleep again.

After the housekeeper had burned up all the books that
were in the house, the curate and the barber thought it
best to safeguard themselves against their friend's fury
when he should find that his treasures had disappeared.
So they decided to wall up and plaster the room where the
books had been. Two days later, when Don Quixote got
up out of bed, he went to look for his library. And it was
nowhere to be found, of course: where the door had been,
there was only a wall. He asked his housekeeper where

his books were, as well as the room they had been kept in; but she had been well instructed and blamed it all on the devil. His niece told him that she believed a magician had taken the room away. She had seen him, she declared, come on a cloud, riding on a serpent; and when he had disappeared, the whole house was full of smoke and there was no trace of either room or books. The niece also declared that she had heard the magician say plainly that he was the Sage Munaton.

The niece's explanation of the magic was heartily approved of by Don Quixote. The only doubt he expressed was about the identity of the magician. "He must have said Friston," he insisted. The housekeeper here came to the niece's aid and stated that she did not know whether he had said "Friston" or "Friton" or what he had said; but one thing she was sure of was that his name ended with "ton."

This convinced Don Quixote that it was no other than the Sage Munaton, a great enemy of his, whose vanity could not tolerate the prophecies that Don Quixote was about to conquer in battle a certain knight whom Munaton had befriended.

After this our worthy knight stuck to his house and home for a fortnight. His two gossiping friends, the curate and the village barber, did everything in their power to divert his thoughts from his fixed idea of a revival of the days of knighthood and chivalry. But the fire in Don Quixote's breast was smouldering: it was an undying flame.

Near Don Quixote there lived a man by the name of Sancho Panza. He was a farm-hand—a poor but honest

fellow who had both wife and children. Sancho Panza
was not overburdened with thoughts derived from reading
books of chivalry—the simple facts being that he could
neither read nor write—nor, for that matter, with thoughts
of any other kind on any other subject, for while Don Quixote' had lost his wits, Sancho had never had any.

To this poor fellow Don Quixote would talk of his adventures by the hour, trying to persuade Sancho that he
was missing much romance by remaining a farm-hand all
his life and that he ought to become the squire of some
noble knight—for instance, himself. And so, after much
persuasion and many promises, Sancho Panza decided to
adopt his noble neighbor as his master. He was told that
he must provide himself with all the necessaries for such
an important and lofty position; and he assured his master
that he would bring along his very best donkey. The mention of this ignoble animal somewhat took the knight aback.
He ransacked his memory for any instance in which any
other mount than a horse had been used, but he could recall none. However, he could not very well have an attendant on foot, so he decided to take him along, mounted on
his donkey. Of course, there was no doubt in his mind that
an opportunity would present itself ere long to appropri-
ate the horse of some rebellious knight.

One night the two sallied forth from the village, unseen.
Sancho Panza sat on his donkey, a picture of grave jovial-
ity, already seeing himself the governor of some conquered
island. Don Quixote was taking the same road he took
on his first campaign, the road that led over the Campo de
Montiel.

ADVENTURE OF THE WINDMILLS

CHAPTERS VIII—IX

OF THE GOOD FORTUNE WHICH THE VALIANT DON QUIXOTE
HAD IN THE TERRIBLE AND UNDREAMT-OF ADVENTURE
OF THE WINDMILLS, WITH OTHER OCCURRENCES
WORTHY TO BE FITLY RECORDED, INCLUDING
THE TERRIBLE BATTLE BETWEEN THE
GALLANT BISCAYAN AND THE
VALIANT MANCHEGAN

WHEN they had traveled a few miles they suddenly saw thirty or forty windmills scattered over a plain. Don Quixote pulled in his horse, his eyes staring out of their sockets.

"Look, friend Sancho Panza!" he exclaimed. "Thirty or more monstrous giants present themselves! I mean to engage them all in battle and slay them; for this is righteous warfare. It is serving God to sweep so evil a breed from off the face of the earth!"

"What giants?" asked Sancho curiously.

"Those with the long arms," replied Don Quixote.

"But, your worship," said Sancho, "those are not giants but windmills, and what seem to be their arms are the sails that make the millstones go."

Hearing his squire make such a foolish remark, Don Quixote could not quite make up his mind whether it was through ignorance, inexperience in the pursuit of adventure, or cowardice, that he spoke like that. So he suggested Sancho would better stay away and pray while he, Don Quixote, fought the giants singlehanded. The honor of conquering in such an unequal combat would be so much greater for him, he thought, if he won victory all by himself.

Don Quixote made ready for the attack by commending himself to his Lady Dulcinea, and then he gave the spur to Rocinante in spite of the pleas and outcries of Sancho Panza. Just at this moment a breeze began to blow and the sails of the windmills commenced to move. The knight charged at his hack's fullest gallop, drove his spear with such force into one of the sails that the spear was shattered to pieces while the poor knight fell over the pommel of his saddle, head over heels in the air, and Rocinante fell stunned to the ground. There they rolled together on the plain, in a battered and bruised condition.

Sancho hurried to his master's side as fast as his donkey could carry him. He was worried beyond words, for he expected to find Don Quixote well nigh dead, and he was not bent on giving up all hopes of governing an island, at so early a stage. The misguided knight was unable to move. Neverthelesss Sancho Panza could not resist the impulse to reprimand his master. "Did I not tell your worship so!" he admonished. But Don Quixote would hear nothing, answering in a sportsmanlike fashion:

"Hush, friend Sancho! The fortunes of war fluctuate, that's all." And then he added his suspicion that the same Sage Friston, the magician who had carried off his room of books, had turned the giants into windmills so that he would be unable to boast of having conquered them—all out of sheer envy and thirst for vengeance. What he most be-wailed, however, was the loss of his lance.

ADVENTURE OF THE WINDMILLS

With much difficulty Sancho succeeded in placing **Don Quixote** on his horse, and they proceeded on their way, following the road to Puerto Lapice. All the while Don Quixote was scanning the woods along the roadside for the branch of an oak-tree that he would deem a worthy substitute for his departed spear. It seemed to him as if he had read somewhere in one of his books that some knight had done such a thing in an emergency.

Having reminded Don Quixote that he must sit straight in the saddle, Sancho was in turn reminded by an inner feeling that it was time to eat. His master, however, scorned this idea, and let Sancho indulge by himself, while he fasted.

Finally night fell, and they passed it in the woods. There Don Quixote chose at last the branch of an oak-tree that was to serve him as a spear, and to one of its ends he attached the head of his broken lance. All night long he lay looking up into the sky, visioning his sweet Dulcinea— all for the purpose of emulating other heroes of the past age of chivalry who could not sleep for thinking of their lady loves.

Sancho Panza, unluckily, was stimulated in no such blessed way. He was supported by no sweet dreams of any beloved one of his. As for his wife, he had forgotten all about her. But as a matter of truth he had no memory of anything, having absorbed too much fluid out of his leather wine-bag, or *bota*, as it is called in Spanish. On getting up in the morning Sancho Panza was grieved to find the contents of his *bota* decidedly diminished.

Don Quixote bravely maintained his self-inflicted hun-

[29]

ger and swallowed his appetite by thoughts of his past valiant deeds. They soon started out, and again took the road leading to Puerto Lapice, whose outlines they sighted in the afternoon. Don Quixote thought this an opportune time for addressing his squire on the etiquette and laws of knighthood, as they were now approaching a very hotbed of adventure.

"Under no pretext," he admonished the faithful one, "must thou put a hand to thy sword in my defense unless it be that I am attacked by mere rabble or base folk; in such case, thou art in duty bound to be my bodyguard. But if my assailants be knights, thou must in no way interfere until thou hast been dubbed a knight thyself."

Sancho promised to obey his master as nearly as his human nature permitted him. He declared that he liked peace and hated strife, yet, if he were assailed, he did not believe in turning the other cheek more than once. Don Quixote saw a certain amount of reason in this; still, he asked his squire to do his utmost to restrain himself against any such rash impulse in the case of members of the knighthood. And Sancho Panza swore that he would keep this precept as religiously as Sunday.

While our noble knight was thus instructing his squire, there appeared on the road two friars of the order of St. Benedict. They were riding mules; and behind them came a coach with an escort numbering nearly half a dozen men on horseback and two men on foot. In the coach, traveling in state, was a lady of Biscay, on her way to Seville.

What could this be except a plot of scheming magicians

to steal away some princess? The friars, innocently traveling by themselves, became in Don Quixote's eyes a pair of evil magicians, and in his thirst for adventure the nearer one assumed stupendous proportions.

"This will be worse than the windmills!" sighed Sancho, who tried in vain to convince his master of the facts in the case.

But Don Quixote cut him short. "Thou knowest nothing of adventures," he said; and that settled it.

Boldly the knight went forward and took position in the middle of the road.

"Devilish and unnatural beings!" he cried in a loud voice, "release instantly the high-born princess whom you are carrying off by force in this coach, else prepare to meet a speedy death as the just punishment of your evil deeds!"

The mules came to a standstill, their ears erect with astonishment at such a figure, and the friars gaped in wonder. At last they recovered sufficiently to declare that they were traveling quite by themselves, and had no knowledge of the identity of the travelers following behind them.

To their meek reply Don Quixote paid no heed, but bellowed forth furiously: "No soft words with me! I know you, you lying rabble!" And with his spurs in Rocinante and his lance lifted he rode against the two friars like a whirlwind, so that if one of them had not quickly thrust himself off his mule, he would certainly have been torn to shreds. The other one saved his skin by setting off across the country at a speed rivaling our hero's charge.

At this stage Sancho Panza began to realize the full extent of his position as squire to a successful knight. Over by the roadside he saw the first friar lying breathless on the ground as a result of his jumping off his mule in such amazing hurry. He proceeded to strip off the friar's gown, using as a moral for doing this his own thoughts on the subject. He reasoned that if he could not share in the honors of battle, he at least ought to share in the spoils.

He was intercepted by some of the men attending the carriage. Unfortunately, they were serious-minded men, and they failed to see the joke. Sancho Panza gave them his views on etiquette pertaining to such matters as these; but it would have been much better for him had he not, for the men set upon him with great fury, beating and kicking him until he was insensible. They left him lying on the ground and then helped the pale and trembling friar to mount his mule. As soon as he was in the saddle, he hastened to join his companion, and the two of them continued their journey, making more crosses than they would if the devil had pursued them.

In the meantime Don Quixote had been trying to persuade the fair occupant of the coach to return to El Toboso that she herself might relate to his beloved Dulcinea the strange adventure from which he had delivered her.

A Biscayan gentleman, who was one of her attendants and rode a hired mule, took offense at his insistence to bother her, and a fight was soon in progress. The Biscayan had no shield, so he snatched a cushion from the carriage and used it to defend himself. The engagement was a most heated one, and Don Quixote lost a piece of his ear early in the combat. This enraged him beyond words; he charged his adversary with such tremendous force and fury that he began to bleed from his mouth, his nose, and his ears. Had the Biscayan not embraced the neck of his mount, he would have been spilled on the ground immediately. It remained for his mule to complete the damage, and when the animal suddenly set off across the plain in great fright, the rider plunged headlong to the ground.

Seeing this, Don Quixote hastened to the man's side and bade him surrender, at the penalty of having his head cut off. Absolutely bewildered, the gentleman from Biscay could say nothing; and had it not been for the ladies in the coach who interceded with prayers for his life, the Biscayan might have been beheaded right then and there. Don Quixote finally agreed to spare his opponent's life on one condition: that he present himself before the matchless Lady Dulcinea in the village of El Toboso, and it would be for her to determine his punishment. The ladies having promised that their protector should do anything and everything that might be asked of him, our hero from La Mancha said that he would harm the gentleman no more.

CHAPTER X

Of the Pleasant Discourse that Passed between Don Quixote and His Squire Sancho Panza

WHEN Sancho Panza had regained consciousness, he saw his master again engaged in battle. He thought that the best thing he could do was to pray, at a distance, for victory; and so he did. Soon he saw Don Quixote emerge from the struggle as victor! Overcome by emotion and gratitude to God, he ran to his master's side and fell on his knees before him. He kissed his hand, then helped him to mount his steed. All the while he did not forget the island of which Don Quixote had promised him he should become governor. He expectantly reminded his master of it now, and Don Quixote said to him that if things continued to go as they had gone, there would be even greater honors in store for him; perhaps he would become a king or an emperor, even.

Much satisfied with this prospect, Sancho lifted himself up into the saddle and trotted after his master, who was galloping ahead at a wild pace. Sancho, seeing him disappear in a wood nearby, steered his ass in the same direction. He yelled to him in a loud voice, begging him to stop.

At last our knight condescended to hear his tired squire, and waited until Sancho caught up with him. Sancho ventured to suggest that they hide in some church, for he was afraid that by this time the friars had reported the happening to the Holy Brotherhood; but his master only laughed at his simplicity and fear; and finally Sancho had to admit that he never in his life had served so brave and valiant a knight. However, he begged his master not to overlook his bleeding ear, and gave him some ointment to apply to the wound. It was only after a long discourse on the merits of the strange balsam of Fierabras, which possessed the enchanted quality of healing bodies cut in twain—he particularly dwelt upon the necessity of fitting the two separated halves evenly and exactly—that Don Quixote deigned to apply Sancho's ointment. In doing so he lamented the absence of the famous balsam.

Now, Sancho Panza saw untold possibilities for making money out of such a remarkable remedy as this balsam. He was even willing to relinquish his rights to any throne in its favor. So what interested him more than anything else was the recipe for making it. But his master told him that he would teach him even greater secrets when the time came, and suddenly changed the subject by cursing the Biscayan, of whom he had just been reminded by a twinge in his bleeding ear. The sight of his shattered helmet brought the climax to his anger, and he swore by the creator and all the four gospels to avenge himself. When Sancho heard this, he reminded his knight of his solemn oath to the ladies. Had he not promised them to refer the Biscayan's punishment to the court of his Dulcinea? Being thus reminded by his squire, Don Quixote nobly declared his oath null and void, and commended Sancho Panza for unknowingly having made him conform with the customs of chivalry.

Then he repeated his vows of knighthood and swore to capture from some other knight a helmet as good as his own. Sancho, by this time, was beginning to wonder whether so many oaths might not be injurious to Don Quixote's salvation. He suggested, for instance, the possibility of meeting with no one wearing a helmet, and asked what his master intended to do to keep his oath in such a case. Don Quixote assured him that they would soon encounter more men in armor than came to Albraca to win the fair Angelica.

Unwittingly Sancho's thoughts went back to his favorite unconquered island, and again his master admonished him to feel no uneasiness on that score. He even bettered his chances, explaining that if the island should disappear or for some reason be out of the question, there were countless other realms to be considered. He mentioned the kingdoms of Denmark and Sobradisa as some of them, and added that these possessed advantages that no island had. These were on the mainland and did not have to be reached by boat or by swimming.

Now Don Quixote was beginning to feel hungry, and he asked Sancho Panza to give him some food out of his *alforjas*. Sancho made apologies for having nothing but onions, cheese, and a few crusts of bread to offer such a valiant knight, but Don Quixote explained that one of the glories of knighthood was self-denial: many a knight had been known to go without food for a month at a time. However, he thought it advisable for Sancho to gather dry fruits from time to time as a safeguard against overwhelming hunger. Sancho feared that his appetite might crave food of a more substantial kind, and added that he would garnish his meals with some poultry. His master made no direct remonstrance to this assertion of his squire, but presumed that not *all* knights at *all* times lived on dry fruit.

As soon as they had finished their repast, they mounted and continued their way, anxious to find some inhabited place before nightfall. When it had grown dark, they found themselves near the huts of some goatherds, and Don Quixote decided that they should spend the night there. Sancho had hoped that they would find some house where he could have a comfortable bed; but his master was pleased to sleep once more in the open. Each act of self-denial made him a more honored and more valuable member of the knighthood.

CHAPTER XI

Of What Befell Don Quixote with Certain Goatherds

THE goatherds were cordial in their greeting to our knight and his squire, and invited them to partake of their meal, which was just being served on a tablecloth of sheepskin spread on the ground. Don Quixote was given a seat of honor on a trough turned upside down. Sancho remained standing to serve him, but his master insisted upon his coming down to his level. To this Sancho objected. He said that he could enjoy his food much better in a corner by himself, where he could chew it as he pleased, without having to take into consideration the formalities inflicted by the presence of one so much above his own state as his worthy master. He called his master's attention to the fact that in company like this, a humble servant like himself would have to suppress all such inclinations as sneezing, coughing and other natural outbursts, and, worst of all, drinking to his heart's content. But

[37]

Don Quixote would listen to no arguments and seated him by force at his side.

All the while the goatherds were marveling at our knight's bombastic speech and flourishing manners, and their interest was only enhanced when Don Quixote suddenly commenced a vast and poetic discourse on the golden age of the past. Some parched acorns he had just eaten had served him as a reminder and this in turn as an inspiration.

Sancho took advantage of his master's long speech by paying numerous visits to the leather wine-bag, which had been suspended from a cork-tree in order to keep the wine cool.

Hardly had Don Quixote finished his discourse when the sound of music was heard in the distance, and soon a good-looking youth of twenty appeared, playing a lute. At the goatherds' request he sang a ballad of love, which was much favored by Don Quixote. Sancho Panza, however, felt the necessity for sleep and slyly suggested consideration on his master's part for the men, who no doubt had to rise with the sun and attend to their labors. This appeal did not fail to move Don Quixote, especially since his ear again began to trouble him with pain. One of the goatherds offered his help. He plucked some leaves of rosemary, put them in his mouth and chewed them well, then mixed them with a pinch of salt and put them as a plaster over the wounded ear, safely attaching it with a bandage. As he had predicted, this proved to be an excellent treatment.

THE STORY THE GOATHERD TOLD

CHAPTER XII

OF WHAT A GOATHERD RELATED TO THOSE WITH DON QUIXOTE

JUST as Don Quixote was about to retire for the night, a young man from the village came to the hut and informed the goatherds of the death of a famous villager named Crysostom. The youth said there was a rumor that Crysostom—who had been a student and had turned shepherd—had died of a broken heart, for love of the daughter of Guillermo the Rich. In his will he had directed that he desired to be buried, like a Moor, at the very place where he first saw her, at the foot of a rock by a spring in the fields. The clergy of the village had been aroused by this and other directions in the will, which they considered smacked of heathenism, and objected to the carrying out of the will. Ambrosio, the bosom friend of Crysostom— and a student who had also become a shepherd—started an opposition to the clergy, and was determined that his dead friend's will should be done. The young man said that the whole village was in an uproar, and he was looking forward to interesting events in the morning, when the burial was to take place.

Don Quixote was eager to learn something of the maiden for whose sake Ambrosio's friend had died. One of the goatherds, named Pedro, related to him all that he knew.

[39]

The parents of Marcela—for that was the maiden's name—and of Crysostom were very rich people, although they were farmers. Marcela's father and mother died when she was a baby, and she was brought up under the care of her uncle, a priest in the village. As she grew up, her beauty was increased with each day that passed, and her uncle had many offers for her hand in marriage; but she would hear of none of them. One day, to the consternation of all in the village, she appeared dressed in the costume of a shepherdess, and declared her intention of turning to that kind of life.

Just about this time the father of Crysostom died, leaving his great fortune to his son, who had just finished his studies in astrology and other learned subjects in the University of Salamanca. Crysostom returned home together with his friend and companion Ambrosio, and both became very well liked in the village. There Crysostom saw Marcela and fell deeply in love with her, and he, like so many others before him, decided to turn shepherd in order to be near her constantly. But she was indifferent to all talk of love; and the sting of her scorn made him take his life.

Having ended his story, Pedro advised our knight not to miss the ceremonies that Crysostom's shepherd friends were to hold at his grave in the morning. Sancho, who had been greatly annoyed by the goatherd's talkativeness, was by this time beginning to think aloud that it might be time for his master to go to bed; and Pedro begged him to sleep in his hut, as he was afraid that the cold night air might hurt his wound.

THE STORY THE GOATHERD TOLD

So Don Quixote retired for the night to the bed given him by his hosts, and dreamed all night of his beloved one in his native village, in imitation of other great lovers. Sancho rested, as comfortable and unemotional as a barrel of settled wine, between his master's charger and his own peaceful donkey.

CHAPTER XIII

In Which Is Ended the Story of the Shepherdess Marcela with Other Incidents

AS soon as the sun was rising in the east, Don Quixote was awakened, and a little later they were on their way to the burial of Crysostom.

They had gone only a short distance, when they met six shepherds, all dressed in black sheepskins and with crowns of bitter oleander and cypress on their heads. In his hand each shepherd carried a staff of holly. Directly behind them came two dignified gentlemen on horseback, followed by three servants on foot. While stopping to exchange greetings, all had learned that they were going in the same direction for the same purpose. The two gentlemen had met the mourning shepherds, and from them had heard the sad story of the love of Crysostom for Marcela. That had aroused their curiosity and sorrow, and they wanted now to do him honor.

The battle-clad Don Quixote, of course, attracted their attention, and one of the gentlemen was eager to learn why any one should be masquerading in armor so early in the morning. To which he got the reply that the danger of his calling made it necessary for him to wear it. The gentlemen could not help then but realize Don Quixote's mental condition. But one of them possessed a restless sense of humor, and when Don Quixote began to discourse on chivalry and knights errant, he asked to know what these things were. Our hero then explained their mysteries at length. He described the deeds of King Arthur, spoke of the famous Round Table, and told the love-story of Don Lancelot and Queen Guinevere.

In the course of these descriptions the jesting gentleman felt that he had fully diagnosed the madness of our knight, and thought it only fair play to beguile the journey to the burial-place by listening to his absurdities. Now and then he would put in a word or ask a question in order not to break the thread. For instance, he suggested cunningly that the calling of a knight errant was as serious as that of a Carthusian monk; and Don Quixote replied that he thought it a much more necessary one. And as to its demands, there was no comparison, he declared, for if ever one rose to become an emperor it was only after tremendous sacrifice of blood and sweat.

The traveling gentleman was agreed with him on that score; but there was one thing he did not approve of: whenever a knight went into battle, he commended himself to his lady, instead of God. This he thought wrong and unchristianlike. Don Quixote, however, saw no wrong in it. It was only human, he contended, to think first of his beloved one at so austere a moment; and, besides, often the knight errant would say things under his breath that would not be understood.   Then only Heaven could know whether he had called upon his lady or God.

The gentleman then soon found another argument. He expressed a doubt that all knights errant were in love, saying that some of them commended themselves to ladies fictitiously.   Don Quixote denied this emphatically; but the traveler thought that he had read somewhere that Don Galaor, the brother of the valiant Amadis of Gaul, never commended himself to any particular lady, yet he was a brave and most illustrious knight errant.   All that Don Quixote replied to this argument was: "Sir, one solitary swallow does not make summer!" and offered, as if in confidence, his conviction that this very knight had been very deeply in love, but secretly.

At that very moment he heaved a sigh of weariness.   The sigh was misinterpreted by the traveler, however, for he asked our knight whether he was reticent about telling the name of *his* lady.

"Dulcinea del Toboso, of La Mancha," answered Don Quixote.   And this time he made her a princess, extolling her virtues and her beauty to the traveler, who found it amusing to hear the knight tell of her ancestry and lineage. First of all Don Quixote named to the traveler the families of Spain that she was *not* connected with, then informed him that she was of the house of El Toboso of La Mancha. And though this was a most modern family, one could never foretell what position it would hold in the future.

The traveler in his turn told Don Quixote of his own family, saying that he of course dared not to compare it

[43]

THE STORY OF DON QUIXOTE

with that of the fair Dulcinea, although he never had heard of hers ere this—a confession that surprised Don Quixote exceedingly.

During this conversation between the knight and the traveling gentleman—who was named Señor Vivaldo—they came in sight of a score of shepherds, all dressed in black sheepskins and crowned with garlands. Six of them were carrying a bier on which lay the body of the dead Crysostom. At his side were scattered some papers and books. When they had found the resting-place that the dead man had chosen for himself, Ambrosio, his dearest friend, spoke some words in his memory. He mentioned how Crysostom's heart had been rent asunder by the cruel treatment of one whom his departed friend would have immortalized to the world in poetry, had Ambrosio not been commissioned by him to consign the verses to the flames after having entrusted his body to the earth.

Señor Vivaldo thought it would be a great pity to do away with such beautiful verses, and he pleaded with Ambrosio against their consignment to oblivion. As he was speaking, he reached out his hand for some of the papers that were close to him, and Ambrosio considerately permitted him to keep them. The remaining ones were burned.

Señor Vivaldo glanced through the papers eagerly and read the title—"Lay of Despair." When Ambrosio heard this, he asked him to read the words aloud that all those assembled might hear the last verses of the dead shepherd. And while Señor Vivaldo spoke the despairing lines, some of the shepherds were digging the grave for their friend.

THE VERSES OF THE DEAD SHEPHERD

CHAPTER XIV

WHEREIN ARE DESCRIBED THE DESPAIRING VERSES OF THE DEAD SHEPHERD

SEÑOR VIVALDO had finished the last verse and was about to glance through the rest of the papers he had saved from the fire, when suddenly on the summit of the rock by the grave he saw a most glorious apparition. It was no other than Marcela, the shepherdess, and everyone was aghast at her presence. The moment Ambrosio saw her, he became indignant beyond words and commanded her to leave. But she remained and asked them all to listen to her. She had come there to defend herself, she said; she knew what people had accused her of: cruelty, scornfulness, arrogance, ingratitude, deception, and hatred. But she hated no one, she declared. She had deceived no one. Crysostom had loved her because of her beauty; but she had loved neither him nor any other man. She had chosen solitude, the woods and the fields, because of her inborn craving for freedom. Should she have forced herself to give that up because any man chose to say, "I love you," while she did not love him? Was she to be blamed for Crysostom's death. For not loving him? Would not that have been to pawn her modesty and her womanly honor and virtue? And why should he have wanted to rob her of them?

So she spoke; and when she had finished she waited for

[45]

no reply but turned and ran like a deer into the woods. All stood gazing after her in silent admiration, not only for her beauty but for her frank speech and good sense also. Some of the men seemed to be about to run after her, having been wellnigh enchanted by her gloriously bright eyes; but they were stopped by Don Quixote, who thundered: "Let no one, whatever his rank or condition, dare to follow the beautiful Marcela, under pain of incurring my fierce indignation! She has shown by clear and satisfactory arguments that no fault is to be found with her for the death of Crysostom. Instead of being followed and persecuted, she should in justice be honored and esteemed by all the good people of the world, for she shows that she is the only woman in it that holds to such a virtuous resolution."

These words Don Quixote uttered in a threatening manner, his hand on the hilt of his sword. Whether because of his threats or because the grave had been dug and Crysostom's remains were about to be lowered into it, they all stayed until the burial was over. The grave was closed with a large stone, and then the shepherds strewed flowers, leaves and branches upon it, and shed many tears.

The two travelers extended an invitation to Don Quixote to accompany them to Seville, where they assured him he would find no end of adventures awaiting him. But he told them that for the present he had his hands full ridding these very regions of highwaymen and robbers. He thanked them, however, and they continued their journey without our hero.

Don Quixote now saw his duty clearly. He would

search the woods and wilds for the beautiful Marcela.   He was certain that she would need his services.

But things did not turn out as he expected.

CHAPTER XV

In Which Is Related the Unfortunate Adventure That Don Quixote Fell in with When He Fell Out with Certain Heartless Yanguesans

WHEN Don Quixote had taken leave of his hosts, he set off with his squire into the woods where he had seen Marcela disappear.   They wandered about for some time and found no trace of the shepherdess.   Then they came to a pasture through which a brook was running, and as they were both thirsty, warm, and tired, they decided to remain there for their noontide meal.   They feasted on the scraps that remained in the *alforjas*, while Rocinante and Sancho's ass were left free to pluck all the grass they desired.

Now, Fate would have it that at that very hour a band of Yanguesans were resting nearby, with their ponies let loose in the pasture.   As soon as the ponies were discovered by Rocinante, he wanted to exchange friendly greetings with them, so he set off at a brisk trot in their direction. But the ponies seemed to have no desire to strike up an acquaintance with an unknown hack, for they arrogantly turned their backs on him and commenced to snort and kick and bite until the saddle fell off Rocinante and he was left quite naked.   By this time the Yanguesans had heard

[47]

the commotion and rushed up, armed with sticks, and with these they thrashed poor Rocinante so soundly that he fell to the ground in a heap.

Just at this time Don Quixote and Sancho, having finished their repast, went to look for their chargers. As soon as Don Quixote had taken in the situation, he realized that these were no knights errant and confided this to his squire, charging him to help him in his battle for Rocinante's honor. Sancho made vehement pleas for abstaining from vengeance, seeing the great numbers of the enemy; but his master's conviction that he alone counted for a hundred eased his mind.

Don Quixote attacked at once and cut off a portion of his opponent's shoulder; Sancho fought bravely too. But when the men saw that they were fighting such a small number they set upon them, all at one time, and after a few thrusts they had unseated our knight and his squire, both sorely battered. Then, fearing the hand of the law, the Yanguesans set off in great haste.

When Sancho came to, he was certain that all his bones were broken, and he feebly turned to his master saying that he only wished that he had at hand the marvelous balsam of Fierabras, of which his master had spoken. Sancho lamented the lack of it no more than Don Quixote, who swore that within two days he would have the potion in his possession. As to his wounds, he took all the blame upon himself: he felt that it was God's punishment for having engaged in battle with ordinary rabble like these carriers, and decided that henceforth he would have Sancho alone chastise those who had not been dubbed knights.

To this Sancho took exception, for he maintained that he had wife and children to support, and was by nature a peaceful, meek and timid man. He called upon God to forgive in advance all the insults man or beast might offer him in the future and for all times; but at this Don Quixote took him to task and admonished him not to lose his valor in attacking and defending himself in all sorts of emergencies.

Sancho's soft heart now turned to Rocinante, who had been the cause of all the trouble. The poor horse was in a sorry plight. So it was considered best that Don Quixote—who could not sit upright—should be slung across his servant's donkey. This decision was reached when Don Quixote remembered that Silenus, the teacher of the God of Laughter, had entered the city of the hundred gates mounted on a handsome ass.

When his master had been secured and Rocinante raised from the ground, Sancho took the two beasts by the halter and led them out to the road, and from there they proceeded on their way. Soon Sancho saw the outlines of an inn, which Don Quixote insisted must be a castle, and before they had finished their dispute, they found themselves at the gate and entered.

CHAPTER XVI

Of What Happened to the Ingenious Gentleman in the Inn Which He Took to Be a Castle

WHEN the keeper of the inn saw the sorry body of the knight on the ass, he became anxious to learn what had happened to him. His wife was a kindly and good-natured woman, and when Sancho had explained that his master had fallen from a rock, she and her pretty daughter offered to care for him. The daughter, and a one-eyed Asturian servant-girl, with turned-up nose and high cheek-bones, made a bed for Don Quixote on four rough boards in a garret, where a carrier was also quartered. Stretched on this bed Don Quixote was attended by the innkeeper's wife, who soon covered him with more plasters than he had quilts. In the meantime she, her daughter, and the Asturian girl, all curious, questioned Sancho about his master.

Sancho told, in as thrilling words as he could command, of their marvelous adventures; to all of which they listened with astonishment. The Asturian servant nearly stared her one eye out of her head. She asked Sancho Panza, trembling with excitement, what a knight errant was. To this Sancho replied that a knight was an adventurer, who one day might be the poorest and meanest of men, and the next day emperor, with crowns and kingdoms in abundance to give away to his squire and underlings. Here the women expressed surprise that he himself, judging by appearance, did not possess even so much as a small strip of land. He then confided to them that he and his master had been going but a short time; that as yet it was much too soon; that the adventures they had met with so far were but a beginning and not worthy of mention.

Don Quixote, who had been listening to everything his squire said, now sat up in bed and informed them of the great honor he had conferred upon them by being in their house; he told them of his indescribable gratitude to them; and of his love for his Dulcinea del Toboso of La Mancha.

The women, not being accustomed to such language, which seemed to them more difficult to understand than Greek, stared at him in bewilderment; then, thanking him for his courtesy, they left him while the Asturian plastered Sancho, who seemed to be in need of treatment as sadly as his master.

CHAPTER XVII

IN WHICH ARE CONTAINED THE INNUMERABLE TROUBLES WHICH THE BRAVE DON QUIXOTE AND HIS GOOD SQUIRE SANCHO PANZA ENDURED AT THE INN, WHICH TO HIS MISFORTUNE HE TOOK TO BE A CASTLE

THE following morning Sancho, feeling his pains even more, reminded his master of the famous balsam he was to make. Don Quixote himself was anxious for it too, so he sent Sancho to an imagined fortress for some oil, wine, rosemary and salt. He mixed these ingredients in a pot, and boiled them. Then he poured the mixture into a tin flask, crossed himself and repeated innumerable pater-nosters and ave-marias. When he had nearly exhausted himself doing that, he swallowed a good portion of the liquid; and immediately he began to vomit and perspire, while his face and body contracted in the most horrible spasms. He asked to be put to bed at once, and they let him sleep for three hours. When he woke he felt so relieved that he really thought he had hit upon the remedy of Fierabras.

Seeing his master's miraculous recovery, Sancho begged to be permitted to drink some of the wonderful liquid, and Don Quixote gave him a dose of it. Unlike his master, Sancho retained what he had drunk for some time before letting it all come up again, but in the meantime his agony was insufferable. He was seized with such gripings and faintness that he was sure his last hour had come. He even cursed his master for having given him such terrible stuff; but Don Quixote said that he had only now come to realize that the remedy was made solely for those who had been dubbed knights: whereupon Sancho, writhing in convulsions cursed him still more. Sancho's agony lasted for several hours.

In the meantime Don Quixote himself, being anxious for new adventures, had saddled Rocinante. He had to help his squire mount the ass, for Sancho still was in a sorry condition. All the folk at the inn had gathered to see them depart, and when Don Quixote's eyes fell on the beautiful young daughter of the inn-keeper, he heaved a heavy sigh; but no one there realized the soul or the reason of it, for they all thought it must be from the pain in his ribs.

As he was about to leave, the valiant knight called the innkeeper and asked him with profound gravity whether he had any enemies that remained unpunished; if so, he, Don Quixote, would chastise them for him. The innkeeper answered shortly that he could take care of his own grudges; all he asked of our knight was payment for lodging and for what he and the beasts and the squire had consumed.

"Then this is an inn?" cried Don Quixote, who could hardly believe his ears. He ransacked his memory for any incident when knight had ever paid for food and lodging, and, unable to remember one, raised his lance, turned Rocinante, and set off at a quick gallop, leaving Sancho behind.

The innkeeper immediately took steps to attach the squire for the unpaid debt; but Sancho's stolid indifference to his representations only tended to prove the truth of the old proverb: like master, like servant. He argued that it was not for him to tear down traditions of noble knighthood.

Unfortunately for Sancho, he was overheard by a good many guests at the inn, rollicking fellows, who were on the alert for amusement. These men seized a blanket, dismounted the squire unceremoniously, placed him in the middle of the blanket, and proceeded to hoist him, not gently, high in the air. This movement no doubt caused a return of Sancho's stomach-ache, for he commenced to groan and scream helplessly. His screams were heard far off by his master, who, believing that some new and glorious adventure was at hand, spurred his hack into a playful gallop and returned to the inn.

The gates were closed, but over the wall the knight could see the tricks that his faithful follower was made to perform in the air and on the blanket, and he boiled with rage, unable to come to the rescue, for he could not dismount because of stiffness. Finally, when the men had been sufficiently amused, they stopped their sport, then mounted Sancho with no little kindness on his ass and bade him godspeed on his journey. The one-eyed Asturian compassionately offered the poor fellow some water to drink; but seeing this, Don Quixote commenced to gesticulate wildly, waving a tin flask in the air, and crying: "Sancho, my son, drink not water, for it will kill thee! See, here I have the blessed balsam: two drops of it will restore thee!"

His master's advice did not appeal to the squire, and he replied rather cuttingly that Don Quixote ought to remember that he was not a knight. Saying this he put the cup the lass had offered him to his lips. But he found that it was not wine but water. He begged her to exchange it, which she did with Christian spirit, paying for it herself. The squire, having drunk the wine, spurred his ass toward the gate, and the innkeeper let him depart without further payment, having, unbeknown to Sancho, appropriated his *alforjas*.

CHAPTER XVIII

In Which Is Related the Discourse Sancho Panza Held with His Master, Don Quixote, Together with Other Adventures Worth Relating

DON QUIXOTE told his squire he was certain that the inn was an enchanted castle, and blamed his transgressions of the laws of chivalry for all their mishaps; for he imagined that, had he abstained from laying hands on the rabble and base folk, these would not have occurred. His being unable to get out of the saddle and climb over the wall, he ascribed to enchantment as well. Sancho thought this might be the moment for reforming his master. He suggested that it was harvest time at home; and reminded the knight of the fact that of all his battles he had come out victorious but once, when he fought with the Biscayan, and then with half of his ear lost, not to speak of all the damage done to his armor.

But Don Quixote was in no mood to contemplate past disasters, for in the distance he suddenly perceived rising clouds of dust, and what could it be but two opposing armies making ready for battle; since the clouds were seen on either side of the road! He made Sancho believe they were the great armies of the mighty emperor Alifanfaron and his enemy, the king of the Garamantas, Pentapolin of the Bare Arm, explaining—on seeing a bare-armed shepherd—that this lord always went into battle in this manner.

THE STORY OF DON QUIXOTE

Sancho Panza asked what they should do. His master replied that their duty was clear: they should, of course, help the weak and needy. Then he went on to explain that the reason for the feud was the pagan Alifanfaron's wish to marry the beautiful and Christian daughter of Pentapolin, and her father's refusal to sanction the marriage unless the emperor became a convert. Immediately Sancho's instinct for righteousness made him declare himself for Pentapolin, and he wanted to fight for him. This spirit pleased Don Quixote tremendously, for, he said, it was not required of dubbed knights to engage in feuds of this sort; thus Sancho would have a chance to distinguish himself all alone.

Scratching his head, Sancho now began to worry about his faithful donkey, for he believed it was not good taste to go into battle mounted on an ass, and if he dismounted, he was afraid his Dapple would be lost in the ensuing tumult. Don Quixote, however, calmed his fears. There would be hundreds of riderless horses after the battle, from which both of them might choose; and he asked Sancho to follow him to a hill nearby that he might point out to his valiant squire the great and illustrious knights of the two armies. He cried out name after name, the last one always more illustrious than the previous one. But Sancho could see nothing but the two flocks of sheep and the shepherds, and he said so.

"How can you say that!" cried Don Quixote. "Do you not hear the neighing of the steeds, the braying of the trumpets, the roll of the drums?"

Sancho answered in despair that he could hear nothing

but the bleating of ewes and sheep. To this his master explained that often fear deranged the senses and made things appear different from what they were. Therefore, being certain that Sancho had suddenly become possessed of fear, he put the spurs in Rocinante and charged down the hill like a flash of lightning, determined to down the pagan emperor.

Lifting his lance, he galloped into the midst of the sheep, and commenced spearing right and left. The shepherds, panicstricken, used their slings. Stones hit his head and body, but it was not until a large one struck him in the ribs that he imagined himself really wounded. He stopped in the midst of the furious battle, and suddenly remembering his flask of balsam, drew it out, put it to his mouth, and was about to swallow a quantity of it when there came a stone that took the flask out of his hand, and another one that smashed out three or four of his teeth. Don Quixote was so astonished and the force of the blow was so sudden that he lost his reins and fell backwards off his horse. When the shepherds came up and saw what they had done to him, they quickly gathered their flocks and hastened away, taking with them the seven sheep that Don Quixote killed with his spear.

During this rampage, Sancho Panza was nearly beside himself where he stood on the hill. He was tearing his hair and beard, wishing he had never laid eyes on his master, and berating himself for ever having joined in his mad adventures. When the shepherds had disappeared, he ran to his master's side.

"Did I not tell your worship," he reproached the prostrate

knight, "that they were not armies, but droves of sheep!"

But again our hero blamed his misfortune on his arch-enemy, that cursed Sage Friston, who had falsified the armies in such a way that they looked like meek and harmless sheep. Then he begged his squire to pursue the enemy by stealth that he might ascertain for himself that what he had said was true; for he was sure that ere they had gone very far they would resume their original shape.

However, before Sancho Panza had time to make up his mind whether to go or not, his master's sip of the balsam during the battle suddenly began to take effect, and Sancho's presence became for the moment a necessity. Having gone through this ordeal, Don Quixote rose and asked his squire for a remedy for hunger. It was then they discovered that the *alforjas* had disappeared, with all its precious contents. Both were dejected. Don Quixote tried to impart, out of the abundance of his optimism for the future, new hope to the discouraged Sancho. It was a difficult task, and he might have failed, had not the loss of his teeth and the sorry plight he was in made Sancho sway from his intentions of home-going. When, at his master's request, the squire put his finger in Don Quixote's mouth in order to learn the extent of the damage done in that region of his body, his heart was touched by the terrible devastation there. He could not, of course, leave his master to shift for himself on the highways in such a condition. So he consented to remain, and they proceeded along the road, hoping that they would soon come to a place where they could find shelter for the night, as well as something with which to still their hunger.

A SHREWD DISCOURSE

CHAPTER XIX

OF THE SHREWD DISCOURSE WHICH SANCHO HELD WITH HIS
MASTER, AND OF THE ADVENTURE THAT BEFELL HIM
WITH A DEAD BODY, TOGETHER WITH OTHER
NOTABLE OCCURRENCES

NIGHT had fallen, yet they had discovered no place
of refuge. Suddenly, in the darkness, they saw a
number of lights that came closer and closer without their
being able to make out what it was. Sancho commenced
to shake like a leaf, and even Don Quixote was frightened
and muttered a pater-noster between his teeth while his
hair stood on end. They withdrew to the roadside, from
where they soon distinguished twenty bodies on horseback,
all dressed in white shirts, and carrying lighted torches in
their hands. With chattering teeth Sancho stared at this
awe-inspiring procession, which was not yet at an end, for
behind the mounted bodies there came others, these in black
and on mule-back, and surrounding a bier, covered with a
large black cloth. All the while a quiet, solemn mumbling
came from the moving figures, and Sancho Panza was now
so stricken with fear that he was almost paralyzed.

Don Quixote's courage—which likewise had been rather
shaky at this passing of ghostlike beings, at such a time of
the night—suddenly revived and mounted to such heights
that he decided he would ask where they were carrying the
wounded king on the bier. This he did without delay.
But such a question seemed silly and out of place to one

[59]

of the guardians of the corpse, and he commanded the knight to move on. This angered Don Quixote beyond measure. He seized the man's mule by the bridle; but this, in turn, annoyed the mule, which rose on its hind legs and flung its rider to the ground. Another man came up to Don Quixote and tried to talk reason to him, but to no avail, and in the disturbance that followed the procession was soon scattered over the fields and plains, with torches glimmering from all points like so many eyes in the black night.

While our knight errant was lunging with his spear in all directions, the meek followers of the dead body became ensnared in their skirts and gowns and long white shirts, and fell head over heels wherever they happened to be, in ditch or field. Moans, groans, and prayers were intermingled, and they all were convinced that the procession had been interrupted by the devil himself, come to carry away the body of the dead man.

When the battle had ceased, Don Quixote approached the man who was flung by his mule, to make him his prisoner. The poor man declared that Don Quixote had made a grave mistake; that the dead man was not a king and had not fallen in battle, but a gentleman who had died from fever; and he himself was a poor servant of the Holy Church who could harm no one. On hearing this confession Don Quixote made a slight apology for having mistaken him in the dark for something evil, if not for the very devil, explaining that since it was his sworn duty to right all wrongs, he had only set out to do so. But the worthy ecclesiastic was not easily appeased, and before making his departure, he unceremoniously excommunicated his attacker in flowing and flourishing Latin.

Sancho, moved by a desire to alleviate the sting of the outburst, called out after him: "If the gentleman should wish to know who was the hero who served them thus, your worship may tell them he is the famous Don Quixote of La Mancha, otherwise called the Knight of the Rueful Countenance."

Don Quixote asked his squire why he called him thus; and Sancho replied that the loss of his teeth had given his master a face so sorry looking that he could find no milder name to describe its ugliness. Don Quixote laughed at the compliment; nevertheless he decided to adopt Sancho's meaning name, and also to have his own rueful face commemorated on his shield at the first opportunity.

After this conversation Sancho persuaded his master to continue their journey; although Don Quixote was eager to view the bones of the deceased man, and Sancho had some difficulty in preventing him from doing so.

Sancho had made his coat into a sack and filled it with the provisions of the clergy; and so, when they arrived in a valley where they found an abundance of grass, they ate all the meals they had been missing. Their repast would have been complete had they had some wine; but they did not have even water.

CHAPTER XX

Of the Unexampled and Unheard-of Adventure Which Was Achieved by the Valiant Don Quixote of La Mancha with Less Peril Than Any Ever Achieved by Any Famous Knight in the World

SANCHO'S thirst drove him to use his instincts in search for drink. He judged by the rank grass that there must be water nearby. So, leading their mounts, Don Quixote and Sancho came in the darkness to a meadow, and they had gone only a short distance when they heard the welcome sound of falling water. Then suddenly a most tremendous, ear-splitting noise came out of the darkness, a din like the beating of gigantic hammers, and added to this a shifting wind. All these furious sounds, the mystery of them, and the blackness of the night, might have intimidated any heart, however stout; but it only made Don Quixote leap like a flash upon his horse. Turning to Sancho, he cried: "I am he who is to revive the Knights of the Round Table, the Twelve of France, and the Nine Worthies; he who is to consign to oblivion the whole herd of famous knights errant of days gone by; he for whom all great perils and mighty deeds are reserved. Therefore, tighten Rocinante's girth a little, and God be with thee! Wait for me three days and no more. If in that time I come not back, thou canst return to our village, and thence thou wilt go to El Toboso, where thou shalt

[62]

say to my imcomparable Lady Dulcinea that her captive knight hath died in attempting things that might make him worthy of being called her own."

These words made Sancho weep copious tears, and he begged his master not to undertake so dreadful an adventure. He even offered to sacrifice himself to such an extent as to go without water for three days, if his master would only return. When Don Quixote was firm in his resolve, Sancho decided that this was a case where the ends justified the means; therefore while tightening Rocinante's girth, he tied the horse's forelegs, so that when Don Quixote was going to ride off, his charger could move only by fits and starts. The more his rider spurred him, the more impossible it became for Rocinante to stir. Sancho had no great difficulty in persuading his master that this was a sign from above that he ought not to pursue any phantom adventure at that hour of the night, but wait until daybreak. Don Quixote resigned himself to do so, although it nearly made him weep, while Sancho tried to soothe his outraged feelings by telling amusing stories in a laborious way.

At daybreak Sancho stole over to Rocinante and untied his legs. The horse immediately became spirited, and when Don Quixote saw this, he believed it a sign from heaven. Again he took a touching leave of his squire—who began to cry, as he had done before—and gave the spur to his steed. Sancho was resolved to follow his master to the end, so he took his donkey by the halter, as was his custom, and led him on foot in pursuit of his knight errant.

They passed through a meadow that was fringed with trees, then came upon some huge rocks with cascades of water pouring over them. Below stood a row of dilapidated houses. It was from these houses that the din and noise emanated. As Rocinante came close to the racket, he began to make hysterical movements, pirouetting backward and forward, and Don Quixote crossed himself, commending himself to God and his Lady Dulcinea.

Coming up cautiously from behind the houses, Don Quixote peered around the corner, and there beheld the cause of the awe-inspiring din—six hammers of the kind that were used in mills.

Sancho could not help himself. He burst into uncontrollable laughter, shaking from head to foot. Don Quixote was mortified with shame and astonishment. And when he heard Sancho's laughter behind him, he broke into a rage, during which he repeated almost every word he had spoken the night before, when he was about to ride away to adventure on a three-legged horse. But Sancho was helpless. Four distinct times he broke into a fit of mirth, and finally his master struck him a blow on the body with his spear. Then he calmed down, and Don Quixote scolded him for his hilarity, saying that no such familiarity would be tolerated in the future. He quoted various chapters from books of chivalry, and cited Gandalin, squire to Amadis of Gaul. There, he said, was a model squire, for he would always address his lord with cap in hand, his head bowed down and his body bent double. And there were many others to look to. He mentioned a few, the most shining examples. Then he decreed that from that day on respect must be the barrier between squire and knight in all their intercourse. He spoke also about his squire's wages and the treasures and islands that were to be his in time to come. He told Sancho not to worry, for if he should not pay him his wages, he had at any rate mentioned him in his will. From the first he had considered everything; he knew the world, and what a hazardous task he had set before himself.

CHAPTER XXI

Which Treats of the Exalted Adventure and Rich Prize of Mambrino's Helmet, Together with Other Things That Happened to Our Invincible Knight

IT started to rain, and Sancho suggested the fulling-mills as a place of refuge; but Don Quixote had taken such an aversion to them that he would not listen to it, and they continued riding, taking the roadway.

Suddenly they saw a man on horseback, who had on his head something that shone like gold, and at once Don Quixote exclaimed: "There comes towards us one who wears on his head the helmet of Mambrino, concerning which I took the oath thou rememberest."

Sancho's only reply to this was that he did not want anything more to do with any fulling-mills; and his master entirely failed to fathom the connection. Sancho then said he could plainly see that the man's horse was an ass and that the man had something on his head that shone.

THE STORY OF DON QUIXOTE

The truth of the matter was that in the neighborhood were two villages so small that the apothecary and barber-shop in one of them had to serve for both. The village barber had just been summoned to shave and bleed a patient in the adjoining community, so he mounted his ass, armed with a brass basin for the bleeding, and set off. He had got about half-way, when it commenced to rain. Having a new hat, he covered it with the clean basin, that glittered like gold.

But Don Quixote had more sense than his squire, of course, and pursued the unknown knight with the helmet at Rocinante's wildest gallop. When the fear-stricken barber realized that Don Quixote's uplifted spear was aimed at him, he promptly threw himself from his ass and ran all the way home without stopping, leaving his brass basin behind as a trophy for our hero, who could not understand why this helmet had no visor.

"That pagan must have had a very large head," remarked Don Quixote, turning the basin round and round, trying to fit it to his own head, now this way, now that.

"It looks exactly like a barber's basin," said Sancho Panza, who had all he could do to keep from bursting into laughter.

Don Quixote treated this blasphemous thought with scorn, and said he would stop at the next smithy to have its shape changed. His next concern was his stomach; and when they found that the barber's ass carried ample supplies, they soon satisfied their appetites. Sancho now turned the conversation to the rest of the spoils of war; but Don Quixote was unable to make up his mind that

[66]

it was chivalrous to exchange a bad ass for a good one, as was his squire's wish; so Sancho had to satisfy himself with the barber's trappings.

Then they set out again. Soon Sancho felt the need of unburdening something he had had on his heart for some time. He suggested that instead of roaming about seeking adventures which no one ever witnessed and which therefore remained unsung and unheralded, they go and serve some great emperor engaged in war, so that their achievements and valor might go down to posterity. This struck a resonant chord in his master's heart. In fact, he went into raptures over it, and commenced to rant about all the great honors the future had in store for the Knight of the Rueful Countenance. He cunningly surmised that their first task would be to find a king who had an uncommonly beautiful daughter, for of course he had to marry a princess first of all. The plan excited him to such an extent that for a moment he forgot about the existence of his Dulcinea. The only thing that worried him was his royal lineage; he could not think of any emperor or king whose second cousin he might be. Yet he decided not to trouble too much about that; for were there not two kinds of lineages in the world? And Love always worked wonders: it had since the beginning of time. What would the princess care, if he *were* a water-carrier's son? And if his future father-in-law should object, all he would have to do would be to carry her off by force.

As Don Quixote went on picturing himself in the most romantic rôles in the history of this as yet unknown kingdom, Sancho began to think it was time for him to be considered as well, when it came to bestowals of honor. Once he had been beadle of a brotherhood, and he had looked so well in a beadle's gown, he said, that he was afraid his wife would burst with pride when she saw him in a duke's robe, with gold and lace and precious stones. Don Quixote thought so, too, but admonished him that he would have to shave his beard oftener, as it was most unkempt. Sancho replied that would be an easy matter, for he would have a barber of his own, as well as an equerry; he knew that all men of fame kept such a man, for once in Madrid he had seen a gentleman followed by a man on horseback as if he had been his tail. He inquired why the gentleman was being followed in that manner and learned it was his equerry. Don Quixote thought Sancho's idea to have a barber was an excellent one, and Sancho urged his master to make haste and find him his island, that he might roll in his glory as a count or a duke.

CHAPTER XXII

OF THE FREEDOM DON QUIXOTE CONFERRED ON SEVERAL UNFORTUNATES WHO AGAINST THEIR WILL WERE BEING CARRIED WHERE THEY HAD NO WISH TO GO

HARDLY had they finished their conversation, when a gang of convicts came along on the road, guarded by two men on horseback and two on foot.

"Galley-slaves," remarked Sancho Panza laconically.

"If they are going against their own free will, it is a case for the exercise of my office," answered Don Quixote.

He approached their custodians and asked to know what crimes these men had committed against his majesty the King. They answered it was not his business.

"Nevertheless, I should like to know," insisted Don Quixote, and he used such choice and magic language that one of the guards was induced to give him permission to ask each one of the men about his crime and sentence.

Don Quixote had questioned every one but the twelfth, and when he came to him he found that he was chained in a way different from the rest. This prisoner was a man of thirty, and crossed-eyed. His body was weighted down by very large irons and especially heavy chains, his hands were padlocked and so secured he could not raise them. Don Quixote asked why he was thus overburdened, and got the reply that he had committed more crimes than all the rest together. The guard then told the knight that the man had written a story of his unfinished life, and that he was no other than the famous Gines de Pasamonte. The culprit strongly objected to hearing his identity mentioned, and there ensued a furious battle of words between him and the guard. The latter lost his temper and was about to strike the slave a blow, when Don Quixote interfered, and pleaded for more kindly treatment. It seemed only fair to him that they, with their hands tied, might be permitted a free tongue. He grew fiery in his defense of them, reminded the guard that there was a God in heaven who would punish all sinners. He ended by requesting their immediate release.

[69]

This demand seemed worse than absurd to the guard, who wished him godspeed on his journey, advised him to put the basin straight on his head, and told him not to go looking for trouble. This was too much for our knight. He set upon his jesting adversary with such speed and suddenness that the musket fell out of the guard's hand. And the other guards were so taken aback at what was going on, and there was such confusion, that they did not notice Sancho untying the arch-criminal Gines. They suddenly saw him free, and with him the rest of the slaves, who had broken the chain; whereupon the guards fled in all directions as fast as their legs could carry them.

When the fray was over, Don Quixote asked the galley-slaves to gather around him, and to show him reverence for the deed he had done. He further demanded that they, armed with their chains, proceed in a body, to El Toboso to pay their respects to the fair Dulcinea. Gines attempted to explain the necessity of each one hiding himself, separately, in order to escape the pursuers, and offered to send up prayers for her instead; but Don Quixote would not listen to any argument. At last Gines decided he was quite mad, and when Don Quixote started to abuse him, he lost his temper, and they all attacked the knight with a rain of stones, until Rocinante and he both fell to the ground. There they belabored him savagely. Sancho had taken refuge behind his donkey, but the convicts found him, stripped him of his jacket, and left him shivering in the cold.

While Don Quixote lay there, fearing the vengeance of the law and the Holy Brotherhood for what he had done, he was also reviewing in rage the ingratitude of mankind and the perversity of the iron age.

CHAPTER XXIII

Of What Befell Don Quixote in the Sierra Morena, Which Is One of the Rarest Adventures Related in This Veracious History

SANCHO at last convinced his master that they had best hide in the Sierra Morena mountains for a few days, in case a search should be made for them; and Don Quixote was pleased to find that the provisions carried by Sancho's ass had not disappeared. When night fell they took refuge under some cork-trees between two rocks. Fate would have it that to this very place should come that night the convict Gines. While Sancho was slumbering peacefully, Gines stole his ass; and by daybreak the thief was already far away. Don Quixote, awakened by sorrowful wailing, in order to console his squire, promised him three of his ass-colts at home in exchange. Then Sancho's tears stopped. But he now had to travel on foot behind his master, and he tried to keep up his humor by munching the provisions it had become his lot to carry.

Suddenly he observed that his master had halted, and was poking with his lance into some object lying on the road. He quickly ran up to him and found an old saddle-pad with a torn knapsack tied to it. Sancho opened it covetously and came upon four shirts of excellent material,

[71]

articles of linen, nearly a hundred gold crowns in a handkerchief, and a richly bound little memorandum book.
The little volume was all that Don Quixote kept for himself. Brimful of curiosity, he read it through and learned
that it contained the bemoanings of a rejected lover.

Meantime Sancho Panza's great discovery of the gold
coins had entirely banished from his memory all the suffering and pain and humiliation he had had to go through
since he had became a squire. But Don Quixote was anxious to find out something about the owner of the knapsack, for he was convinced there was some very strange
adventure connected with his disappearance. And as he
was planning what to do, he perceived on the summit of a
great height, a man, half-naked, jumping with remarkable
swiftness and agility from rock to rock.

Don Quixote saw no way of getting there, so he stood
for some time pondering what to do. Then he saw above
him on the mountainside a flock of goats, tended by an
elderly goatherd. Calling to him, the knight asked him to
come down, and the old man descended, amazed at seeing
human beings there. Don Quixote immediately began to
ask about the strange half-naked man he had seen, and the
goatherd told what he knew of him and the mystery of the
knapsack.

The stranger, he said, was a youth of good looks and no
doubt of high birth, who had lost his wits because of the
faithlessness of a friend. His behavior was such that they
had never seen the like of it. In fits of madness he would
approach people, snatch away food offered him out of their
hands, and then run away with the speed of a deer. Then

again he would come begging for food, the tears flowing down his cheeks.

Now, while they were standing there discussing the young man, chance would have it that he came along, and greeted them courteously. Don Quixote returned his greeting with grand gestures, descended from Rocinante's tired back, and advanced to the youth with open arms. He held him in his embrace for some time, as if he had known him forever. Finally the youth tore away and, placing his hands on the shoulders of the Knight of the Rueful Countenance, the youth, who might be called the Ragged One of the Sorry Countenance, looked into his eyes and spoke to him.

CHAPTER XXIV

In Which Is Continued the Adventure of the Sierra Morena

THE Ragged One thanked Don Quixote for being so kind and courteous; and Don Quixote replied that his duty to the world consisted in giving succor to those in despair and need. He implored the youth to tell him the name of the one who had caused his misfortune, that he might revenge him. The Ragged One stared at him strangely and said: "If you will give me to eat, I will tell you my story."

Sancho and the goatherd gave the youth something to appease his hunger; and he ate it ravenously. When he had finished, he motioned to them to follow him, and they came to a spot where green grass grew and all stretched themselves on the ground in silence. Before he began his story, the youth warned them not to interrupt him, for then it would come to an end. Don Quixote promised solemnly for all of them.

The youth told of his love for one Luscinda, and how his best friend, Don Fernando, son of a grandee of Spain, had stolen her love away from him; but suddenly he was interrupted by Don Quixote, and refused to continue. Whereupon Don Quixote nearly lost his senses—for his curiosity was aroused beyond words—and called the Ragged One a villain.

The Ragged One broke into a violent fit when he heard himself called names and picked up a stone which he hurled against the knight errant's breast with such force that it placed him flat on his back. Seeing this, Sancho Panza flew at the madman; but the youth seemed to possess supernatural strength, for he felled Sancho to the ground with one single blow, and then jumped on his chest and buckled his ribs. Having also beaten the old goatherd, he went into the woods again.

When Sancho had seen the last of him, he turned loose his rage on the poor old goatherd, whom he cursed for not having warned them that the youth might be taken with fits. Words led to blows; the two grabbed each other by their beards, and had it not been for Don Quixote, their fray might have had a sad ending. He calmed his squire by absolving the old man of all blame. Then he asked him— for he was still aching with curiosity to learn the end of the story—whether he knew where he might find Cardenio (that being the youth's name). The goatherd answered that if he remained in the neighborhood long enough he could not help meeting him; but as to his mood, he could not answer for that.

CHAPTER XXV

WHICH TREATS OF THE STRANGE THINGS THAT HAPPENED TO THE STOUT KNIGHT OF LA MANCHA IN THE SIERRA MORENA

DON QUIXOTE and Sancho Panza now made their way into unknown regions of the mountains, Sancho trailing behind his master, on foot, silent, and in bad humor. Finally he requested his master's permission to say what was in his heart, and Don Quixote removed the ban under which his squire was suffering. Sancho asked for the knight's blessing and begged leave to return to his wife and home; but his master could not make up his mind until he hit upon a great inspiration, the carrying out of which made necessary his using Sancho as a messenger to his incomparable Dulcinea.

Don Quixote, in short, had decided to go mad, in emulation of other bold knights, such as Roland and Amadis—a decision that extracted from Sancho Panza some muttered words to the effect that any one who could mistake a barber's basin for a gold helmet could not go much madder. And then Don Quixote explained to what sufferings, sorrow, penance, and folly he would subject himself; and quite unintentionally he revealed to Sancho the real identity of his famous Lady Dulcinea, whom Sancho had always thought a princess. Now the good squire learned to his dismay that the famous Dulcinea was no other than Lorenzo Corchuelo's daughter, Aldonza Lorenzo, a lady with manners like a man, and a man's ability to handle a crowbar easily.

When Don Quixote had determined upon his penance in the wilderness, all for the sake of Dulcinea, he thought it would be a good idea to make known to her the sacrifices and sufferings he was about to undergo for her sake. Therefore he granted his squire the requested permission to return to his family, and bade him speed homeward on Rocinante, so that he himself, horseless, might undergo an even greater penance. He sent a letter by Sancho to his fair one, relating to her the pain of his wounded heart; a pain enhanced by self-inflicted absence and to be ended only by death, to satisfy her cruelty.

Sancho's covetousness did not permit his master to forget the three promised ass-colts; so Don Quixote wrote an order to his niece in the notebook of the ill-starred Cardenio.

Before they parted, Don Quixote asked Sancho to stay and see some of the insanities he meant to perform in his absence. He then stripped to the skin and went through some remarkable capers before his squire. This exhibition nearly brought tears to Sancho's eyes, and he besought him to stop. And when he expressed a fear that he would not be able to find his way back, Don Quixote assured him that he would remain in that very spot, or thereabouts, until the squire returned from El Toboso; and he told him also to cut some branches and strew them in his path. Furthermore he said he would be on the lookout for him from the peak of the highest cliff.

When Sancho finally took leave of his master, he felt that he could swear with unprotesting conscience that his beloved master was quite mad.

CHAPTER XXVI

In Which Are Continued the Refinements Wherewith Don Quixote Played the Part of a Lover in the Sierra Morena

SOON after Sancho had gone, Don Quixote came to the conclusion that the exercises he was putting himself through were much too hard and troublesome. So he decided to change them, and instead of imitating Roland and his fury, he turned to the more melancholy Amadis, whose madness was of a much milder form and needed a less strenuous outlet. But to imitate Amadis, he had to have a rosary, and he had none. For a moment he was in a quandary; but a miracle gave him the inspiration to use the tail of his shirt—which was too long anyhow—and tearing off a long piece, on which he made eleven knots, he repeated quantities of credos and ave-marias on it, there in the wilderness. His love would at times drive him to write verses to his cruel and beloved one on the bark of

[77]

the trees, all the while he would make moaning sounds of lovesickness. Again he would go about sighing, singing, calling to the nymphs and fauns and satyrs, and, of course, looking for herbs to nourish himself with.

But while Don Quixote exiled himself in the wilds, his servant Sancho Panza was making for El Toboso. On the second day he found himself at the inn at which the incident of his blanket journey had taken place. The smell of food reminded him that it was dinner time; yet he hesitated about entering. As he was standing there, along came two men; and one of them was heard to say: "Is not that Sancho Panza?" "So it is," said the other one; and it turned out to be the curate and the barber of Don Quixote's own village.

At once they approached him. They asked him about his master, but it was not until they had threatened to believe that he had robbed and murdered Don Quixote—for was he not mounted on Rocinante?—that he divulged the secret of his master's hiding-place. He told them of everything; even about his master's strange and unbounded love for the daughter of Lorenzo Corchuelo and the letter he had written to her. When the curate asked to see it, Sancho could not find it; and then he suddenly remembered that Don Quixote had given him neither the letter nor the order for the ass-colts. He turned pale and green, and beat his chest frantically, but it produced no miracle. The curate and the barber told him that the only thing to do was to find Don Quixote and get him to write them anew; and the thought of losing the ass-colts made Sancho only too anxious to return.

HIS EPISTLE OF LOVE

When the squire had been comforted somewhat, he tried to recite Don Quixote's epistle of love; and his recital amused the two friends to such a degree that he had to repeat it thrice, each time adding new absurdities. Finally they invited him to come into the inn and eat, while they talked over the journey to their friend's wilderness paradise of penitence. Sancho was quick to refuse; but he gave no reason for so doing. He said he preferred to eat outside and asked that they bring him the food, and also some barley for Rocinante.

While the barber was serving Sancho and Rocinante, the curate was developing a plan of strategy which was unanimously adopted by all concerned. It was arranged that the curate should invade the region of knightly penitence, dressed as an innocent-looking maiden with a masked countenance; while his friend the barber should appear on the scene behaving like a squire. The bogus maiden should be in great distress and ask for protection, when Don Quixote, valiant knight that he was, would be sure to give it. She would then beg him to shield her on her journey, and, as a favor, to ask her no questions regarding her identity, until she was safely at home. Once they had him there, they would try to find a cure for his strange madness.

CHAPTER XXVII

Of How the Curate and the Barber Proceeded with Their Scheme; Together with Matters Worthy of Record in This Great History

THE curate proceeded to borrow the needed dress from the landlady, whose curiosity he satisfied by explaining Don Quixote's madness and their mission in the mountains. The landlady recognized Don Quixote by the description the curate gave, and willingly furnished the clothes, and an ox-tail out of which the barber made himself a beard. As security for these things the curate left behind a brand-new cassock.

When the curate's transfiguration was completed, however, his conscience began to trouble him; so it was agreed that he and the barber were to change rôles. The curate shed his female attire, and the barber decided not to don it until they approached the mountainside. Meanwhile Sancho was instructed as to how to act and what to say, when he saw his master.

The day after they set out, they came to the place where Sancho's branches were strewn. The curate thought it best that they send Sancho ahead to take to his master Lady Dulcinea's reply; this was agreed to, and Sancho left.

While the two conspirators were resting in the shade of some trees they were suddenly startled by hearing a man singing in the distance. It was clearly a voice trained in the art of singing, and the verses he sang were not of rustic origin. Soon they perceived the singer, and it was no other than Cardenio, the Ragged One. Now he was untouched by madness, for he spoke quite sanely, telling them of his woeful misfortune, the memory of which, he said, would sometimes overpower and strangle his senses. The curate and the barber were both eager to know the story of the comely youth's life, and he then told them of the faithlessness of his friend. This time he was not interrupted, and he finished his story, which was one of a great love as much as one of misfortune. He had just reached the end, when from no great distance came the sound of a lamenting voice.

CHAPTER XXVIII

WHICH TREATS OF THE STRANGE AND DELIGHTFUL ADVENTURE
THAT BEFELL THE CURATE AND THE BARBER
IN THE SAME SIERRA

WHEN Cardenio and the curate and the barber looked about they discovered a youth with exquisite, delicate features bathing his feet in the brook below them. His garb was that of a peasant lad; on his head he had a *montera*. Having finished bathing, he took from under the *montera* a cloth with which he dried his feet. In removing the cap there fell from under it a mass of auburn hair, and all were amazed to find that instead of a youth, it was a most lovely maiden. In their astonishment either the curate or the barber uttered a cry; and frightened at the sight of them, the girl took to flight, but soon stumbled and fell.

The curate was the first one to reach her. He spoke some kind words and told her that they were there to help her, to fulfill any wish she might express. And he begged her to cast away any pretence, for he was certain that she was there because of some misery that had befallen her.

At first the maiden seemed bewildered, but after a while she showed that the curate had gained her confidence, and she spoke to him in a beautiful, melancholy voice. She seated herself on a stone, while the three gathered around her, and confided to them with tears in her eyes the reasons for her being there. She told them of a certain grandee of Spain, living in Andalusia, of whom her father, lowly in birth but rich in fortune, was a vassal. This grandee had two sons. She had been betrothed to the younger one of these, Don Fernando, and he had jilted her in favor of a lady of noble birth, whose name was Luscinda.

When Cardenio heard his own lady's name, he bit his lips and tears came to his eyes. Dorothea—for that was the maiden's name—wondered at such interest and such emotion, but she continued her story. She told of how, upon Don Fernando's marriage to lady Luscinda, she had fled in despair from house and home. A herdsman in the heart of the Sierra had given her employment as a servant; but when he had discovered that she was a woman, she was forced to leave. While she was bemoaning her evil fate, and praying to God in the woods, she had cut her feet on the stones; and she was bathing them in the brook when she encountered the present gathering.

"ALL WERE AMAZED TO FIND THAT INSTEAD OF A YOUTH,
IT WAS A MOST LOVELY MAIDEN."

—Page 81

CHAPTER XXIX

WHICH TREATS OF THE DROLL DEVICE AND METHOD ADOPTED
TO EXTRICATE OUR LOVE-STRICKEN KNIGHT
FROM THE SEVERE PENANCE HE HAD
IMPOSED UPON HIMSELF

DOROTHEA had told her story with great simplicity. When she had ended it, the curate arose to console her; but Cardenio was already at her side.

"Are you not the daughter of the rich Clenardo?" he asked of her eagerly.

She gazed at him in wonder, for she had not spoken her father's name. She asked the youth who he might be, and he told her that he was the Cardenio who had been wronged by Don Fernando, the faithless friend and faithless lover; and he swore then and there a holy oath that he should see her married to Don Fernando or the latter would perish by his, Cardenio's, sword. Dorothea was moved to tears by the youth's words and thanked him profusely. The curate then made the suggestion that both of them return with him and the barber to their village where they could make further plans as to what to do to set things aright. And Dorothea and Cardenio accepted this kind offer gratefully.

Sancho was now seen arriving, and the curate told the youth and the maiden the reason for his being there. He explained to them the curious nature of Don Quixote's madness, and Cardenio mentioned to the curate his meeting with the knight.

Sancho had found Don Quixote nearly dead with hunger, crying aloud for his Dulcinea; and when his squire entreated him in her name to return to El Toboso, he refused, declaring that his penitence was not yet complete; that he was not yet worthy of her favor. Sancho was quite worried lest he should lose his island and his titles and all the other honors he had expected, and the curate did his best to calm his fears. The good man then explained to Cardenio and Dorothea how they had planned to take Don Quixote back to his home by persuading him to go there on an adventure in aid of a distressed damsel.

Dorothea at once offered to play the part of the damsel. Having read a good many books of chivalry, herself, she thought she could qualify in asking favors of our knight. She had brought with her a complete woman's dress, with lace and rich embroidery, and when Sancho Panza saw her in her new array, he asked, in astonishment, what great lady she might be. The curate replied that she was the ruler of the great kingdom of Micomicon, and after having been dethroned by an evil giant had come all the way from Guinea to seek the aid of Don Quixote. Immediately Sancho's hope for his titles and possessions was revived, for the thought of his master's fame having spread to such distant parts seemed most encouraging.

While Sancho Panza was entertaining these visions, Dorothea mounted the curate's mule, and the barber decorated himself with the ox-tail for a beard. Sancho was told to lead the way, and the curate explained to him that the success of their mission depended on him. He was warned that he must not give away the identity of the curate and the barber; if he did, the empire would be lost. And then they started out, leaving the curate and Cardenio behind, as that was thought best.

They had gone almost a league when they saw Don Quixote on a rock, clothed, but wearing no armor. Dorothea was helped from her horse. She walked over to Don Quixote and knelt before him; and she told him the errand that had brought her there, saying that she would not rise until he had granted her the boon she was asking. While she was kneeling before him, Sancho Panza was anxiously whispering to Don Quixote bits of information about her and her kingdom, afraid that his master might refuse her; but, demented though he was, rank and riches mattered little to Don Quixote, for he drew his sword, he said, in defense of anything that was righteous, and the meek and down-trodden always found in him a ready and courteous defendant. When he learned from the Princess that a big giant had invaded her kingdom, he at once granted her the promise of his services. Dorothea wanted to kiss his hand as a proof of her gratitude; but Don Quixote would not permit her to do this, being ever a respectful and courteous knight. He commanded his squire to saddle his horse immediately, while he put on his armor, mounted, and was ready for the crusade.

They set out, Sancho on foot, cheerfully grinning to himself at the covetous thought of all the possessions that would be his in a short time. Soon they passed the place where Cardenio and the curate were hiding. The curate had by this time conceived the idea of shearing Cardenio of his beard that Don Quixote would be unable to recognize him; and he had furnished him with his own grey jerkin and a black cloak, so that he himself appeared in breeches and doublet only. Having effected the change, they took a short-cut through the woods and came out on the open road ahead of Don Quixote.

As he approached them, the curate feigned astonishment beyond words at seeing his old friend; and Don Quixote was so surprised that he hardly recognized the curate. He courteously offered Rocinante to him, but the curate remonstrated and finally accepted the long-bearded squire's mule, inviting the squire to sit behind him. This arrangement did not please the mule, however, for he commenced to kick with his hind legs. Luckily the beast did not damage the barber, but the demonstration frightened him so that he turned a somersault in a ditch. In so doing, his beard came off, but he had enough presence of mind to cover his face at the same moment, crying that his teeth were knocked out. When Don Quixote saw the beard on the ground without any sign of flesh or blood, he was struck with amazement, and thought that the barber had been shaved by a miracle.

The curate hastened breathlessly to the barber's side, and began to mumble incomprehensible words, while the barber was groaning on the ground in an uncomfortable position. When the barber finally rose, Don Quixote's eyes nearly fell out of their sockets, for he beheld the barber bearded again. He begged the curate to teach him the charm that could produce such a miracle, and the curate promised he would. Then they proceeded on the journey.

The curate now began to wonder about the road (all this

was pre-arranged) and said that in order to go to the kingdom of Micomicon, they had to take the road to Cartagena, where they would embark on a ship. That, he said, would take them through his own village, and from there it was a journey of nine years to Micomicon. Here the Princess corrected him, saying that it had taken her only two years to make the journey here, in quest of the noble and famous knight who had now sworn to restore her kingdom to her.

Don Quixote at this moment happened to observe the light attire of the curate, and was curious to know the reason for it. Whereupon the curate (having learned of the incident through Sancho) related how he and Master Nicholas, on their way to Seville, had been held up by a gang of liberated galley-slaves. These criminals, it was said, had been set free by a man on horseback, as brave as he was bold, for he had fought off all the guards, single-handed. The curate criticized this man heartlessly, called him a knave and a criminal for having set himself against law and order and his king, and expressed a belief that he could not have been in his right mind. The Holy Brotherhood, he said further, was searching for him now, and he himself was afraid that the man's soul would be lost. He finished his story by calling upon the Lord to pardon this unregenerate being who had taken away the galley-slaves from the punishment that had been meted out to them by justice.

Don Quixote seemed to take the curate's sermon to heart, and bent his head humbly, not daring to admit that he was the culprit, and not knowing that the curate knew it.

CHAPTER XXX

WHEN Sancho heard the harsh sermon of the curate, he, being a good Christian, became afraid that his own soul might be lost too; for was he not an accomplice? So he confessed then and there his own and his master's guilt, much to the shame and anger of Don Quixote. The Princess was quick to sense the danger, and she calmed our hero before his anger had risen to any great height, by reminding him of his promise, and how he had sworn to engage in no conflict of any kind until her kingdom had been saved. He answered her with infinite courtesy and expressed his regrets for having let his anger get the better of him; he would stand by his word. Then he asked her to tell him all that she could about herself and her kingdom. She would willingly do that, she said, and began her story.

But she came very near ending it then and there, for she could not remember the name she had assumed. Luckily the curate—who had invented her long and difficult name—was there to prompt her, and the situation was saved. Having told Don Quixote that her name was Princess Micomicona, she continued her story, relating how she was left an orphan, how a certain giant and lord

[88]

of an island near her kingdom had asked for her hand in marriage and she had refused, how his forces had overrun her country and she had fled to Spain, where it had been predicted by a magician she would find a certain great knight errant by the name of Don Quixote, otherwise called the Knight of the Rueful Countenance, who would be recognized by a gray mole with hairs like bristles under the left shoulder.

Immediately upon hearing this, Don Quixote wanted to strip, but Sancho assured them that he did have just such a mark. Dorothea said she was quite sure he must, for in other respects the description that the magician had given fitted him; and she hastened to relate to him how she had first heard of him on her landing at Osuna. But evidently the pretended Princess had not been as careful a student of geography as Don Quixote, who was quick to ask her: "But how did you land at Osuna, señorita, when it is not a seaport?" Again the curate displayed proof of rare presence of mind, for he broke in: "The Princess meant to say that after having landed at Malaga, the first place where she heard of your worship was Osuna." And Dorothea immediately corroborated the curate's explanation with great self-assurance.

However, she thought it best to end her story here, for fear of complications, and only added how happy she was to have found him so soon. She also pointed out, demurely enough, that it had been predicted if after having cut off the giant's head the knight should ask her to marry him, she would accept. But Don Quixote said he would be true to his Dulcinea; and this made Sancho exclaim with

[89]

dismay that he was out of his head, for Dulcinea could never come up to this fair princess.

Sancho's remark angered his master so intensely that he knocked him to the ground with his spear; and if the Princess had not interfered the unfortunate squire might never again have been able to say his ave-marias or credos or, more to the point, have eaten another square meal. He was quick to cry out that he had meant no ill by what he said, and acting upon the suggestion of the Princess, he kissed his master's hand.

At this moment a man, mounted on an ass, was seen on the road, and Sancho, no doubt feeling instinctively the proximity of his beloved animal, recognized in the man Gines de Pasamonte. Wildly shouting, he set out after the galley-slave, who threw himself off the ass at Sancho's first shout. Sancho, crying with joy, was so glad to have his faithful donkey returned to him that he did not pursue the thief. And Don Quixote himself was so pleased that he entirely forgot about his quarrel with Sancho. He called him to his side, and asked him to repeat everything his Dulcinea had told him, over and over again.

CHAPTER XXXI

Of the Delectable Discussion Between Don Quixote and Sancho Panza, His Squire, Together with Other Incidents

DON QUIXOTE was anxious to know what jewel his fair one had bestowed on Sancho before the leave-taking. Sancho replied that the only jewel Dulcinea had given him was some bread and cheese; whereupon Don Quixote remarked that no doubt she had had no jewels at hand. He expressed wonder at the speedy trip Sancho had made, to which Sancho replied that Rocinante had gone like lightning; and Don Quixote then was sure some friendly enchanter had carried him through the air.

CHAPTERS XXXII–XXXIV

WHICH TREATS OF WHAT BEFELL ALL DON QUIXOTE'S PARTY AT THE INN

THE following day they reached the inn. The landlady at once wanted her ox-tail back, so it was decided that the barber should hereafter appear in his own true character, having supposedly arrived at the inn after the galley-slaves' hold-up.

Don Quixote was tired, and was given a bed in the garret where he had slept once before. While the others were having dinner, the landlady was confidentially telling all who would listen of Don Quixote's absurdities during his previous visit, and also of Sancho Panza's being juggled in the blanket. And while the curate was discussing Don Quixote's madness, the innkeeper confided to him that he himself had a weakness for reading about deeds of the past, particularly stories of chivalry. Often, he said, he would read aloud from these books to his family and servants. He had just read a novel entitled "Ill-Advised Curiosity," which he had found very interesting.

He showed the manuscript of it to the curate, who seemed
to think it might make very good reading and expressed
a desire to copy it.   Whereupon the innkeeper asked him
whether he would not read it aloud to them; and as they
were all eager to hear it, the curate commenced the reading
of the manuscript.

CHAPTER XXXV

WHICH TREATS OF THE HEROIC AND PRODIGIOUS BATTLE
DON QUIXOTE HAD WITH CERTAIN SKINS OF
RED WINE, AND BRINGS THE NOVEL OF THE
"ILL-ADVISED CURIOSITY" TO AN END

THE curate had almost finished the reading of the
novel, (which consumed all of the two chapters
which are omitted here) when Sancho Panza burst into the
room, excitedly shouting that his master was having the
wildest battle he had ever seen, up in the garret.   He
pleaded for reinforcements, and wanted them all to join
in conquering the enemy who, he declared, was no other
than the fierce giant that had invaded the kingdom of
Micomicon.   He said he had left just as his master had
cut the giant's head clean off with his sword, leaving the
beast to bleed like a stuffed pig.

While Sancho was relating his blood-curdling story, a
tremendous noise and loud exclamations poured forth from
the garret, and the innkeeper, suddenly remembering all
the many wine-skins he had hung up there on the previous

night sprang out of his chair and toward the scene of action, followed by the rest.

The worst that the innkeeper might have feared was true; for there, on the garret floor, was a sea of red wine, with hosts of empty skins floating about upon it. In the middle of the sea stood Don Quixote, sword in hand, slashing right and left, dressed in nothing but his shirt. But the strangest thing of all was not his attire, but the fact that he was fast asleep, his eyes shut tightly, dreaming that he had already arrived in the distant realm of the Princess Micomicona and had encountered the giant enemy.

Seeing all his precious wine floating away, the innkeeper became enraged and set upon Don Quixote with his bare fists; but the beating had no effect on the knight except, perhaps, that it made him sleep more soundly. It was not until the barber had drenched him in cold water that he came to his senses.

The Princess Micomicona, who had been listening to the saving of her kingdom outside the door, became eager, after she had heard the tempest subside, to enter and see the conquered giant; but she retired hastily and with a slight exclamation of horrified modesty on seeing the abbreviated length of her defender's night-shirt, the tail of which had been sacrificed to his prayers in the wilderness.

The landlord, cursing his luck, swore that this time the knight errant and his squire should not escape without paying. But Don Quixote, whose hand the curate was holding in an endeavor to calm him, merely fell on his knees before the curate, exclaiming: "Exalted and beautiful Princess! Your Highness' may now live in peace; for I have slain the giant!" He imagined that he was at the feet of Micomicona. Soon after having spoken thus, he showed signs of great weariness, and the curate, the barber and Cardenio carried him to his bed, where he fell asleep.

Next they had to console Sancho, who was grief-stricken because he had been unable to find the giant's head. He swore he had seen it falling when his master cut it off, and imagined that if it could not be produced there would be no reward for either him or his master; but Dorothea, in her rôle of Princess, calmed and comforted him.

All this time the innkeeper's wife was crying about the ox-tail, which, she said, had lost its usefulness after having served as beard, and the innkeeper was demanding that he be paid for the spilt wine and other losses. The curate assured them that he himself would see to it that they were reimbursed for everything; and when the excitement in the inn had simmered down, and everybody had gathered again in the room where they had heard the curate read from "Ill-Advised Curiosity," he was asked to resume the reading. This he did; and they all thought it a very entertaining story and listened intensely to what the curate was reading.

MORE CURIOUS INCIDENTS AT THE INN

CHAPTER XXXVI

WHICH TREATS OF MORE CURIOUS INCIDENTS THAT OCCURRED
AT THE INN

AT this moment there was a sound of people approaching on horseback, and the innkeeper rushed to the gate to receive the guests. There were four men, with lances and bucklers, and black veils for their faces; a woman, dressed in white and also veiled, and two attendants on foot. One of the four, a gentleman of distinction, helped the lady to dismount, and they entered the inn.

As they came into the room where the curate had just finished reading the novel of "Ill-Advised Curiosity," Dorothea covered her face, and Cardenio left and went to the garret. As the gentleman seated the lady in a chair, she heaved a deep sigh. Her arms fell limply by her side. The curate was curious to know who these people were, so he asked one of the servants that accompanied them. But none of them knew, for they had met the travelers on the road, they said, and had been offered employment at good pay. They added that they feared the lady was being taken somewhere against her will, as she had done nothing but sigh all through the journey, and had exchanged no words whatever with her escort.

Dorothea, hearing the lady sigh repeatedly, felt compassion for her, and asked her whether there was anything that she could do for her. But although she asked her the question several times, she got no reply.

THE STORY OF DON QUIXOTE

When the gentleman with the distinguished bearing observed that Dorothea was interested in this lady, he told her it was useless to bother with her, for her answers were all lies and anything done for her would be rewarded with ingratitude. This remark was speedily answered by the lady, who retorted. "I have never told a lie. On the contrary, it is because I am truthful and cannot lie that I am now in this miserable condition. And you are the lying one!"

Cardenio was in the adjoining room, just returning from the garret, and when he heard these words he exclaimed: "Good God! What is this I hear! It is her voice!"

The lady heard the exclamation, and seeing no one, she became agitated and rose, but was held back by the gentleman. Her veil suddenly fell off, and every one could see her face, which was one of alabaster-like whiteness and great beauty. And while the gentleman was struggling to keep her from leaving the room, his own veil became unfastened and Dorothea saw that he was no other than her own lover, Don Fernando. The moment she recognized him she fainted, and the barber caught her, or she would have fallen to the floor. The curate was quick to throw some water on her face, and she soon came to. As soon as Cardenio heard the commotion, he rushed in from the other room, imagining that the worst had happened to his Luscinda—for it was no other than she—and it was a curious thing to see the four suddenly finding themselves face to face.

Luscinda was the first one to speak, and she implored Don Fernando to take her life, so that her beloved Cardenio might believe that she had been true and loyal and faithful to him until the very last.

When Dorothea heard Luscinda speak thus, she fell on her knees before Don Fernando and implored him to reconsider everything that he had done that was base and wrong and sinful. She pleaded with tears in her eyes, begging him to give up Luscinda to her faithful Cardenio, told him how much she still loved him in spite of his wrongdoing, and said she would forgive him everything if he would only let his real and better nature come into its own. And her tears and sincerity moved Don Fernando so that he himself wept, and he promised to abide by the ending which Fate itself seemed to have provided for by bringing them all together in this strange way.

He told Luscinda that when he had found the paper in which she declared she could never be the wife of any other man than Cardenio, he was tempted to kill her, but was prevented by chance. He had left the house in a rage, and had not returned home till the following day, when he found that she had disappeared. Some months later he learned that she had taken refuge in a convent. He gathered the companions they had seen at the inn, and with their help he carried her from the convent. Now he repented of what he had done, prayed he might be permitted forever to live with his Dorothea, and asked them all for forgiveness. Then he gave his blessing to the overjoyed Cardenio and Luscinda, who were both so affected at their reunion that they shed tears. Even Sancho was weeping, although for quite another reason. He was grieved to find his Princess Micomicona suddenly lose her royal identity and turn out to be a mere lady.

CHAPTER XXXVII

IN WHICH IS CONTINUED THE STORY OF THE FAMOUS
PRINCESS MICOMICONA, WITH OTHER DROLL
ADVENTURES

SANCHO thought it his solemn duty to go to his master
at once and inform him of the catastrophe. Dejected, he approached Don Quixote, who had just awakened, and said: "Sir Rueful Countenance, your Worship
may as well sleep on, without troubling yourself about
killing or restoring her kingdom to the Princess; for that
is all over and settled now."

Don Quixote agreed with his squire enthusiastically,
and then told him of the tremendous battle he had just
had with the giant, dwelling particularly upon the great
amount of blood that flowed when the giant's head was
cut off.

"Red wine, your Worship means," said Sancho, "and no
less than twenty-four gallons, all of which has to be paid
for! The Princess your Worship will find turned into a
private lady named Dorothea; and there is much more that
will astonish your Worship."

Whereupon there ensued a rich and varied conversation between master and servant. When Don Quixote
heard his squire confound blood with wine, he called him
a fool. And when he heard that his Princess had turned
into a simple Dorothea, the fears he had entertained dur-

ing his past visit to the inn, began to return, and he decided that the place was enchanted. But of that his squire could not be convinced, for the episode of the blanketing still remained a most vivid reality to him. Had it not been for that, he repeated, he could have believed it readily.

Meanwhile the curate had been telling Don Fernando and the others of Don Quixote's strange malady; he described how they had succeeded in taking him away from the wilderness and his self-inflicted penance, and told them all the strange adventures he had heard Sancho relate. They were greatly amused and thought it the most remarkable craze they had ever heard of. Don Fernando was eager that Dorothea should continue playing her part, and they all decided to come along on the journey to the village in La Mancha.

At this moment Don Quixote entered in his regalia, the barber's basin on his head, spear in hand, and with the buckler on his arm. Don Fernando was struck with astonishment and laughter at the sight of the mixed armament and the peculiar long yellow face of the knight. After a silence, Don Quixote turned to Dorothea and repeated his vow to regain her kingdom for her. He said he approved heartily of the magic interference of the spirit of the king, her father, who had devised this new state of hers, that of a private maiden, in which guise she would no doubt be more secure from evil influence on her journey to her home.

His ignorant squire broke in when his master related of his battle in the garret, and inferred irreverently and rather loudly that he had attacked wine-skins instead of giants, but Don Fernando quickly made him be quiet. Dorothea rose and thanked our rueful knight at the end of his speech for the renewed offer of his sword.

Having listened to her lovely voice, Don Quixote turned angrily to his squire and reprimanded him for being a disbeliever, saying that he could now judge for himself what a fool he had made of himself. Sancho replied that he hoped he had made a mistake about the Princess not being a princess, but that as to the wine-skins, there could be no doubt, for the punctured skins he had seen himself at the head of Don Quixote's bed—and had not the garret floor been turned into a lake of wine? Whereupon his master swore, at his stupidity, until Don Fernando interrupted and proposed that they spend the evening in pleasant conversation at the inn instead of continuing their journey that night.

While that was being agreed upon, two travelers, a man and a woman, dressed in Moorish fashion, came to the inn. They asked for rooms overnight, but were told there were none to be had. Dorothea felt sorry for the strange lady—whose face was covered with a veil—and told her that she and Luscinda would gladly share their room with her. The lady rose from her chair, bowed her head and made a sign with her hands as if to thank them; and they concluded, because of her silence, that she could not speak their language. At this moment her companion returned to her and, seeing her surrounded by the guests at the inn, he confirmed what they had thought, for he made the remark that it was useless to address any questions to her as she could speak no other tongue than her own. They explained that they had asked no questions, but had only offered her quarters for the night. When the stranger learned this, it seemed to please him very much, and he thanked them profusely.

As they were all curious to know who the lady was, they asked the stranger whether or not she was a Christian. He replied that while she was not, she wished to become one; and he informed them that she was a lady of high rank from Algiers. This excited a desire to see her face as well as to know whom she might be, and Dorothea could not resist the temptation of asking her to remove her veil. When her companion had told her Dorothea's desire, and the Moorish lady had removed her veil, they all stood in awe, for they beheld a face that seemed to them lovelier than any they had ever beheld before. Don Fernando asked her name, and the stranger replied it was Lela Zoraida; but when the fair lady heard him speak this name, she exclaimed emphatically that she was called Maria and not Zoraida. Luscinda embraced her in a loving way and said they would call her by that name.

The supper was now ready and all placed themselves at a long table, at the head of which Don Quixote was asked to seat himself. At his request Dorothea—as the Princess Micomicona in disguise—sat on his right. All were merry and content and many pleasantries were passed. But suddenly Don Quixote stopped eating, rose, and with inspiration in his eyes and voice, began a long discourse on knight-errantry, reviewing the great good it had done for mankind. The language he used was so perfect, his manners so free and easy, and his delivery possessed of such charm, that his listeners could hardly make themselves believe they were in the presence of one who was demented.

CHAPTER XXXVIII

WHICH TREATS OF THE CURIOUS DISCOURSE DON QUIXOTE DELIVERED ON ARMS AND LETTERS

DON QUIXOTE told them in his discourse of that age in which victory in battle depended on personal courage and good swordsmanship, before the use of such devilish contrivances as lead and powder. These things almost made him despair of success for his revival of chivalry in this age, he said; for while guns and artillery could instill no fear in his breast, they did make him feel uneasy, as one never knew when a bullet, intended for some one else, might cut off one's life. The very worst of such a death, he maintained, was that the bullet might have been discharged by a fleeing coward. And so he pledged himself again, in spite of all the things he had to struggle against, not to give up what he had undertaken to do: to set the world aright in accordance with the principles of knight-errantry.

All the while that Don Quixote was discoursing, Sancho was much concerned because he neglected his food. He broke in whenever he had an opportunity, and admonished his master that he would have much time for talking after he had eaten.

HIS DISCOURSE ON ARMS AND LETTERS

When they had finished their supper, the landlord informed them that he had re-arranged their quarters in order to accommodate all, and that the three women might sleep in the garret, as Don Quixote gallantly had given up his quarters to them. Their interest then turned again to the stranger. Don Fernando asked him some questions about his life, and he replied that while his life-story would be interesting, it might not afford them much enjoyment. However, he said, he would tell it if they so wished. The curate begged that he do so; and, seeing the interest of all, the stranger mentioned by way of introduction that while his was a true story, many a story of fiction would seem tame and less strange in comparison. And while all of the company expectantly turned their eyes toward the strange traveler in Moorish garb, he began the following tale.

CHAPTERS XXXIX—XLI

WHEREIN THE CAPTIVE RELATES HIS LIFE AND ADVENTURES

AS a young man, the stranger said, he had left Spain, bent on adventure and on becoming a soldier. He had served with the Duke of Alva in Flanders, and in the wars of the Christians against the Turks, the Moors, and the Arabs. In one of these wars he was taken prisoner by King El Uchali of Algiers; he had previously advanced to the rank of captain. He was held a captive for a long time, first at Constantinople, then at Tunis, then at Algiers. At Constantinople he encountered a good many other Christian prisoners. Particularly he remembered one Don Pedro de Augilar, a brave soldier and a native of Andalusia, who, he said, had written some very excellent poetry. He especially spoke of two sonnets which he had liked so well that he had learned them by heart. One day Don Pedro succeeded in making his escape, but what had become of him he had never heard.

As soon as the captive had spoken Don Pedro's name, the ladies and Don Fernando exchanged glances and smiled, and Don Fernando could not refrain from informing the narrator that Don Pedro was his brother. Furthermore, he said, he was safe in Andalusia, where he was happily married, in the best of health, and had three robust children. Then he touched on his brother's gift for composing poetry, and said that the very two sonnets the captive had mentioned, he himself knew by heart. Whereupon every one asked him to recite them, and so he did with fine feeling and intelligence. Then the captive resumed his story.

At Algiers, he said, there lived, overlooking the prison, a great alcaide named Hadji Morato, a very rich man, who had but one child, a daughter of great beauty. She had learned the Christian prayer from a slave of her father's, when she was a child; the things that this Christian woman had taught her had made her long to know more about the religion and to become a Christian herself. This beautiful Algerian maiden had seen the captive from her window, and she liked him, and one day she managed to get a message to him, begging him to escape and to take her with him. From time to time she would throw to him gold coins wrapped in cloth, and these he would hide until finally he had enough to buy not only himself but some other prisoners free from their slavery.

However, in order to effect the escape of the maiden, the captive was obliged to take into his confidence an old Algerian renegade who turned out to be a believer in Christ. With this man the captive sent messages to Zoraida. Now, this renegade was a sly fellow, and he bought a small vessel with which he began to ply to and fro between the city and some islands nearby, bringing back fruit each time, in order to alleviate all suspicions of his having acquired the vessel for any other purpose than trading. Finally it was decided the time had come for the escape, and the captive had himself ransomed.

That night the renegade had the ship anchored opposite the prison and Zoraida's garden, and, with the help of a number of Christians whom they had gathered as rowers, and who were eager to return to Spain, they secured the ship and put the Moorish crew in irons and chains.

Zoraida witnessed the proceedings from her window, and when she saw her captive and the renegade return in the skiff of the vessel, she hastened below into the garden. She was bedecked with a fortune in pearls and precious stones. She asked the renegade to follow her into the house, and when they returned, they brought with them a chest laden with gold. Just then her father was awakened and he began to shout in Arabic as loudly as he could that he was being robbed by Christians. Had it not been for the quick action of the renegade all might have been lost. He bound and gagged the father and carried him downstairs, where Zoraida had fainted in the captive's arms. Then they hastened back to the ship and set sail for Majorca.

It was some time before the old alcaide realized that his daughter had gone with the captive of her own free will, and when he learned it, he flung himself into the sea, but was rescued by one of the rowers. When he found himself then on board the ship, he began to curse his daughter, calling her a Christian dog and other vile names. Finally it was deemed best to set him and the other Moors ashore; and when the old man saw the ship sail away with his daughter, he began to sob and cry aloud in the most heart-rending way, threatening to kill himself if she did not return to him. The last words that she heard were, "I forgive you all!" and they made her weep so bitterly that it seemed as if her tears would never cease flowing.

They were then less than a day's voyage from the coast of Spain. As they were breezing along with all sails set, over a moonlit sea, they saw a large ship appear in the distance. It turned out to be a French corsair from Rochelle out for plunder, for when it came closer it suddenly fired two guns that took terrible effect and wrecked their vessel. As the ship began to sink, they begged to be taken aboard the corsair, to which the captain was not averse. Once aboard they were told that if they had been courteous enough to reply to the question shouted from the corsair as to what port they were bound for, their own vessel would still have been intact. The covetous crew stripped them of all their valuable belongings, the pearls and jewels, money and adornments of Zoraida. The chest of gold, however, the renegade stealthily lowered into the sea without any one seeing it.

The next day when the Spanish coast was sighted the captain put them all in a skiff, gave them some bread and water for their voyage, and set out to sea. Before letting them depart, moved by some strange impulse, he gave Zoraida forty crowns; and he had not robbed her of her beautiful gown. They steered their skiff towards the shore, where they landed soon after midnight. Immediately they left the shore, eager to know where they were. They climbed the mountain—for the shore was a rocky one —and there they rested until dawn, then went on into the country.

Soon they met a young shepherd; but when he saw their strange garbs, he ran away from them like a frightened lamb, crying that the Moors had invaded the country. And not so long after that they encountered fifty mounted men of the coast guard, but as soon as these saw their Moorish costumes and had heard the captive's explanation, they realized that the boy's vivid imagination had disturbed them needlessly. And when one of the Christian captives recognized in one of the guards an uncle of his, these men could not do enough for the returned slaves. They gave them their horses, some of them went to rescue the skiff for them, and when they arrived at the nearby city they were welcomed by all the inhabitants.

At once they went to the church to return thanks to the Lord for their marvelous escape, and Zoraida was impressed beyond expression with the hosts of praying worshippers. She, the renegade, and the captive stayed at the house of the returned Christian, and the rest were quartered throughout the town. After six days the renegade departed for Granada to restore himself to the Church through the means of the Holy Inquisition. One by one the other captives left for their own homes, and finally only Zoraida and he himself remained. He then decided to go in search of his father, whom he had not seen for so many years, and he did not know whether he was alive or not. His journey had brought him to this inn, and it was here that his story came to an end.

CHAPTER XLII

WHICH TREATS OF WHAT FURTHER TOOK PLACE IN THE INN, AND OF SEVERAL OTHER THINGS WORTH KNOWING

THE captive having finished his strange and interesting story, Don Fernando rose and thanked him, and all were eager for an opportunity to show him their goodwill. Don Fernando begged the stranger to allow him to provide for his comfort, and offered to take him to his brother, the Marquis, who, he said, would be most eager to act as Zoraida's godfather at her baptism. But the stranger declined graciously all the offers that were made.

Night was now setting in, and each one was contemplating going to his room, when suddenly a coach with attend-

ants on horseback arrived at the inn. The landlady told
the one demanding lodging that there was none to be
had at any price. Whereupon the man replied that
room *must* be found for his lordship, the Judge, his master.
As soon as the landlady learned she was dealing with the
law, she nearly fainted from exertion to please, and offered
to give up their own room and bed to his lordship. By
this time the Judge, attired in a long robe with ruffled
sleeves, had stepped out of the coach, accompanied by a
beautiful girl of about sixteen years of age. There were
exclamations from all when they saw the young lady, for
she possessed beauty and grace that were really rare.

The first one to greet the strangers was no other than
Don Quixote, who, with a grave air and the most exalted
and flowery language, bade them welcome to the castle.
He finished his speech by saying: "Enter, your worship,
into this paradise, for here you will find stars and suns to
accompany the heaven your Worship brings with you.
Here you will find arms in their supreme excellence, and
beauty in its highest perfection."

The Judge looked for a moment as if he hesitated about
entering with his daughter after such an unusual reception;
he seemed to wonder whether he was at an inn or an asy-
lum. He scrutinized Don Quixote's curious armor, then
turned his attention to the rest of the company, which evidently made him feel more at ease.

It was arranged that the young lady should sleep with
the other ladies; which pleased her greatly, for it was evident that she was very much taken with them and their
beauty. The Judge was as much pleased with the pres-

ence of so many people of quality as he was puzzled by
Don Quixote and his strange appearance and behavior.

The moment the former captive and captain had laid
eyes on the Judge, he was stirred by the conviction that here
was his own younger brother. He asked the Judge's name
of one of the servants, and was told he was called the Li-
centiate Juan Perez de Viedma, lately appointed Judge of
the Supreme Court of Mexico, to which country he was
now on his way. The Captain inquired whether the servant knew from which part of Spain the Judge came, and
got the reply that he had heard it rumored he was a native
of a little village in the mountains of Leon. The Captain was then certain it was his brother, and he hastened to
tell the curate, Don Fernando, and Cardenio, saying he
felt diffident about making himself known too abruptly
for fear his brother might refuse to acknowledge him because of his poverty and ill-fortune.

The curate understood the Captain's way of thinking,
and asked that he trust him to manage it in a discreet way.
So when the Judge invited them all to keep him company
while he supped, the curate told the story of the captive
at the table. In telling it he pretended to have been a
captive in the hands of the Turks and the Algerians and a
comrade-in-arms of the Captain. When he had finished
the story, tears rolled down the Judge's cheeks, and he
begged the curate to help him to find his beloved brother,
for whom their aged father was ever praying, ever asking,
hoping that he might see him once more before he closed
his eyes in death. It was then that the Captain, himself
in tears, stepped forward and, the Judge having recog-

nized him, embraced his brother. Then the Judge embraced Zoraida, offering her all the worldly goods he possessed. His daughter, the lovely young girl, now joined them, and all the others were moved to tears by the brothers' happiness in finding each other after so many years of separation.

Don Quixote stood gazing in silence at what passed before his eyes, ascribing the two brothers' luck to magic.

When the first emotion of the unexpected meeting had subsided, the Judge asked his brother and Zoraida to return with him to Seville, from where he would send a messenger to the father, telling him of the good news and begging him to come to the joint marriage and baptismal ceremony. As the Judge was obliged to leave for New Spain within a month, it was agreed that a speedy return to Seville was necessary.

It was now early morning, though still dark, and all were tired, so it was decided that every one should go to bed. But Don Quixote, sacrificing himself in spite of his fatigue, appointed himself to keep guard for the remainder of the night, fearing attack of some evil giant or beast upon all the beauty that was slumbering within. They, who were aware of his peculiar weakness, returned thanks in their most gracious manner; and when they were alone with the Judge they hastened to explain the knight's mental state. The Judge was much amused by the accounts of his adventures and his attempts to revive knight errantry in Spain.

There was only one unhappy being in the inn that night: that was Sancho Panza. He was not at all pleased with his master's staying up at such a late hour. But there seemed nothing he could do about it, so he retired and spread himself comfortably on the trappings of his donkey.

While Don Quixote was guarding the castle, and dawn was approaching, Dorothea, who had lain awake, was suddenly stirred by the sound of a man's voice, a voice so beautiful that it seemed to her there could be none sweeter in the world. Then Cardenio was awakened by it, and he felt that he ought to share the joy of hearing it with the ladies, so he went to the garret to call their attention to it. When he knocked on the door and told them, Dorothea called out that they were already listening. The only one not awake at that time was Doña Clara, the Judge's fair daughter.

CHAPTER XLIII

WHEREIN IS RELATED THE PLEASANT STORY OF THE MULETEER,
TOGETHER WITH OTHER STRANGE THINGS
THAT CAME TO PASS IN THE INN

DOROTHEA and the other ladies were in a quandary as to whether to awake Doña Clara or not. Finally they decided that she would be sorry if she had to learn what she had missed and would regret that they had not a-wakened her; so they shook her until she opened her eyes and then asked her to sit up in bed and listen. But scarcely had she heard one note, before she began to sob hysterically. She threw her arms around Dorothea and cried: "Why, oh, why did you wake me, dear lady?" The greatest kindness fortune could do me now would be to close my eyes and ears so that I could neither see nor hear that unhappy musician!"

Dorothea was at a loss to know what had happened to the child. All the while she was trying to soothe her, the tears were streaming down the young girl's face, and she was trembling like a leaf. Finally she quieted her feelings sufficiently to be able to confide to Dorothea in a whispering voice the story of her romance with the singer, who, she said, was not a muleteer as his garb would indicate, but the only son and heir of a rich noble of Aragon. This gentleman's house in Madrid was situated directly opposite her father's, and having once seen Doña Clara the youth proceeded to declare his love for her. She, being motherless and having no one to whom she could confide her love secrets, had to leave Madrid with her father, when he was given his appointment to New Spain, without an opportunity to see her lover. But as soon as the youth, who was not much older than herself, learned of their departure, he dressed himself up as a muleteer and set out on foot to pursue her. At every inn where they had stopped overnight she had found him awaiting their departure in the morning, and she was always in dread, she said, lest her father learn of their love for each other.

With her arms tight around Dorothea, she confessed to her how great her love was for the youth, saying that she could never live without him. Dorothea kissed the girl, and promised her that with God's help all would end well, telling her to put her trust in Him; and before another day had passed she hoped to have good news for Doña Clara.

Dorothea's assurances calmed and put new faith in the young girl's heart; and soon they all were fast asleep again.

Now, all this time the one-eyed Asturian maid, and the landlady's daughter, both bent on deviltry, were keeping their eyes open. It was impossible for them to forget Don Quixote, and they were determined to play a joke on him before the night was over. They posted themselves in the hayloft, where there was a hole in the wall; and when Don Quixote passed on Rocinante, he heard some one calling: "Pst! Come here, señor!"

As Don Quixote turned to see who it might be, he discovered the hole in the wall and it seemed very much like a marvelously decorated window, in keeping with the beautiful castle he had made out of the inn. He beheld at this window the two maidens, and immediately they became to him the daughter of the lord of the castle and her attendant. Wistfully he gazed at them, certain, however, that they had designed to destroy his faithful and stubborn allegiance to Dulcinea, to whom he had just been sending up prayers and salutations under the influence of the moon. Then he spoke to them, regretting that they should let themselves be so overcome by love for him that they could no longer master their feelings. He told them of that great and only mistress of his soul, the incomparable one of El Toboso of La Mancha, to whom he had sworn eternal love and undying admiration. And at last he admonished the innkeeper's daughter to retire to her beauteous apartment, lest he should be forced to prove himself ungrateful. If, he said, she would demand any other thing than love, he would willingly grant her the favor, even unto a lock of Medusa's hair.

The wench immediately realized that her opportunity had come, so she quickly said that she cared for no lock of Medusa's or any other, but would be satisfied to feel the touch of his hand.

Before sanctioning this demand, Don Quixote asserted his virtuousness again by stipulating that she must not kiss it, only touch it. He understood, of course, that any woman would be likely to ask such a favor of him at any time (for who would not be proud to have touched the sinewy hand of so remarkable and famous a knight errant as himself?) but he insisted on being discreet at all times. So he climbed up and stood on the saddle of his hack, reaching his lean arm through the hole in the wall.

By this time the Asturian maid had procured from the stable the halter of Sancho's donkey, on which her young mistress quickly made a running knot and passed it over Don Quixote's wrist. As soon as she had proceeded thus far in her deviltry, she jumped down from the hole and made fast the other end of the halter to the bolt of the door. Then she and her maid swiftly made off, bursting with laughter, leaving the knight to complain of the roughness of her touch.

But after a while Don Quixote began to realize that no one was there to listen to his complaints, and also that he was not standing too securely on his Rocinante's back; for should Rocinante move without being urged—a most unusual event—he would be left to hang in the air by one arm. It suddenly came to him that he was a victim of enchantment, and he called on all the saints, and Dulcinea, and Sancho Panza, on all kind magicians and sages, and every one else he could think of, to come to his aid.

But no one came, until the morning brought four travelers on horseback. They found the gate still shut, so they called to Don Quixote, who by this time was almost exhausted. But although wearied, his spirit had not left him. He reprimanded the strangers for their insolence; asked whether they were so stupid they failed to realize that as yet the castle gates were not open, that all were asleep. He commanded them to withdraw to a distance and to approach the fortress after daylight; then he could better tell whether they should be permitted to enter or not.

One of the travelers mistook Don Quixote for the innkeeper, and was immediately reprimanded for this. The offended knight then began to talk about knight errantry and its revival in the world, until finally the men tired of his discourse. Again they knocked at the gate, this time with such force and fury that the innkeeper woke up and came out and admitted them in a hurry. They entered violently on their horses, enraged because of their long waiting at the gate, and dismounted, leaving their horses free. The moment the horses saw Rocinante and the curious position of his master, they went to investigate him, and the unsuspecting Rocinante leaped from under Don Quixote with such suddenness that the poor knight's arm was nearly wrenched from his body. There he was left to dangle, while the shouts that forced their way from his throat rent the air fiercely.

CHAPTER XLIV

In Which Are Continued the Unheard-of Adventures at the Inn

WHEN the landlord heard the terrible outcries of Don Quixote, he ran, greatly excited, to see who could be giving vent to such agony. The travelers joined him; and the Asturian maid was stirred to quick action by a bad conscience, as well as by the excited state of her master. She untied the halter, and Don Quixote fell so suddenly that his meager body landed like a dead weight on the ground.

The landlord and the travelers found him there, and asked him impatiently why he was making such a tremendous noise. He ignored their question entirely, pulled the rope off his wrist, and mounted his charger with as much nonchalance and elegance as his stiff limbs would permit. Then he haughtily raised his head, after having adjusted all his knightly paraphernalia, and circled down the field, returning in a canter. Having halted Rocinante, he bellowed out to those assembled "Whoever shall say that I have been enchanted with just cause, provided my lady the Princess Micomicona grants me permission to do so, I give him the lie, challenge him and defy him to single combat."

THE STORY OF DON QUIXOTE

The landlord saw at once the effect these words of the poor demented knight had on his newly arrived guests, so he hastened to explain Don Quixote's condition to them. They then asked whether the innkeeper had seen a youth dressed like a muleteer. He replied that he had not; but just then one of the men exclaimed that the youth must be there, since the Judge's coach—which he had suddenly observed—was there. They then decided to dissemble, each one going to a different entrance of the inn, so there would be no chance for the youth to escape.

The landlord was curious to know what it was all about, but could arrive at no conclusion. The truth was that these men were servants of the young muleteer's father. And it was not long ere they had discovered him, lying asleep, never thinking that he would himself be pursued. The servant who roused him made a few caustic remarks to the young Don Luis—for this was his name—about his bed and the luxury of his surroundings, as particularly befitting a youth of his rank and breeding.

Don Luis could not at first believe that he was really awake. He rubbed his eyes in astonishment, and failed to find a reply to the servant's remarks. The man then continued, advising his young master to return to his home at once, saying that his father, as a result of his disappearance, was dangerously ill. The youth was curious to learn how his father had found out what road he had taken and that he had disguised himself as a muleteer. The servant answered that a student to whom Don Luis had confided his love for Doña Clara, had told his master everything, when he saw how he suffered.

OTHER ADVENTURES AT THE INN

Now, it chanced that another muleteer, who had been sleeping with Don Luis, could not keep what he was hearing to himself; besides, he deemed it best to disappear from the scene. He informed some of the guests of what had occurred, and thus it happened that Don Fernando and Cardenio learned of the plight of the young singer, whose voice they had so admired a short time before; and when the muleteer told them that his comrade was a young nobleman in disguise, they decided to go and help him in his quandary.

They found the four men entreating Don Luis to return to his father; and the youth emphatically refusing to do so, saying that they might take him dead, but never alive.

At this moment Dorothea saw Cardenio from her window, and she called him and told him the story of the lad and Doña Clara. He in turn related to her how the servants of the youth's father had come to take him back to his home. In telling Dorothea this news Cardenio was overheard by Doña Clara who would have swooned had not Dorothea supported her.

By this time the servants had brought Don Luis into the inn, threatening to take him back by force should he not go willingly. Again he protested, and at last the argument attracted all the guests, including Don Quixote, who had ceased his duties as guard for the present. The Judge was there too, and when one of the servants recognized in him their neighbor in Madrid, he pleaded with him to do all he could to make the young man return to his ill father.

The Judge turned to the young muleteer, and saw that it was his neighbor's son; whereupon he embraced him and asked in a fatherly way what had brought him there dressed in such a manner. With his arm around the youth's neck, the Judge withdrew with the lad to discuss the reasons for his disguise and for his leaving his father.

While the kindly Judge was thus occupied with Don Luis, a tumult suddenly arose at the gate of the inn. It was the landlord, trying to hold back two guests who had attempted to get away without paying. The innkeeper was stubbornly clinging to the garb of one of the adventurers, and in return was being pummeled mercilessly, until his face was a study in dark and fast colors, except his nose, which was tinted a running red. As soon as the landlady perceived her mate's distress, the thought struck her that this would be a most worthy opportunity for our valiant knight errant to show his skill as a swordsman and a wielder of the lance. So she dispatched her daughter, the fair young lady of the castle, to bring the knight her message of distress.

Don Quixote received the young lady calmly and courteously, but said that he was in honor bound to engage in no combat except by the express permission of her Royal Highness the Princess Micomicona; she having granted it, there could be no doubt as to the outcome of any battle in which he chose to draw his sword. Seeing this, in her opinion, ill-timed hesitancy, the one-eyed Asturian muttered that by the time the Princess was found, her master would have passed the heavenly border. The Princess, however, was quickly summoned, and Don Quixote knelt on his stiff knees before her; but ere he had finished his long harangue of request, she—having been advised of the urgency of the situation—had already given him permission and wished him godspeed.

Don Quixote arose and drew his sword, paced toward the gate, and then suddenly stopped short. All wondered what had happened to cause his hesitating thus, and the Asturian maid expressed her wonder aloud. Don Quixote was not long about the answer. He replied at once that this was no business for him; they had best call his squire. It was for Sancho, he said, that he reserved the task and joy of fighting such lowly people as the ones he saw before him here and now.

Now, while all of this was taking place, Don Luis, with tears in his eyes, was confessing to Doña Clara's father his great and indomitable love for her. This placed the Judge in a curious predicament, for he found himself forced to sit in judgment on the welfare of his own child. He was so taken with the charm and intelligence of the youth that he was anxious to have him for a son-in-law, particularly as his family was one of distinction, and extremely rich. Yet his better judgment told him that it would be wise to wait another day before giving his consent. He would have preferred to have Don Luis' father approve of the marriage, although he thought it almost certain that this gentleman would like to see his son married to a titled lady.

And while the fate of the young lovers was being weighed by the Judge, peace had been declared between the inn-keeper and the two travelers who, persuaded by the chivalrous words of Don Quixote, and the summoning of Sancho, had been made to see the light and pay the bill. By this time everything was settled amicably, the landlord having demanded no special indemnity for his battered, many-colored face.

But who should loom up on the scene, now that everything was peaceful again, but the owner of Mambrino's golden helmet! This particular barber was now leading his donkey to the stable, when he suddenly discovered Sancho Panza hard at work repairing the barber's own trappings, which our Sancho had taken as booty at the time his master fell heir to the helmet. The barber left his donkey at no slow speed and ran towards Sancho, to whom he exclaimed threateningly "There, you thief, I have caught you! Give me my basin and my pack-saddle, and everything you robbed me of!"

But Sancho was not willing to give up so easily things that he had gained as spoils in righteous warfare. He refuted with his fists, as well as by argument, the barber's coarse suggestion that he was a common highwayman; and his master, coming up at this instant, was proud and pleased to hear his faithful squire talk like that, and also to see the barber's teeth gone, which the force of Sancho's blow evidently had carried away. As a matter of fact, Sancho's demonstration of physical strength made such a profound impression on Don Quixote, that he decided his squire was not far from being eligible to knighthood.

As soon as the barber was able to make himself heard again, he began to arraign both master and squire. He was not to be subdued. He told all that quickly gathered round them that they could assure themselves of the truth of what he said by fitting Sancho's saddle to his own steed; furthermore, he said, they had plundered him of a basin.

When Don Quixote heard this ridiculous accusation, his lips twisted into a scornful smile. He dispatched Sancho to fetch the helmet—which seemed to Sancho a dangerous move—and when Sancho returned with the basin, Don Quixote held it up with great self-assurance before everybody.

"Your worships," said he, "may see with what face this squire can assert that this is a basin and not the helmet I told you of; and I swear by the order of chivalry I profess, that this helmet is the identical one I took from him, without anything added to or removed."

This statement was corroborated in detail by Sancho, who added: "Since that battle my master has fought in the helmet only once. That was when he let loose the unfortunate ones in chains. And if it had not been for this basin-helmet he might have been killed in that engagement, for there were plenty of stones raining down on him at that time."

CHAPTER XLV

In Which the Doubtful Question of Mambrino's Helmet
and the Pack-Saddle Is Finally Settled,
with Other Adventures That Occurred
in Truth and Earnest

THE barber appealed to those present and asked them what they thought about Don Quixote's nonsense; and it was then that it occurred to Don Quixote's friend, the barber of his village to play a joke on his fellow barber. He solemnly asked the other barber whether he was out of his head, for of course anybody could see that it was a helmet, although, he admitted, not a complete one.

The poor barber was so taken aback, so perplexed that a learned barber, and a seemingly sane one otherwise, could not tell the difference between a basin and a helmet that he nearly toppled over. But when the worthy curate, Cardenio, Don Fernando, and all—for they realized at once the barber's joke—insisted that he was wrong, and that it was not a basin, the perspiration began to trickle down his face, and he exclaimed: "God bless me! Is it possible that such an honorable company can say that this is not a basin but a helmet? Why, this is a thing that would astonish a whole university, however wise it might be! And if this basin is a helmet, then the pack-saddle must be a horse's caparison!"

Some one present was quick to assert that it most certainly was a caparison and not a pack-saddle at all; that no one but a fool could take it for a pack-saddle. And when a gentleman of quality like Don Fernando offered to take the votes of those present and they turned out to be in favor of the pack-saddle's remaining a caparison, the barber thought he had gone completely mad.

By this time the group of spectators had been increased by the arrival of the four servants of Don Luis, Don Luis himself, and three new guests—officers of the Holy Brotherhood, to whom the proceedings and the amusement of those present seemed utter foolishness. One of these uninitiated newcomers, one of the officers of the Brotherhood, dared to

say that any one who maintained that it was a helmet instead of a basin must be drunk. But he should not have
said it, for our knight lifted his lance and let it fly out of
his hand with such ferocity and such sure aim that if the
officer had not been lucky enough to be able to dodge it, it
would have pierced his body.

The tumult that followed was indescribable. The landlord came to the rescue of his Brotherhood comrades. His
wife fell into hysterics for fear he would be beheaded by
Don Quixote's vicious sword. The women were all
screaming, wailing, weeping and fainting. Then this
tremendous din and noise was suddenly rent by the voice
of Don Quixote; and like a flash there was peace, when the
knight errant began to appeal in soft lucid tones for a
cessation of hostilities. It was a curious thing to observe
how willingly the demented man's appeal to reason was
listened to by all. The confusion had struck most of them
with terror and they were glad to heed in such a moment
even the will of unreason.

But as soon as there was quiet again, the grudge against
Don Quixote that had established itself in the heart of one
of the Brotherhood, began to assert itself. It suddenly
came to his mind that among his warrants he had one for
a man of Don Quixote's description who was accused of
having set free a chain of galley-slaves. As soon as he
had convinced himself that there could be no mistake about
the identity, he strode forth and seized Don Quixote so
abruptly by the collar that the knight nearly choked.

"Help for the Holy Brotherhood!" the officer yelled a-
loud. "And that you may see that I demand it in earnest,

read this warrant which says this highwayman is to be arrested!"

Hardly did Don Quixote feel himself handled in so undignified a manner, when he clutched the villain's throat, foaming at the mouth like a wild beast. Luckily they were separated in time by Don Fernando and the rest, or they would have torn each other to pieces. Yet the officer was not willing to give up his claim on Don Quixote's person: a claim that our knight errant laughed at, for who had ever heard of members of the knighthood being dependent on jurisdiction? Did he, this base knave, this ill-born scoundrel, not know that the law of knights was in their swords, their charter in their prowess, and their edicts in their will? And then he calmly rambled on, his speech of denunciation culminating in this last crushing remark: "What knight errant has there been, is there, or will there ever be in the world, not bold enough to give, single-handed, four hundred cudgellings to four hundred officers of the Holy Brotherhood if they come in his way?"

While his master was thus discoursing in his usual vein, Sancho was reviewing past events at the inn, and he could not help but make this sad exclamation: "By the Lord, it is quite true what my master says about the enchantments of this castle, for it is impossible to live an hour in peace in it!"

CHAPTER XLVI

OF THE END OF THE NOTABLE ADVENTURE OF THE OFFICERS OF THE HOLY BROTHERHOOD; AND OF THE GREAT FEROCITY OF OUR WORTHY KNIGHT, DON QUIXOTE

THE curate had to argue for some time with the officers of the Brotherhood before he could finally persuade them that it would serve no purpose to arrest Don Quixote, for, being out of his senses, he would in the end be released as a madman. Furthermore, he warned them, Don Quixote would never submit to force.

Sancho Panza and the barber were still quarreling over the pack-saddle and the other booty, and at last the officers agreed to act as mediators, and the differences were adjusted by arbitration. The curate settled for the basin by paying eight reals, and received a receipt for payment in full from the barber.

Don Fernando, in the meantime, extracted a promise from three of the servants of Don Luis to return to Madrid, while the other one agreed to remain and accompany his young master to where Don Fernando wanted him to go. Doña Clara was sparkling with happiness; and Zoraida seemed to feel at home with the Christians, in spite of the noise and tumult she had had to live through during her short stay at the inn.

The landlord did not forget the reckoning for the wine-skins and all the other things whose loss he could attribute to Don Quixote, for he had witnessed the curate's paying off the debt for the barber's helmet. Don Fernando paid all the innkeeper's demands generously, after the curate had decided the claims were just.

But when Don Quixote felt no discord in the air, he betook himself to the presence of Dorothea, knelt before her, and told her how willing and anxious he was to serve her and conquer her giant. And he requested that they make ready to leave. Her reply was simple and direct, for she told him that his will was hers. So Don Quixote ordered his squire to saddle Rocinante and his own donkey; but Sancho only shook his head in sorry fashion.

"Master," he said, "there is more mischief in the village than one hears of." And as his master begged him to speak freely, he burst out: "This lady, who calls herself ruler of the great kingdom of Micomicon, is no more so than my mother; for, if she was what she says, she would not go rubbing noses with one that is here every instant and behind every door."

Though it was merely with her husband, Don Fernando, that she had, as Sancho said, rubbed noses, the crimson in her royal blood came to the surface, and her face turned as red as a beet. Sancho, fearing that the Princess was a courtesan, wanted to save his master the two years' journey to Micomicon, if at the end of it it should turn out that another one than Don Quixote or himself should reap the fruits of their labor.

It is impossible to describe the terrible wrath of the knight when he heard the Princess thus slandered. His indignation and fury knew no bounds. He began to stammer and stutter, inarticulate with rage, until Sancho was scared out of his wits, afraid of being cut open by his raving master's sword. He was just about to turn his back on his master and disappear till the storm had passed, when Dorothea came to his rescue. She suggested that Sancho's strange behavior could only be ascribed to one thing: enchantment. How else could he have seen such diabolical things as he described, how could he have been made to bear false witness against her, and how could he have spoken words so offensive to her modesty? Knowing the heart of Sancho, Don Quixote at once thought her explanation a most ingenious one, for what else could have put into Sancho's head such disrespect for a royal personage? Don Fernando, too, pleaded in Sancho's behalf; and Sancho meekly stumbled to his knees before his master, and kissed his hand frantically, begging him for forgiveness. Whereupon our knight errant with many gestures pardoned and blessed him.

"Now, Sancho, my son," he said, "thou wilt be convinced of the truth of what I have many a time told thee, that everything in this castle is done by means of enchantment."

To which Sancho Panza replied meekly but firmly: "So it is, I believe, except the affair of the blanket, which came to pass in reality by ordinary means."

But Don Quixote as usual was not in a mood to listen to nonsense, and he replied that if such were the case he would have avenged him, but seeing no one to avenge himself upon, how could it have been anything else but enchantment?

THE STORY OF DON QUIXOTE

Those who were there were eager to know what had happened to Sancho, and the landlord was most obliging in giving a graphic description of all that had occurred. They all seemed to enjoy the account enormously, for they laughed hilarously. Had Don Quixote not again assured Sancho that it most certainly had happened by enchantment, there is no doubt that he would have interrupted their hilarity.

It was now two days since they had arrived at the inn, and Don Fernando and Dorothea were becoming anxious to depart. In order that they might not have to go out of their way, it was arranged that they should go by themselves; meanwhile a scheme was devised whereby the curate and the barber could restore Don Quixote to his native village.

An ox-cart passed that day, and the curate, hearing it was going in the direction of El Toboso, made arrangements with the owner to make the journey with him. Then he ordered some of the servants to make a cage, large enough to hold Don Quixote, and provided it with bars. He then asked Don Fernando and his companions, the officers of the Holy Brotherhood, the servants of Don Luis, and the innkeeper to cover their faces and change their appearance so that Don Quixote would think they were quite different people.

When this had been done they tiptoed to the valiant knight errant's room, where they found him fast asleep, bound him, without waking him, hand and foot; then they stood about the room silently. When the knight awoke, he was startled to find that he could not move, and seeing

all these strangely conjured-up figures before him, it struck
him they must be phantoms of the enchanted castle. He
was absolutely helpless, and the men had no difficulty in
stuffing him into the cage. The bars were nailed on securely, and the cage was then carried out of the inn and
placed in the ox-cart.

While the procession slowly proceeded from the inn to
the ox-cart, the men supporting the cage on their shoulders,
the barber chanted strange words in a weird and hollow
voice. The barber took it upon himself to become the prophet of the occasion, and he proclaimed to the Knight of
the Rueful Countenance that he ought not to consider his
present imprisonment an affliction. It was in a way a
sort of penance, he said, through which he would be hum-
bled to be in readiness for a still greater, sweeter imprisonment, the bond of matrimony. This prediction would
come true, he avowed, when the fierce Manchegan lion and
the tender Tobosan dove met again. They would be
joined in one, and the offspring of this union would be of
such stuff as to set the world aflame.

When Don Quixote heard these words, he was stirred
into an exalted emotion. Had he not been well bound it
would have been expressed by kneeling. He raised his
eyes toward Heaven and thanked the Lord for having sent
this prophet to him in this needy moment. He prayed
that he should not be left to perish in the cage, and also
implored of the prophet not to let his faithful Sancho Panza
abandon him, saying that if by chance the promise of the
island should not come true, he had made provision for him
in his will. Sancho was much moved by what his encaged

and enchanted master had said, and he bent down and kissed his hands—he had to kiss both since they were tied together. By that time the procession had arrived at the oxcart, and all was ready for the departure.

CHAPTER XLVII

Of the Strange Manner in Which Don Quixote of La Mancha Was Carried Away Enchanted, Together with Other Remarkable Incidents

DON QUIXOTE was greatly perplexed and, indeed, somewhat impatient with the slow speed of the cart carrying away this enchanted knight. The cart had rolled only a few paces and then stopped; there was nothing exciting or heroic in being carried off in such a way! Never had he read anywhere of so ridiculously slow and tame a proceeding. And on an ox-cart! However, times had changed, and he realized that until he had established the new era of knight-errantry, the most plebeian ways of being captured by enchantment would have to serve. Yet, he did not consider it beneath his dignity to ask Sancho what he thought on the subject.

"I don't know what to think," answered Sancho, "not being as well read as your Worship in errant writings; but for all that, I venture to say and swear that these apparitions that are about us are not quite Catholic."

Don Quixote could not refrain from laughing aloud at his squire's simplicity. How could they be Catholics

"HE PRAYED THAT HE SHOULD NOT BE LEFT TO PERISH IN THE CAGE."

—*Page 131*

when they were devils, made of no substance whatever, nothing but air?

"By the Lord, Master," interrupted Sancho excitedly, "I have touched them already, and one of the devils, I swear, has firm flesh. Furthermore, I have always heard it said that all devils smelled of sulphur and brimstone, but this one smells of amber half a league off."

Here Sancho was referring to Don Fernando, who, like most nobles, used a perfume; but Don Quixote explained to his squire that this particular devil was so besprinkled in order to give people the impression he was not a devil.

While Don Quixote and his squire were thus exchanging thoughts on the subject of devils and their religion and what stuff they were made of, the curate and the barber were saying farewell to Don Fernando, his bride, Dorothea, Cardenio, Luscinda, the Judge and Doña Clara, as well as to the Captain and the Captain's bride, Zoraida. All of them promised to write to the curate, so that he in return might let them know how his and Don Quixote's journey had ended.

After many embraces, the curate and the barber were ready to make their departure when the landlord came running out with some papers which he handed to the curate as a gift. The landlord said it was the manuscript of the novel, "Rinconete and Cortadillo," a part of the contents of the valise in which he had found the story of "Ill-Advised Curiosity," which the curate had read aloud at the inn.

The curate thanked the innkeeper, saying that he hoped it was as good as the other novel. Then he and the barber

covered their faces that they might not be recognized by
Don Quixote, and took their places behind the cart,
mounted on their mules. The three officers of the Brotherhood had been brought by the curate to escort them to El
Toboso, armed with muskets. And then Sancho Panza,
mounted on his donkey, led Rocinante by the reins. As
the procession started, the landlady came out to weep make-
believe tears for Don Quixote, who begged her to shed
none, for in the end, he said, virtue would triumph.

At the head of the procession came the ox-cart, the officers of the Brotherhood marching beside it, then followed
Sancho Panza on his ass, leading Rocinante by the bridle,
and in the rear trailed the curate and the barber on their
mules. The slow pace of the oxen had to be imitated by the
rest, so the whole procession took on a solemn and mysterious aspect, which was enhanced by the encaged Don Quixote's stiff and stone-like form leaning against the wooden
bars.

They had traveled several leagues, when the curate
heard the sound of riders approaching from behind. Turning in his saddle he perceived six or seven men, mounted
on mules, and riding at a quick pace. They had soon over-
taken the procession, and exchanged greetings with the
curate and the barber. One of the travelers was a canon
of Toledo, and on observing the fettered Don Quixote,
with the armed officers of the Brotherhood as an escort, he
took it for granted that the knight was some dangerous
highwayman. Yet, scrutinizing the strange parade, he
could not help asking questions. So when he inquired of
one of the officers why Don Quixote was being transported

in that way, the officer did not know what to say but referred him for an explanation to Don Quixote himself.

The knight errant had heard the canon's question, and he offered to give him the information if he knew anything about errantry. As the canon said he had read a good deal about knights errant and their deeds, Don Quixote was quick to tell of his misfortune—how he had been encaged and made helpless by enchantment. At this moment the curate, seeing that the canon was talking to Don Quixote, and fearing a mishap in the carrying out of their plan, came up and joined in the conversation. He corroborated what the knight errant had just said, and added that it was not for his sins that he was enchanted, but because of his enemies' hatred of virtuous deeds, of which this famous Knight of the Rueful Countenance was the strongest champion in their age.

When the good canon heard the two of them talk like that, he was at a loss for words and felt he had to cross himself, in which action his attendants joined him. But as luck would have it, Sancho Panza had been listening, and seeing the curate disguised by a mask, the suspicion crept into his head that he was trying to play a joke on his master. So he burst into the conversation with a grudge against them all.

"Well, sirs, you may like it or not," he declared, "but my master is as much enchanted as my mother! He is in his full senses; he can eat, and sleep, and drink. Then why do they want me to believe that he is enchanted? I have heard it said that when you are enchanted you cannot do any of these things, nor talk. And my master will talk more than thirty lawyers would if you do not stop him." Then turning to the curate, he exclaimed: "And, señor curate, señor curate! Do you think I do not know you? Well, I can tell you I do, for all your face is covered; and I can tell you I am up to you, however you may hide your tricks. If it had not been for your Worship, my master would be married to the Princess Micomicona this minute, and I should be a Count at least—for no less was to be expected."

And then the faithful Sancho went on to say that he had told all this that the curate might weigh in his conscience the pranks he had played on Don Quixote, and for which he would have to pay in heaven (if he ever should come there) unless he did penance now. Here the barber thought it best to put an end to Sancho's communications, and offered him a place in the cage beside his master, but Sancho was quick to retort: "Mind how you talk, master barber, for shaving is not everything; and as to the enchantment of my master, God knows the truth!"

Soon after Sancho had commenced his tirade, the curate thought it best, having listened to his own denunciation, to explain everything concerning the knight errant and his squire to the canon. Therefore he asked him to ride on ahead with him. When the canon had heard the whole story, he remarked that he thought that books of chivalry were really harmful, for not one of them was truthful. He was amused when the curate related how he and the barber had burned nearly all of Don Quixote's treasures in literature of this sort.

"But what mind," asked the canon, "that is not wholly

barbarous and uncultured can find pleasure in reading of how a great tower full of knights sails away across the sea like a ship with a fair wind, and will be to-night in Lombardy and to-morrow morning in the land of Prester John of the Indies?"

CHAPTER XLVIII

In Which the Canon Pursues the Subject of the Books of Chivalry, with Other Matters Worthy of His Wit

THE curate and the canon had become very much interested in their subject, and the canon after a while confided to the curate that he himself had once started to write a book on chivalry, with the intention of making each incident in it a plausible one. It was his view that fiction was all the better the more it resembled the truth. Furthermore, he believed in adhering to good taste and to the rules of art; these things, it seemed to him, had been ignored in the writing of these books. From fiction the conversation drifted to playwriting, and here again the curate and the canon were of the same mind. The actors of their age chose plays that appealed to people of nonsense and with bad taste. Instead of trying to improve the national taste, they produced tawdry plays. The canon cited three excellent plays, however, that he had seen at Madrid, which had earned great profits for their producers; this proved to the canon that the great mass of the public did appreciate a really good play if it was only produced.

While the two clergymen were thus whiling away the time, the barber approached and told the curate they had reached a place which to him seemed a good pasture for the oxen. It was now noon, and the canon decided to join them in their rest. He offered them food out of the provisions that he had brought along on a pack-mule. The rest of the canon's mules were sent to an inn, which was seen nearby, to be fed there.

Seeing his master unguarded, Sancho decided the time had come when he could speak undisturbedly to him, so he hastened to tell him of the plot that the curate and the barber had hit upon. He told his master he was certain it was out of envy and malice, for his having surpassed them in fame and brave deeds. Don Quixote, however, calmly told his squire that if he saw two shapes that resembled the barber and the curate there, they could be nothing but devils having taken on the appearance of his friends in order to be able to do their black deeds so much the more safely and cruelly.

CHAPTER XLIX

WHICH TREATS OF HOW OUR KNIGHT IS PERMITTED TO DESCEND FROM HIS CAGE, AND OF THE CANON'S ATTEMPT TO CONVERT HIM FROM HIS ILLUSIONS

DURING his conversation with Sancho, Don Quixote suddenly felt it an absolute necessity to leave the cage, and to stretch himself in the open. So Sancho went to the curate to ask his permission, which he received upon promising to answer for his master's not disappearing. The curate and the canon went to the cage, and Don Quixote swore as a knight that he would not run away, whereupon they untied his hands and feet.

The first thing Don Quixote did was to go to his Rocinante; and then the canon thought he would try to talk sense into him, to see whether he could not persuade him to give up his crazy notions and ideas. Don Quixote listened courteously and attentively, but when the canon had finished, he turned to him and said he rather thought it was the canon and not he who was afflicted and out of his wits, since he had the audacity to blaspheme the order of knighthood. And then he went on, describing the deeds of all the famous knights he had read of; and the canon was really amazed at the great ease and clearness of mind with which he related these tales of adventure. He thought it a pity that so much knowledge of a wrong kind should be heaped into one brain.

CHAPTERS L—LI

OF THE SHREWD CONTROVERSY WHICH DON QUIXOTE AND THE CANON HELD, TOGETHER WITH OTHER INCIDENTS

WHAT the canon had tried on the knight, Don Quixote now decided to try on him. Was that not the great mission he had undertaken in the world—to revive the spirit of chivalry? So he told the canon of the many fine qualities he had developed since he was dubbed a knight, such as courtesy, generosity, valor, good breeding, patience, and many others that he mentioned; how he had learned to bear hardships of all kinds, and now, of late, enchantment. He ended his long discourse by expressing a desire that he might soon be an emperor, for, he said, he wished to do good to some of his faithful friends, especially his squire Sancho Panza.

Sancho heard his master's last words, and reminded him again of the island that he was to govern. On hearing this, the canon broke in with a few remarks about administration and government, and their difficulties, and Sancho interrupted the canon to say it would be very easy to find some one to do all that for him. In reply to this the canon came forward with a good many arguments phrased in philosophical language which the squire could make neither head nor tail of. So he took up the thread of his own mind, and replied: "I have as much soul as another, and as much body as any one, and I shall be as much king of my realm as any other of his; so let the country come, and God be with you, and let us see one another, as one blind man said to the other."

All the canon could do when he realized how badly both master and servant were in the clutch of their beliefs and superstitions, was to wonder at it. But by the time Sancho had finished his words, the repast was being served on the grass.

As they were about to seat themselves, a goat came running from between the trees, pursued by a man whose clear voice could be heard distinctly from the distance. Soon he came up, and he caught the goat by the horns and began to talk to her, calling her daughter, as if she had been a child. The goat seemed to understand everything, and the canon was so impressed with the scene that he asked the goatherd not to be in a hurry, but to sit down and eat with them.

The goatherd accepted the invitation; and when they had finished the repast, they had found that he was by no means a fool. When he asked them if they would like to hear a true story, they were all anxious to have him tell it to them. Only Sancho Panza withdrew, that he might get a chance to load himself brimful of food; for he had heard his master once say that a knight errant's squire should eat until he could hold no more. The goatherd began his story, after having told the goat to lie down beside him. She did so, and while the goatherd was telling the story of his unfortunate love for Leandra, a rich farmer's daughter, who had jilted both him and his rival Anselmo for the good looks of a braggard by the name of Vicente de la Roca, the goat was looking up into his face with an expression as it seemed of understanding and sympathy.

THE STORY OF DON QUIXOTE

CHAPTER LII

OF THE QUARREL THAT DON QUIXOTE HAD WITH THE GOAT-
HERD, TOGETHER WITH THE RARE ADVENTURE OF THE
PENITENTS, WHICH WITH AN EXPENDITURE OF
SWEAT HE BROUGHT TO A HAPPY
CONCLUSION

ALL had enjoyed the goatherd's story, and they thanked him for it. Don Quixote offered him the aid of his sword for the future, and said that if he had not been enchanted at this moment he would at once set out to free his Leandra. When the goatherd perceived Don Quixote's strange behavior and appearance and heard his remarkable language, he was struck with amazement, and asked the barber what madness was his, who talked like the knights he had read about in the books of knight-er-rantry. Scarcely had Don Quixote heard that he was being taken for a madman by the goatherd than he flew at him in a raging fit. The most fierce battle ensued, during which the faces of both men were scratched until they could hardly be recognized. They fought in the midst of the setting for the meal, and plates and glasses were smashed and up-set. Both were urged on like dogs by the rest of the company, and soon blood began to flow. Finally Don Quixote stumbled, and the goatherd managed to get him on his back, while Sancho was held off by one of the canon's servants, moaning all the while because he could not go to his master's rescue.

Just then a trumpet blew a solemn note, and all listened

[142]

in surprise. Don Quixote was all eagerness: there was no doubt in his mind but that he was being summoned by one in distress, so he asked for and received an hour's truce from the goatherd. As soon as he was on his feet, he ran to Rocinante, whom he bridled in great haste, and set off, armed with lance, buckler, sword and helmet, in the direction of the sound.

What Don Quixote saw when he had ridden a short distance at his charger's usual comfortable canter was a procession of penitents, clad in white, some of whom were carrying an image, draped in black. The procession had been called for by the priests who desired to bring relief to the country, which had been suffering that year from a terrific heat and a lack of rain. They were now marching to a nearby hermitage, where they wanted to do penance, praying in silence to God that he might have pity on them.

But what could such a procession have suggested to an imaginative mind like Don Quixote's but one of the many incidents that he had read of in his books of chivalry, where some great and worthy lady was being carried away by evil forces? To the knight the covered image easily became the worthy lady. Violently kicking Rocinante in the sides, for he had not had time to put on his spurs, he tried to increase his steed's canter to a gallop that he might attack in real knight errant fashion.

The faithful squire, the curate, the canon and the barber all did their best to stop the knight by their yells. Sancho was frantic, and cried after him: "Where are you going, Señor Don Quixote? What devils have possessed you

to set you against our Catholic faith? Plague take me!
It is a procession of penitents!" And then he asked him,
filled with horror and almost choking with tears, whether
he knew what he was doing. Why, he was charging the
blessed image of the immaculate and holy Virgin Mary!
Sancho, seeing his master's lifted lance, could not know
that his master wanted to release her.

When Don Quixote had reached the penitents, he abruptly halted his horse and demanded in no uncertain,
though flowery, language that the fair lady—whom, he
said, he could plainly see they were carrying away against
her will—be released at once.

One of four priests, who had just begun to chant the
Litany, stopped on a high note and answered the knight
that he must not hold up the singing or the procession, for
the marchers were doing penitence by whipping themselves and could not stop once they had commenced the
ceremony. Again Don Quixote put forth his demand, this
time in language that seemed much more ludicrous to the
penitents so that some of them could not resist bursting
into laughter. This sign of disrespect was too much for our
errant, who started his attack but was prevented from finishing it by the blow of a stick carried by one of the penitents. With one thwack of it he was felled to the ground.

Sancho had now come up, and when he saw his master
stretched out, with no sign of life, his eyes filled with tears,
and he thrust himself over his master's body, crying and
wailing like a little child. It was pitiful to see the sorrow
and the devotion of the poor, simple-minded fellow, bewailing his master's fall from the blow of a mere stick.

THE QUARREL WITH THE GOATHERD

And he ended his tribute by thanking him for the great generosity he had always shown; for Don Quixote, for but eight months of service, had given him the best island that was afloat in the sea.

Sancho was suddenly called from his grief by the weak voice of the knight, who implored his squire to mount him on the ox-cart, as his shoulder was in a dilapidated condition. Then he commended himself to his Lady Dulcinea, while Sancho recommended that they return with their friends to their village, where they could prepare for another sally at a more favorable time. The knight seemed inclined to take his squire's advice, for he remarked that it was not a bad idea: that in the meantime the prevailing evil influence of the stars might disappear.

By this time the curate, the canon and the officers of the Brotherhood had arrived at the spot, and the curate found that he knew one of the priests in the procession. This simplified matters considerably, for he found it easy to explain to his friend the malady and peculiarities of Don Quixote, which had been the cause of so much disturbance in so short a time. After the curate had taken leave of the canon, the goatherd and those in the procession, he paid off the officers, who considered it unwise to accompany the party any further. The canon begged the curate to keep him informed of any change in Don Quixote's behavior, as he was most interested in his case. Then Don Quixote was heaved into the cart where a stack of hay served as a softer resting-place this time; and after six days of travel, the oxen and the cart and the whole procession entered the La Mancha village. When they passed the square, it being Sunday, the people crowded around them, and all were amazed at what they saw.

Soon Don Quixote's niece and his housekeeper got word of his homecoming. When they saw him, and observed his pallor and leanness, they began to weep and beat their breasts, and curse all books of chivalry.

Then Sancho Panza's wife learned the news, and as soon as she saw her husband the first thing she asked him was whether the donkey was well. To this greeting he replied that the donkey was better than he himself. And then she pestered him with questions as to what he had brought back with him for her and the children; to which he impatiently remarked that she would have to wait until he got his island or empire, when she would be called Her Ladyship. Of course, it was not to be expected that Teresa Panza should understand this; and she did not. Sancho attempted to give her an insight into the intricacies of knight-errantry by telling her of some of his remarkable experiences, such as the blanketing, which stood out in his mind's eye as the culmination of suffering in his career as a squire.

While this was going on in the Panza household, Don Quixote had been undressed and put to bed by his niece and the housekeeper. The curate had told them what troubles and tribulations he had been forced to undergo in order to restore him to his community and his loved ones. So they decided, with fear in their hearts, to be ever watchful, lest he escape and depart on another rampage. And again and again they would curse the books that they had burned too late.

VOLUME II

CHAPTER I

OF THE INTERVIEW THE CURATE AND THE BARBER HAD WITH
DON QUIXOTE ABOUT HIS MALADY

DON QUIXOTE had been at home almost a month.
During that time neither the curate nor the barber
had been to see him for fear that the sight of them would
remind him of his days of knight-errantry and make him
long for another campaign. They did visit the niece and
housekeeper, however, and advised them from time to
time what to do; and at last the women began to think that
there was hope for our knight's being restored to his right
mind, for his conversation never touched upon deeds of
chivalry, and when he spoke on other subjects he always
talked most sanely.

Finally the curate and the barber decided to pay their
friend a visit, firmly resolved not to let the subject of conversation turn to knight-errantry. They found him in bed,
with a red Toledo cap on his head. His face had changed
greatly; it was so withered and yellow that it resembled
parchment rather than human flesh. He greeted them
cordially, however, and soon they engaged in an animated
conversation, which finally turned to such an intricate subject as government. So unusually sane and clear was
Don Quixote's reasoning that his friends were amazed at
the change that had taken place, and they felt quite certain

[147]

that he was cured. Then they began to discuss the news from the capital, and the curate mentioned that the Turk was expected to attack. Nobody knew when, he said, but in order to safeguard the island of Malta and the coasts of Naples and Sicily, His Majesty had already made provisions for the defense of these provinces.

Here Don Quixote interrupted and said that His Majesty could easily settle the whole thing if he would only follow his advice. Both the curate and the barber began to wonder and worry about what his plan might be, but before divulging it Don Quixote insisted upon absolute secrecy, which of course they promised. And then he began in the old, familiar strain, citing the examples of the innumerable heroes of his condemned books of chivalry, heroes who, single-handed, had conquered armies of millions. He finished with a tirade about God's providing such a knight errant to-day to save the nation and Christianity against the onslaught of the heathen Turk, with an inference in his last words that he was to be the chosen savior.

When the two women heard Don Quixote again rave in this manner, they burst into tears, and the curate and the barber were as sorry and concerned as the women. The curate turned in bewilderment to his poor friend and asked him whether he truly believed that the heroes of these tales of chivalry were men of flesh and blood. He himself, he said, was convinced that these stories were nothing but fables and falsehoods, and that none of the personages in them ever lived. Whereupon Don Quixote began to ridicule the curate, and went on to describe his heroes, saying that his faith was so strong that he could almost swear he had seen Amadis of Gaul and some of the others he worshiped. Then he embarked on a description of these knights, giving the color of their eyes, of their beards and hair, their height, complexion, all according to his own crazy imagination. Much of what he said seemed so amusing to his two friends that they nearly went into hysterics from laughter. His mind's image of Roland was particularly laughable, for he saw him as a bow-legged, swarthy-complexioned gentleman with a hairy body, courteous and well-bred.

On hearing Roland so pictured, the curate remarked it was no wonder that he was jilted by the fair lady Angelica. To this Don Quixote retorted that lady Angelica was a giddy and frivolous damsel with desires that smacked of wantonness. He only regretted that Roland had not been a poet that he might have libeled her in poetry for all eternity.

Here the knight was interrupted by the sound of loud talking in the courtyard, intermingled with screams, and when he and the curate came running they saw the two women struggling to keep a man from entering the house.

CHAPTER II

WHICH TREATS OF THE NOTABLE ALTERCATION WHICH
SANCHO PANZA HAD WITH DON QUIXOTE'S NIECE
AND HIS HOUSEKEEPER, TOGETHER WITH OTHER
DROLL MATTERS

THE man turned out to be no other than Sancho, who wanted to see his master. But the housekeeper and the niece were bent on not admitting him, for they considered Sancho the arch enticer and felt that he was to blame for Don Quixote's expeditions into the country. When Sancho heard himself thus accused, he defended himself with accusations against Don Quixote, who, he said, had been the one to hypnotize him; and then he added that he had come to find out about his island.

As soon as Don Quixote recognized his squire, he quickly took him inside, being afraid that he would tell the women all the little details of the knight's adventures, such as the galley-slave episode and others not tending to reflect honor on his shield. Whereupon the barber and the curate left, both of them in despair of their friend's ever being cured. The curate remarked that it would not surprise him to learn before many moons that Don Quixote and Sancho had set off again on another sally. They were curious to know what the master and the servant might be discussing at that very moment. However, the curate was of the firm belief that they could rely upon the two women to keep their ears to the door. They would learn from

[150]

them what had been the topic, and what had been said.

When Don Quixote was alone with his squire, he expressed dismay over his having told the housekeeper the knight had taken him from house and home, when he knew perfectly well that he had gone of his own free will. They had shared everything, he said; everything except blows, where he had had a distinct advantage over his squire, having taken ninety-nine out of a hundred beatings. This dividing of fortune, Sancho thought, was quite as it should be, for of course knights errant ought to share the greater benefits of the battle. Here Don Quixote interrupted with a Latin quotation, which had an evil effect on Sancho, for it made him retaliate with the blanket episode which to him still seemed the height of all his suffering in the world. But this attempt to belittle the fairness of his master's division of honors in battle was speedily parried by Don Quixote, who maintained that his squire's bodily suffering in the blanket was as nothing compared with the painful agony of his own heart and soul when he had seen his squire in such a predicament. And then he proceeded to question Sancho as to public opinion of his deeds and valor.

Sancho was inclined to be reticent; but urged by Don Quixote—and having been forgiven in advance for any vexation he might cause him by telling the truth—he told of the variety of opinions that existed in the village. This his master thought only natural; for when had the world ever given full recognition to a genius or a great hero until after he was dead? He pointed to all the great names he could recollect in history that had been persecuted.

But Sancho had not come to the worst; and at last he found sufficient courage to tell his master of a book entitled "The Ingenious Gentleman, Don Quixote of La Mancha," which had already, he said, been spread abroad. In this book not only Don Quixote, but he himself—under his own name!—and the Lady Dulcinea del Toboso figured; and he was so stupefied that he had to cross himself, for he could not imagine how everything that had been told in the book—the most intimate happenings between Don Quixote and himself—had come to be known to the author. Don Quixote thought it was very plain that the adventures must have been reported by some sage and enchanter; but Sancho told him that the author was one Cid Hamet Berengena (meaning eggplant). It was no other than the son of Bartholomew Carrasco, who had been a student at Salamanca, who had told him all this, he said. He asked his master whether he should like to see the young bachelor, and Don Quixote begged him to run and fetch him at once, for, he said, he would be unable to digest a thing until he had had a talk with him.

"Cid Hamet Berengena," repeated Don Quixote to himself. "That is a Moorish name."

"Yes, I have heard the Moors like eggplant," added Sancho.

And then his lord and master asked: "Didst thou not mistake the surname of this 'Cid,' which means in Arabic 'lord,' Sancho?"

"Perhaps," said Sancho; "but the bachelor can tell you that."

And he ran to fetch him.

CHAPTER III

OF THE LAUGHABLE CONVERSATION THAT PASSED BETWEEN
DON QUIXOTE, SANCHO PANZA, AND THE
BACHELOR SAMSON CARRASCO

WHILE Sancho was gone, Don Quixote sat and worried about what the book might be like; for what justice could be expected from the pen of a Moor writing history? But perhaps it was not true that such a chronicle had been written. It seemed almost an impossibility, for it was only a short time since he returned from his achievements. What worried him most was the thought that this Cid Hamet Berengena might have made public in some odious way that great love and sacred passion of his for the beautiful and virtuous Lady Dulcinea del Toboso.

As he was thus meditating Sancho returned, bringing with him the younger Carrasco, who went by the strong name of Samson, in defiance of his unpretentious size. But what he lacked in this respect, he made up for in wit and humor. He was about twenty-four years of age, had a round jovial face, a large mouth and a flat nose. What more need one know to be inclined to think he might be mischievous? He gave proof of it as soon as he entered, for he fell on his knees and kissed the hero's hand respect-

[153]

fully, pronouncing him the first and foremost warrior and knight of the age. Then he called down a blessing on the name of Cid Hamet Benengeli, his noble biographer, and on the worthy, learned man who had translated the work from the difficult Arabic into their pure Castilian for the edification of all the Spanish people who knew how to read their own language.

"So then there *is* a history of me—and written by a Moor and a sage?" asked Don Quixote, as he bade Samson rise.

The bachelor assented and went on to tell how the world was clamoring for this remarkable chronicle of heroism and sacrifices. Don Quixote remarked here what a great source of joy and inspiration it should prove to a man with achievements to his credit to see himself in print before being dead. The bachelor's opinion on the subject coincided with his own; and Samson took the opportunity to pay homage to the marvelous courage, intrepidity, gallantry, gentleness and patience of Don Quixote, as the author had described it in the book. He also spoke feelingly of the beautiful, platonic courtship of our knight errant; and the mention of this caused Don Quixote to ask which of his many acts of chivalry were most appealing to the reader. The bachelor replied that that depended greatly upon the reader's taste: some liked the adventure of the windmills that were enchanted giants; others preferred reading about the two armies that suddenly turned into droves of sheep; then again there were those who seemed to think the victorious assault on the Biscayan made a thrilling chapter; while many would swear they had never read anything that excited them quite as much as the account of the liberation of the galley slaves.

Sancho interrupted him here, asking what was said of their experience with the Yanguesans, when the good Rocinante went looking for adventure and was bitten by the ponies. Samson replied that the sage had forgotten nothing; not even the capers that Sancho himself had cut in the blanket. Whereupon Sancho said: "I cut no capers in the blanket. In the air I did, and more of them than I liked!" But Don Quixote interposed here, saying that history must of necessity be more than one-sided. It must take into its pages adversities as well as good fortune.

Some people, the bachelor held forth, had expressed a desire that the author might have eliminated some of the cruel thrashings he had given the hero; but Sancho differed with these people and supported the author unqualifiedly, saying, with a glance at Don Quixote, "That is where the truth of the history comes in!"

Of course Don Quixote saw it in a different light, for he thought that the thrashings tended to bring the hero of the book into contempt. The author should have passed them over in silence, he said. Sancho muttered something to himself, and Don Quixote admonished him to be quiet so that the bachelor might tell him more of what was said of him in the book.

"And about me!" broke in Sancho, "for they say that I am one of the principal presonages in it."

"Personages," corrected Samson, adding that Sancho was the second person in the chronicle, although many thought he was even first. He also remarked that the author had been criticized for having inserted a story called "Ill-Advised Curiosity," which had nothing to do with Don Quixote whatever. This Don Quixote thought was an infringement on the hero's rights, and corroborated the justification of the criticism.

Thus Don Quixote learned from the bachelor all about his own deeds and exploits, as they had been given to the world by the great Moorish sage Cid Hamet Benengeli. And when he had asked about himself again and again, and had been satisfied by the replies of Samson, he found it was nearly dinner time. Sancho took a hurried leave, fearing the wrath of his wife if he were late for his meal, and Don Quixote asked the bachelor to stay and keep him company.

All the while they were eating, Don Quixote entertained his guest with tales of chivalry. When they finished their repast, they took a nap, and when they awoke, Sancho was there waiting for them to return to their conversation concerning the famous chronicle.

CHAPTER IV

In Which Sancho Panza gives a Satisfactory Reply to the Doubts and Questions of the Bachelor Samson Carrasco Together with other Matters Worth Knowing and Mentioning

SAMSON was anxious to learn what Sancho had done with the hundred crowns he had found in the knapsack. Sancho replied that he had spent them for the benefit of himself, his wife and children, adding that, had he come back to his wife without riches of any sort, he would have had a doubtful reward waiting for him. Now, he said, if anybody wanted to know anything about him, he was ready to answer the King himself.

"It is no one's business," said he, "whether I took the money, or did not; whether I spent it or did not spend it, for if every beating I have received in my master's service were to be valued at no more than four maravedis, another hundred crowns would not pay me for half of them. Let each look to himself and not try to make out white, black; and black, white; for each of us is as God made us—aye, and often worse."

Don Quixote was curious to know whether there was to be a second part to the book; and Samson replied that the author was diligently looking for one, but had as yet found none; so it remained only a possibility. Yet, inspired by the profits he had made out of the first book, he was anxious to find a second part, he said.

"The author looks for money and profit, does he?" asked Sancho. "Well, let Master Moor, or whoever he is, pay attention to what he is doing, and I and my master will give him adventures and accidents of all sorts, enough to make up not only a second part but a hundred. The good man fancies, no doubt, we are asleep in the straw here, but let him hold up our feet to be shod and he will see which foot it is we go lame on. All I say is, that if my master would take my advice, we would now be afield, redressing outrages and righting wrongs, as is the use and custom of good knights errant."

Scarcely had Sancho spoken these words, when Rocinante commenced to neigh; and how could this be interpreted to be anything else than a good omen? In an instant Don Quixote had resolved to sally forth again in a
few days. The bachelor warned him this time to expose
himself to no such tremendous risks as on his previous
sallies, and begged him to remember always, his life was no
longer his own, but was dedicated to those in need and in
despair.

"There is what I abominate, Señor Samson," Sancho sus-
tained him. "My master will attack a hundred men as a
greedy boy would half a dozen melons. Body of the
world, Señor bachelor, there is a time to attack and a time
to retreat!"

And here it was that Sancho felt it a solemn duty to himself and his wife and offspring to come to a definite understanding with his master regarding his position in battle.
He wanted it stipulated that his master was to do all the
fighting. He would willingly look after his master's and
Rocinante's comfort, and keep them clean, but when it
came to drawing sword, he would leave that honor to Don
Quixote, he declared. He would do his duty so well that
it would be worth a kingdom as well as an island, both of
which he would gladly accept.

The bachelor, having recommended Saragossa and the
kingdom of Aragon as hotbeds of adventure, Don Quixote
thanked him and asked him whether he was a poet; to which
the bachelor replied that he was not one of the famous ones.
Don Quixote explained that he wanted a most original
idea of his carried out in poetry. Could Samson write a

poem of love in such a manner as to have the first letters of each line, reading downward, form the name of his beloved one, the peerless Dulcinea del Toboso? Samson promised he would try, but Don Quixote replied: "It must be done by some means or other, for unless the name stands there plain and manifest, no woman would believe the verses were made for her." And so the bachelor promised to do it, and to have them ready before the day of the departure, which would be on the third day.

Don Quixote extracted a promise from Samson to keep his intentions a secret; and he and Sancho took leave of him, Don Quixote promising he would not fail to send him word of his conquests. Sancho in the meantime went home and began preparations for their second quest of adventure.

CHAPTER V

Of the Shrewd and Droll Conversation That Passed
Between Sancho Panza and His Wife,
Teresa Panza, and Other Matters
Worthy of Being Duly Recorded

WHEN Sancho came home that evening, his wife noticed at once by his mood that something out of the ordinary had happened to him. After much persuasion, he finally told her that he had made up his mind to go out in the world again with his master, looking for strange adventures, during which, he said, he hoped to come across another hundred crowns that he would bring home to her.   Then Sancho proceeded to tell his wife of his great plans for the future, when he became ruler of his island.   Their daughter, Maria, he was was going to marry off to some great count; his wife would be Doña Teresa Panza, and he pictured her already, dressed according to richest fashion, sitting in her pew in church, surrounded by cushions and pillows, and walking on a red plush carpet. And as to his son, he should, of course, as was the custom, follow his father's trade; so what was he to do but be a ruler?

But everything that her illustrious husband proposed, Teresa Panza only sneered at; and this angered Sancho, who thought she might be more appreciative.   Certainly not every husband in their village offered to do as much for his wife and family.   And so they began to quarrel with each other, Sancho using—as he invariably did with his master—all the proverbs he had ever heard, to defeat the arguments his wife put forward, enforced in the same manner.   But when her good Sancho finally lost his patience with her entirely, she gave in and promised to go so far as to send their young son to him—that his father might train him in the business of government—as soon as Sancho, as the governor of the island, should send his wife the necessary money.   Sancho charged her particularly with the task of seeing that the son on his departure should be dressed as a prince of the blood.

And all the while poor Teresa Panza was receiving her husband's instructions as to herself and her two children, she was bemoaning and struggling against their fate in her heart; and at last she burst into bitter tears. Seeing her in such agony because he had predestined that their daughter Maria was to marry a mighty count instead of a poor peasant boy, Sancho tried to soothe her feelings by telling her that he would try to put off the day of the wedding as long as possible; and this promise seemed to cheer Teresa Panza to some extent, for she dried her tears.

Having accomplished so much, Sancho then went back to his master's house to talk over some things of importance with him.

CHAPTER VI

Of What Took Place Between Don Quixote and His Niece and His Housekeeper; One of the Most Important Chapters in the Whole History

WHILE Sancho and his wife were flinging proverbs at each other at home, there was another scene of unrest at Don Quixote's house. The housekeeper had had a premonition of her master's impending expedition, and soon perceived by his actions that she had not been alarmed in vain. She and the niece employed all possible means to restrain him from faring forth; but to all their admonitions and advice and prayers he made the same reply: that there must be knights errant in the world to defend the weak and virtuous and to punish arrogance and sin, and that he was the one to set the world aright on that score. And when his niece began to bewail his stubborn-

[161]

ness and called down the wrath of heaven upon all tales of chivalry, he threatened to chastise her for uttering such blasphemies. Then he burst into a tirade on things and usages pertaining to chivalry, a discourse so saturated with knowledge that it called forth a cry of astonishment, a wail of disappointment, and a sigh of pity from the niece, to whom it suddenly seemed that her uncle had missed his vocation in life when he did not become a preacher.

This drove Don Quixote to discourse on almost everything under the sun, and he finished up by reciting poetry, at which the niece became terror-stricken from superstition, and exclaimed that her uncle knew everything in the world. She even dared to suppose he knew something about masonry and could build a house. This daring thought of hers he immediately corroborated by saying that if he were not so occupied with dealing out justice to the world, there would be nothing he could not do, from building cages to making toothpicks.

Just then there was a knock at the door. It was Sancho Panza. As soon as the housekeeper learned it was he, she fled from the room, for she had grown to detest him like sin itself. The niece opened the door for him, and he hastened to his master's room, where he was welcomed by Don Quixote. And soon they were in the midst of a conversation, which took place behind locked doors.

THE SECRETS OF MASTER AND SQUIRE

CHAPTER VII

Of What Passed Between Don Quixote and His Squire, Together with Other Very Notable Incidents

AS soon as the housekeeper heard Don Quixote turn the key in the door, she realized the urgency of the situation, put on her shawl, and ran to the house of the bachelor Samson Carrasco. She knew that her master had taken a fancy to this learned young man and thought he might be able to persuade him to give up the crazy idea. She fell on her knees before Samson and told him in excited language that her master had broken out again.

"Where is he breaking out?" asked the roguish bachelor.

"He is breaking out at the door of his madness," replied the bewildered housekeeper. "I mean he is going to break out again, for the third time, to hunt all over the world for what he calls adventures."

And then she went on to say that his first sally ended in his being brought back home, slung across the back of a donkey. The second time he made his entry into the village in an ox-cart, shut up in a cage, and looking so worn and emaciated that his own mother would not have known him. The last escapade had been an extremely expensive one, for it had taken no less than six hundred eggs to cover up his bones again.

The bachelor quieted the housekeeper, and promised her

[163]

to do all he could for her master. Then he advised her to return home and prepare something hot for breakfast, and on her way home to repeat the prayer of Santa Appolonia. He himself would be there in time for breakfast, he said. The housekeeper remonstrated with the bachelor for prescribing the prayer of Santa Appolonia, which, she declared, was for toothache and not for brains; but Samson told her to do as he bade her, reminding her that he was a learned bachelor of Salamanca and knew what he was talking about. The housekeeper then left, saying her prayer, and the bachelor went to look for the curate that they might decide what to do.

In the meantime Don Quixote and Sancho were discussing what the future was holding for them, and Sancho gave the glad news to his master that he had induced his wife to sanction his departure and his becoming governor. Sancho was very much annoyed by his master's continual interruptions and corrections. Whenever Sancho would misuse or abuse a word, as he did in almost every sentence, Don Quixote would stop and ask him what he meant, until poor Sancho was so confused that he did not know what he had meant. Finally Don Quixote asked him to tell him all that his wife had said, and as soon as Sancho had a chance to use proverbs again, he felt more at home. "Teresa says," he repeated, "that I should make sure with your Worship, and let papers speak and beards be still. One *take* is better than two *I'll give thee's.*"

"And so say I," said Don Quixote. "Continue, Sancho my friend. Go on; thou talkest pearls to-day."

"The fact is," continued Sancho, "that, as your Worship

knows better than I do, we are all of us liable to death, and to-day we are, and to-morrow we are not. The lamb goes as soon as the sheep, and nobody can promise himself more hours of life in this world than God may be pleased to give him; for death is deaf, and when it comes to knock at our life's door, it is always insistent, and neither prayers, nor struggles, nor scepters, nor miters, can keep it back, as they tell us from the pulpits every day."

Here Don Quixote felt he ought to ask a question. "Sancho," said he, "all that is true; but what art thou driving at?"

And then came the reason for all these long-winded preliminaries. Sancho wanted his master to make definite arrangements with him for compensation. But here was the drawback. Don Quixote could recall no incident in any of the many books he had read, when a knight errant had given his squire fixed wages. How could he possibly establish a precedent now? And so it became his sad and solemn duty to refuse his squire's miserly request, and inform him that his services were no longer wanted. Not only that, but our valiant hero was cruel enough to remark that there would be any number of people who would be only too eager to serve him; and, what was more, he was convinced that no one could be less careful and diligent, or more thick-headed and talkative than Sancho.

Poor Sancho stood thunderstruck. He had expected his master would address him in a much more gracious manner; and had taken for granted that his own person was indispensable to his master. As he stood there gaping in amazement, the bachelor, Samson, suddenly entered, followed by the niece and the housekeeper. Samson threw himself on his knees before the knight, passionately declaiming:

"O flower of knight-errantry! O shining light of arms! O honor and mirror of the Spanish nation! May God Almighty grant that any person or persons who would impede or hinder thy third sally, may find no way out of the labyrinth of their schemes, nor ever accomplish what they most desire!"

Then he rose and turned to the housekeeper, who was distressed and astonished beyond words, telling her it was no use gainsaying her master; that he had made up his mind, and no Santa Appolonia or any other prayer would cause him to change it. Whereupon he addressed Don Quixote again in the same lofty way, and slyly asked him whether he would deign to accept him as his squire or as his meanest servant.

Sancho's eyes nearly bulged out of his head at this, and filled with tears. Fearing that he might lose both his master and his island, he embraced Don Quixote's knees and kissed his hand, begging Don Quixote not to give him up. Then he began to plead with him to leave the village at once. Don Quixote, having taken the squire into his fold again, embraced him, and then conferred with the bachelor and decided that they would set out three days hence. Samson promised to obtain a helmet for Don Quixote before the departure.

In the meantime the bachelor had daily conferences with the curate and the barber. The niece and the housekeeper were cursing the evil and learned bachelor of Salamanca, and hardly slept at night for fear that Don Quixote would steal away in the darkness.

Finally the night of the third day arrived, and Don Quixote and Sancho, accompanied by Samson, quietly and secretly stole out of the village, in the direction of El Toboso. When they had ridden half a league, Samson wished the knight errant godspeed, embraced him tenderly, begged him to let him hear of his good fortune, and then he returned to the village.

CHAPTER VIII

Wherein Is Related What Befell Don Quixote on His Way to See His Lady Dulcinea Del Toboso

SCARCELY had Samson departed before Rocinante began to neigh, and Dapple, Sancho's donkey, to bray; and these animal expressions, considering the time, and the road they were taking, were interpreted by their respective masters to be omens of good luck. But it so happened that Dapple kept up his braying. As a matter of fact he brayed so much louder than the emaciated Rocinante could neigh that the superstitious Sancho took it for a sign that his own good fortune would be ever so much greater than that of his master, though he was considerate enough to say nothing about it to him.

Night soon began to fall, and the conversation between master and squire turned to Don Quixote's incomparable love, whom he had never seen in the flesh, and to whose abode he was now making this pilgrimage in the dark, that he might be blessed by her before going into new battles.

Sancho was beginning to worry that his imagination, with which he was not overburdened, would give out; for with every new question of his master's he had to give a fresh answer, and he was in a deadly fear that Don Quixote might discover that he had never been at El Toboso with the letter to his Lady Dulcinea. Again Don Quixote asked his squire to repeat how he had been received when he had brought her the message of his master's penance in the wilderness, but it infuriated him that Sancho should insist on her having been sifting wheat instead of pearls on that occasion. The courtyard wall mentioned by his squire must, of course, have been a portico, or corridor, or gallery of some rich and royal palace, only Sancho's language was so limited he could not express himself or describe things properly. Or perhaps that infernal enchanter had been busy again, and made things appear in different shapes before his squire's eyes.

What his master said made Sancho's thought suddenly turn to the book which the bachelor Samson had spoken of, and he began to worry that some enchanter might have misrepresented his true character in its pages. He felt it his place and duty to defend himself aloud against any such evil; and having his master as audience, he proceeded to carry out this thought, which, however, he abandoned towards the end in favor of a careless independence: "But let them say what they like; naked was I born, naked I find myself. I neither lose nor gain. When I see myself put into a book and passed on from hand to hand all over the world, I don't care a fig. Let them say what they like of me!"

Perhaps what Sancho had just said made Don Quixote's thoughts drift out into the world, which was now being stirred by the accounts of his greatness, for he fell into contemplation on all the tombs and monuments to the great men of past ages. He touched upon the tombs of some who had become saints, when suddenly Sancho shot this question to him out of a clear sky: "Tell me, which is the greater work, to bring a dead man to life or to kill a giant?"

Don Quixote was dumfounded by his squire's suddenness, but replied: "The answer is easy. It is a greater work to bring to life a dead man.

"Now I have got you!" Sancho exclaimed. Then he divulged his longing, which he wanted his master to share, to become a saint; viewing a saint's life from all sides, he had come to the conclusion that it was a much more peaceful life than that of a roving knight errant, who had to be up at all hours and out in all sorts of weather.

But his master answered laconically: "We cannot all be friars." And then he went on to say that the number of knights errant in the world, deserving that name, was a very small one; that, as a matter of truth, knight-errantry, was a religion. But Sancho, stubborn as usual, insisted that there were more friars in heaven than knights errant. In this way they passed that night and the following day, without any trace of excitement or adventure.

Finally, at daybreak on the second day, they approached

the great city of El Toboso; and Sancho's worries increased as they came closer to the place where the heart of the peerless Dulcinea was beating—for what was he going to say or do when his master wanted to meet his beloved one? Don Quixote decided to await dusk before entering the city, and they spent the day resting in the shade of some oak-trees outside the town.

CHAPTER IX

WHEREIN IS RELATED WHAT WILL BE SEEN THERE

IT was midnight when they rode into El Toboso. It was a very dark night, so Sancho could not be blamed for not finding the house in the darkness. They were greeted by a multitude of noises: barking dogs, braying asses, mewing cats, and grunting pigs; noises that seemed like an ill ómen to Don Quixote. He suddenly turned to Sancho and said: "Sancho, my son, lead on to the place of Dulcinea. It may be that we shall find her awake."

"Body of the sun! What palace am I to lead to, when what I saw Her Highness in was only a very little house?" exclaimed the squire.

"Most likely she had then withdrawn into some small apartment of her palace," said Don Quixote, "to amuse herself with her damsels, as great ladies and princesses are accustomed to do."

"Here Sancho told his master to have it his own way,

but asked him whether he thought it in conformity with the behavior of a gentleman to go around in the middle of the night knocking at people's doors. Don Quixote dispensed with the discussion of this particular point; all he wanted to do, he said, was to find the house. Then they could discuss how to proceed. So they roamed about the city, Don Quixote insisting that first one house and then another was the palace of his love, until they finally hit upon the great tower of the church. At last he had found it, he declared. Here was where she dwelt, he was quite sure.

But Sancho, hearing this and seeing it was a church, began to feel ill at ease, for his superstitious soul did not like the idea of walking across a graveyard at such an hour of the night. He quickly told his master, he was now certain that the Lady Dulcinea lived in an alley, a kind thought which was rewarded by a fierce outburst from Don Quixote.

"The curse of God on thee for a blockhead!" he exclaimed. "Where hast thou ever heard of castles and royal palaces being built in alleys?"

"I wish I saw the dogs eating it for leading us such a dance," was all that Sancho said in reply.

But evidently this was not a pleasing answer to Don Quixote, for he admonished his squire: "Speak respectfully of what belongs to my lady; let us keep the feast in peace, and not throw the rope after the bucket!"

Sancho muttered something about how he could be expected to find, in the dark of night, a house he had only seen once in his lifetime, when his master, who must have seen it hundreds of times, could not recognize it. To this his master retorted wearily that he had told him a thousand times that he was enamored only by hearsay, and had never visited Dulcinea in her palace.

At this moment a laborer on his way to his work came along on the road, singing a dreary song. It was only another omen to Don Quixote that his efforts to approach his lady would not be crowned with success that night. He asked the man to direct him to the palace of his princess, but the laborer turned out to be a stranger, having only just come to the city.

Don Quixote was grieved that he could not find Dulcinea, and when Sancho suggested that they withdraw from the city and develop a plan for seeing her, he was ready to accept it. So they left El Toboso and hid in a forest nearby. There it was decided that Sancho should return to the city as the messenger of love for his master.

CHAPTER X

WHEREIN IS RELATED THE CRAFTY DEVICE SANCHO ADOPTED TO ENCHANT THE LADY DULCINEA, AND OTHER INCIDENTS AS LUDICROUS AS THEY ARE TRUE

DON QUIXOTE instructed Sancho to ask his lady for an audience for him, and he begged his squire to observe every little change in her expression and demeanor, that he might tell him about it afterward. Sancho then set off on Dapple; but as soon as he was out of sight, he dismounted, seated himself on the ground, and took measure of the situation aloud. In a meditative soliloquy he discussed with himself the problem that was his, and he finally reasoned that there was a remedy for everything except death. If his master could take windmills for giants, and a flock of sheep for an army, why could he not take black for white, and any country lass that came along, for his princess? Having reached this satisfactory conclusion, he decided to remain where he was till in the afternoon, in which time he could reasonably have gone to El Toboso and returned.

As the afternoon arrived, three country girls came along on their donkeys, on the road from the city. The moment Sancho saw them, he mounted his ass and returned to find his master, who nearly went out of his head with joy, and promised Sancho the three next foals from his three mares, when his squire told him that the Lady Dulcinea was coming to see him, accompanied by two of her ladies-in-waiting. And then the lying Sancho went on to describe them: how they were robed in richest brocade, and weighted down with jewels—precious stones and pearls. But when Don Quixote saw the three peasant girls approach, he said he could see nothing but three jackasses and three girls. Any princess, or any one like one, he failed to see. Finally Sancho persuaded him to believe that those he saw were really three ladies, one of them being the Peerless One, who had come to bestow her blessing upon him. And so Don Quixote fell on his knees in the dust of the road before the girls, giving vent to his immeasurable gratitude to her, his queen, who had come all this distance to give him her blessing.

When the ugly peasant girl heard herself called a queen and Dulcinea, she thought that Don Quixote was trying to play a joke on her, so she got angry, and yelled to him: "Get out of the way, bad luck to you, and let us pass, for we are in a hurry!" and left the astonished knight crawling in the dust.

Sancho had also fallen to his knees, to help his master in his plea for blessing, and he called out after the peasant girls: "Oh, princess and universal lady of El Toboso, is not your heart softened by seeing the pillar and prop of knight-errantry on his knees before your sublimated presence?"

When the wenches were out of sight, Don Quixote turned to his squire and bemoaned, cast-down, his evil fate, and the length his sage enemy would go to gain his ends. The very worst thing of all, he said, was that the evil enchanter had turned his Dulcinea into an ugly peasant, who smelled of garlic. And while Don Quixote was thus complaining, Sancho struggled to hide his laughter, happy to have saved himself and to have played such a joke on his master.

At last Don Quixote was ready to mount his hack, and they steered their beasts in the direction of Saragossa.

HE MEETS DEATH AND THE DEVIL

CHAPTER XI

Of the Strange Adventure Which the Valiant Don Quixote Had with the Car or Cart of "The Cortes of Death"

SANCHO did his best to imbue his master with a new inspiration; for Don Quixote was a sorry sight as he was riding along on his hack. The enchantment of his Dulcinea had been a great blow to him. He fell into a sort of meditative slumber, from which he would rouse himself only now and then. Suddenly, however, he was fully awake, for on the road he saw before his very eyes a cart with Death on the front seat, and drawn by mules that were being led by the Devil himself.

As soon as the knight could gather his senses, he distinguished the rest of the strange company that occupied the cart. Next to Death sat an ugly angel with wings, and on the other side Don Quixote observed an emperor with a crown of gold on his head. Then he discovered Cupid—who was a god—and a knight with plumes in his hat. There were a number of other figures, all weird and awe-inspiring, in strange costumes and with curious faces, and when Sancho saw them he turned as pale as Death himself, and his teeth began to chatter from fright. Even Don Quixote was more than startled, but his heroism soon asserted itself, and he was quickly himself again, glad to sense another adventure. He gave Rocinante the spur, the lean hack sprang forward to the cart at a sickly gallop, and Don Quixote exclaimed: "Carter or coachman, or devil or whatever thou art, tell me at once who thou art, whither thou art going, and who these folk are thou carriest in thy wagon, which looks more like Charon's boat than an ordinary cart!"

To this challenge the devil responded on behalf of himself and his fellow-travelers, explaining that they were harmless players of Angulo el Malo's company; that they had been acting the play of "The Cortes of Death" in the village from which they had just come; and since they had to act the same play in a village nearby in the afternoon, they wished to save themselves the trouble of making up twice, by remaining in their costumes. The devil was extremely polite and offered to give Don Quixote any information he could, adding that, being the devil, he was up to everything; besides he played the leading parts, he said. Don Quixote told them how disappointed he was that this had not turned out to be another adventure; then he wished them a happy journey, saying that ever since he was a child he had been an admirer of the actor and fond of his art.

As they were about to take leave, one of the mummers, with three blown ox-bladders at the end of a stick, came up and banged them against the ground under Rocinante's nose; and the frightened animal set off across the plain as if he had been shot out of a cannon, taking the bit in his teeth. Sancho was so certain his master would be thrown that he left his donkey and ran as fast as he could after Rocinante. But when he reached Don Quixote, the knight was already on the ground and with him Rocinante, whose legs always seemed to give away after a sudden strain.

Now, as soon as Sancho had run away from Dapple, the crazy devil with the bladders was on his back tickling his ears with them, and the donkey flew across the fields toward the village as if beset.

Seeing his faithful one running away, Sancho was in mortal agony, as well as in a quandary, for he did not know whether to attend to the donkey or his master first. Finally he found his love for human beings was the greater, and rushed to his master's side. When he had helped him to mount, he told him that the devil had run away with Dapple. Immediately Don Quixote was ready to pursue the enemy; but just then the squire saw his Dapple come running back, and cautioned his master to be meek.

But Don Quixote was eager to give the mummer a lesson in courtesy, even, as he said, if he had to visit his sin upon the rest of the company, not barring the Emperor himself. Sancho did his best to warn his master that there was great danger in meddling with actors, as they were a favored class; but had the King himself interfered in their behalf, it would not have stayed the hand of the errant revenger.

So Don Quixote drew forth, and caught up with the cart as it was close to the village. He commanded the players to halt, saying he wanted to teach them how to be courteous to donkeys and animals that served squires and knights errant for steeds. The merrymakers could tell by his stentorian tone that he was not jesting, so they all quickly jumped out of the cart and armed themselves with stones.

By this time Sancho had reached the scene of action,

[177]

and as soon as he saw the threatening attitude of the strollers, he begged his master not to fight against either Death or the angels, particularly since neither one of them was a knight errant; nor was there any one in the whole company who was. This point Don Quixote thought was wisely taken, and he ordered his squire to fight the battle himself. · But Sancho said he preferred to show a Christian spirit and forgive, and promised his master he would come to an agreement with his donkey to leave *his* end of the grievance to the squire's goodwill.

Don Quixote let Sancho have his way; and when they had seen the caravan of mountebanks disappear, Sancho was happy in the thought that he had averted a great calamity for himself and his master.

CHAPTER XII

OF THE STRANGE ADVENTURE WHICH BEFELL THE VALIANT DON QUIXOTE WITH THE BOLD KNIGHT OF THE GROVE

THEY passed that night under some cork-trees, and while they were eating their supper, Sancho as usual became talkative and again gave proof of his chronic weakness for proverbs. Every phrase abounded with them. As ever, he would use them to fit the wrong case, or twist them so as to fit what he wanted them to fit. Don Quixote had to laugh at his squire's simplicity, and at the way he tried to imitate his master's manner of speaking. His words and expressions were indeed a strange mixture.

THE KNIGHT OF THE GROVE

One moment he would use the most abominable grammar and the next he would borrow the language of Don Quixote, repeating in stilted fashion the polite phrases he had heard Don Quixote use in his flowery discourses on knighthood and chivalry.

Soon after they had fallen asleep, Don Quixote was awakened by the sound of men's voices. He quickly rose, curious and anxious to learn who the disturbers were, and was amazed to behold a real knight, clad in full armor, dismount from his horse, while speaking words that indicated he was lovesick and in despair. Don Quixote hastened to call Sancho, who awoke to the tune of a love sonnet sung by the strange knight, and was as startled as his master had been, though, perhaps, not greatly thrilled at this promise of a new adventure in the middle of the night.

But if Don Quixote was surprised when he was awakened, what was his amazement when he suddenly heard such words as these: "O fairest and most ungrateful woman on earth! Can it be possible, most serene Casildea de Vandalia, that thou wilt suffer this thy captive knight to waste away and perish in ceaseless wanderings and rude and arduous toils? Is it not enough that I have compelled all the knights of Navarre, the Leonese, the Tartesians, and the Castilians, and finally all the knights of La Mancha to confess thee the most beautiful in the world?"

Don Quixote took exception to this last statement in silence, knowing that his chance to correct it was at no great distance. But Sancho soon gave himself and his master away to the Knight of the Grove by becoming too talkative, and they were hailed by the knight, who greeted them in the most courteous manner, when he learned who they were.

The two knights errant soon were engaged in a friendly conversation, which Sancho could not restrain himself from breaking into; but the Knight of the Grove was quick to reprimand him, saying he never permitted his squire to open his mouth. Whereupon Sancho persuaded himself and the squire of the Grove to remove to a spot where they could talk between themselves without being overheard by their superiors, and where they might be undisturbed by any yoke of knighthood etiquette.

CHAPTERS XIII—XIV

In Which Is Continued the Adventure of the Knight of the Grove, Together with the Sensible and Tranquil Colloquy That Passed Between the Two Squires

THE two squires drank and talked most of the night, bemoaning the fate of squires in general. Before they finally fell asleep, the squire of the Grove suggested that, since they both were tired of knight-errantry, they give up the life. To this Sancho replied that he would remain in his master's service until he arrived at Saragossa, when he might decide to leave him.

In the meantime the two knights also were exchanging confidences; and the Knight of the Grove told Don Quixote of all the great and famous errants he had conquered in single combat. Don Quixote was all ear, but nearly gasped for breath when he heard the knight say that he had vanquished the famous Don Quixote of La Mancha, and had made him confess that his own Casildea was more beautiful by far than the La Mancha knight's Dulcinea. Don Quixote suppressed a scornful smile that threatened to betray him, and controlled the feelings that the boasting errant's words provoked, while wondering at the braggart's audacity. He slyly expressed a doubt, however, that the valiant knight Don Quixote of La Mancha had let himself be vanquished by any living being. The Knight of the Grove then gave a description of Don Quixote which in every detail fitted him.

That drew Don Quixote out of his originally assumed indifference. He told the knight that he himself was no other than that famed and illustrious errant, and declared that any other one that had appeared as Don Quixote, must have been some enchanter who had disguised himself to resemble him, in order to defraud him of the honor that was rightly due to him. Then he proceeded to tell the knight how his enemy had transformed the Lady Dulcinea, and challenged the Knight of the Grove to single combat if he dared to question what Don Quixote maintained to be the truth.

To this challenge the Knight of the Grove retorted that since he had once vanquished the semblance of Don Quixote, he would now welcome the opportunity of meeting him in combat in his own proper shape. Being a cautious and cold-blooded knight, however, he suggested to Don Quixote that they should rest until the morning, when the mighty struggle could ensue in the light of day. It was further agreed that the vanquished knight should place himself at the command of the victor, to fulfill any desire of his within the bounds of chivalry.

Each one was eager to inform his own squire of what the morning was to behold, so they awoke Sancho and the squire of the Grove and told them. Sancho was scared that his master might not be the gainer, for the squire of the Grove had been feeding him with stories of his master's conquests all that night until they had fallen asleep, drunk with wine.

The squires went to get the horses ready, and on the way Sancho was aghast to learn that he would have to fight the friendly squire of the Grove in cold blood, this squire maintaining that such was a rule among knights errant. Sancho said he would rather give two pounds of wax to the church than fight with him; furthermore, he said, he could not, for he had no sword, and never had had one. Whereupon the friendly squire told him that did not matter, and proceeded to make ready two linen bags, both of the same size, saying they could fight their duel in this fashion. This was most pleasing to Sancho, until he perceived the other squire filling the bags with pebbles, when he remonstrated, saying he thought their masters could settle the whole affair without their interference. But his friend the squire insisted that they fight, even if it should be only for half an hour, and offered—if he should have any difficulty in rousing himself to the occasion—to give Sancho a few cudgels and whacks to act as an inspiration.

By this time it was beginning to dawn, and Sancho was

watching the sunrise. As he looked around, the first object that he saw the sunrays strike was the nose of the squire of the Grove, protruding out of the opened visor of his helmet. It was an object so fearful to look at that Sancho Panza was paralyzed with fright. The nose was so large it seemed uncanny. It was covered with warts and was bent at a tremendous angle, and it hung down way beneath his chin, while its color was that of an eggplant. It was a face so horrible and ugly to look at that Sancho's eyes nearly rolled out of his head. He acted as if he were about to have convulsions, for he began to tremble from head to foot. When Don Quixote beheld the squire's countenance, even he began to show signs of feebleness, but his bravery overcame his fears. He shrugged his shoulders as if shaking off an evil spirit, and was ready for the combat with his adversary.

Before the battle began, Sancho pleaded with his master to help him up into a tree; so afraid was he of this monstrous squire with the awful nose. But while Don Quixote was hoisting his faithful one up into a cork-tree, he suddenly heard the knight approach on his steed behind him, and not knowing whether it was squire or master, and being subconsciously afraid of the nose, one blow of which might have felled him, it seemed, he turned around and made straight for the knight.

The facts were that this gentleman was trying to limber up the joints of his charger—a hack of the same caliber as Rocinante—and was just taking his horse on a tour of exercise, making him skip hither and thither, wherever his master's agonized spurring would carry him. Each time he would land heavily on his stiff legs, and it was when Don Quixote suddenly heard the sound of such a landing behind him that he turned. But by the time Rocinante had completed the turn, which was a movement of much contemplation and hesitation on his part, the back of the Knight of the Grove shone in the distance. Charging by sound and instinct rather than by sight, not seeing whether the knight was coming or going, Don Quixote set upon him with such blind fury that with one thrust of his lance he sent the bespangled gentleman flying out of his saddle, so that he fell flat on the ground, seemingly dead.

Now, when Sancho saw what an auspicious beginning and ending the adventure had had for his master, he heaved a sigh of relief and contentment and climbed down from his tree, approaching the lifeless monster with caution and superstitious awe. But he had taken only one look into his face, when he began to cross himself with so many motions and contortions that Don Quixote thought his squire had gone insane. Turning to his master, who had been contemplating his victory with pride from the back of Rocinante, Sancho begged him to thrust his sword into the mouth of his vanquished foe. Scarcely had he made this suggestion before Don Quixote drew his sword and advanced to carry it out, when the squire of the Grove, now minus the drooping nose, ran forward, wildly exclaiming: "Mind what you are about to do, Señor Don Quixote! That is your friend the bachelor, Samson Carrasco, you have at your feet, and I am his squire!"

"And the nose?" Sancho broke in, unable to restrain his amazed senses.

"I have it here in my pocket," answered the squire of the Grove, as he pulled out and showed him a false nose of immense proportions.

Whereupon Sancho eyed the squire more carefully, and suddenly cried out: "Holy Mary be good to me! Isn't it Tom Cecial, my neighbor and gossip!"

And Tom was only too glad to confess that he was.

At this very moment the bachelor returned from the dead, and when Don Quixote saw him open his eyes, he pointed his sword at his face and swore that the Knight of the Mirrors—thus he called the Knight of the Grove because of his shining regalia—would be a dead man if he did not pronounce the Lady Dulcinea del Toboso the most beautiful woman in the world. Furthermore, he demanded that he swear to present himself before the Peerless One in the city of El Toboso, that she might deal out judgment upon him. Having been dealt with by her, the Knight of the Grove was to return to inform him of the punishment, giving a full account of what had passed between them.

The fallen Samson gladly confessed to everything, including his belief in the true identity of his conqueror. He felt an urgent need for medicine and plaster, and he and his squire departed quickly to seek such aid in the nearest village, while Don Quixote and Sancho took the road which lead to Saragossa.

CHAPTER XV

WHEREIN IT IS MADE KNOWN HOW THE KNIGHT OF THE MIRROR
AND HIS SQUIRE EMERGED FROM THEIR ADVENTURE

AS Don Quixote was bumping along on his lean Rocinante, he was dreaming of the return of the Knight of the Mirrors, who would bring him word about his beloved one. He was anxious to know whether she was still enchanted. Then he thought of the great victory he had won over this bold knight, and it was perhaps only pardonable if it aroused some conceit in his breast.

But while Don Quixote was contemplating thus, the bachelor-knight kept bemoaning the fate he had brought upon himself. He had dubbed himself Knight at his own instigation, for the kindly and unselfish purpose of unseating and vanquishing Don Quixote in battle, thinking, of course, that that would be an easy matter to accomplish. It was for good reasons he had proposed that the vanquished one should place himself at the disposal of the victor. The bachelor, the curate, and the barber had conferred after Don Quixote's departure as to what to do, and when the bachelor Samson offered to go crusading and to bring back Don Quixote, the two gossips were pleased beyond words. A neighbor of Sancho's, Tom Cecial by name, was induced to become the squire of the knight Samson.

Both knight and squire were now contemplating in a sorry mood the disastrous outcome of their encounter with the Knight of the Rueful Countenance. As they were staggering along on their decrepit mounts, the squire summed up the thoughts of his master Samson in this question: "I'd like to know now which is the madder, he who is so because he can not help it, or he who is so of his own choice?"

While the learned bachelor was thoroughly in accord with the good reason for asking such a question, he could not at the same time help acknowledging the fact that the thrashing he had received was paining him. The desire he had had when he started out looking for Don Quixote —to bring him back to his home and his wits—was now changed into a wild inner cry for revenge.

At last some of the physical agony of the Knight of the Mirrors was stilled by a quack, whom they found in a town along the road. Tom Cecial, the squire for a day and a night, had been cured of knight-errantry and returned to his less venturesome occupation in his La Mancha village; but the thoughts of evilness would not leave his master, who stayed behind, bent on having his revenge.

CHAPTER XVI

Of What Befell Don Quixote with a Discreet Gentleman of La Mancha

WHILE Don Quixote was contemplating his own greatness as a reviver of knight-errantry, the monstrous nose of the squire kept coming before Sancho in his fancies. When he told his master, Don Quixote asked him whether he ever for a moment doubted that the knight of the Mirrors and his squire were anything but enchanted and made to appear like the two village friends of theirs. The idea that Samson, who was such a devoted friend of his, should be envious of his deeds in battle and have wanted to steal away honors from him as a knight, was too absurd; and with this he dismissed the subject.

While they were discussing these matters and the enchantment of the Lady Dulcinea, they were passed by a gentleman on horseback, and Don Quixote called to him and asked him politely whether he would not join company with them. The traveler accepted the knight's invitation, and both were soon scrutinizing each other. The gentleman, a man about fifty years of age, with handsome features, wondered at the strange appearance of Don Quixote; and when our knight saw his wonder, he told him why he was so attired and what he had set out to accomplish in the world. This confession drew forth still more astonishment on the gentleman's countenance, but he finally found words to ask whether he could really believe his own ears, for he had thought knight-errantry extinct. It was not long, however, before he realized that he was talking to a madman; and then Sancho Panza came under his observation, and he was deemed a simpleton.

Don Quixote had asked the newcomer's name, and learned it was Don Diego de Miranda; and then the knight was curious to know what he did with his life. Whereupon Don Diego proceeded to tell his fellow-travelers of his tame and godly life in the country with his wife and children; and he pronounced in the course of his description some very beautiful thoughts and principles, which so took Sancho's fancy that he jumped off Dapple, embraced the gentleman's leg, and began to kiss his feet in the most passionate and ardent way.

Astonished, the good gentleman inquired what all this display meant; and Sancho begged of him between his transports: "Let me kiss, for I think your Worship is the first saint in the saddle I ever saw!"

Of course, the gentleman confessed his sinfulness to Sancho, who refused to change his opinion, in spite of his master's honest laughter. Then the gentleman told Don Quixote about his great pride, his son, who was eighteen years old, had been a student at Salamanca, and wrote divine poems. This immediately inspired Don Quixote to a discourse on poetry, in which he dwelt on the dishonor of commercializing this great gift of the gods. He finished his speech with the advice to Don Diego that he bring up his son to write discourses in which all vice was flayed and all sin chided and rebuked. Above all, he said, a poet must never let envy or personal grudge and hatred guide his pen. When the traveler heard Don Quixote speak in so wise and discerning manner, he was aghast; and he was entirely at a loss to know how to judge him. He was inclined to think that what he had taken for madness in him was nothing but eccentricity.

But while Don Quixote was discoursing on poetry, Sancho, on seeing some shepherds, had fled to beg some ewe milk of them. When his master had finished his discourse, and the gentleman was silently considering his madness, Sancho suddenly heard himself called to battle. Having in his possession his master's helmet, he spurred his donkey to further increase his efforts toward speed, and when he reached the valiant knight, he discovered the reason for the call: a cart bedecked with royal flags approaching on the road.

CHAPTER XVII

WHEREIN IS SHOWN THE FARTHEST AND HIGHEST POINT WHICH THE UNEXAMPLED COURAGE OF DON QUIXOTE REACHED OR COULD REACH; TOGETHER WITH THE HAPPILY ACHIEVED ADVENTURE OF THE LIONS

WHEN Sancho was summoned by his master, he had just bought some curds from the goatherd, and not knowing what to do with them at such a moment, he hastily deposited them in his master's helmet. The first thing Don Quixote did when Sancho had caught up with him, was to snatch the helmet from him, exclaiming that he had to make ready for what promised to be an exciting adventure; while all Sancho could see was the cart with the royal flags, probably carrying some treasure of the kings. As Sancho stood watching the cart, Don Quixote resolutely put on the helmet, which he proceeded to press down on his head in order to make it sit fast; but as he did so, the curds were squeezed, and the whey began to run down over his face, so that Don Quixote imagined that he had been taken with softening of the brain.

Sancho said nothing but gave his master something to

wipe his face with, and Don Quixote muttered that if this was sweat he was certain it was going to be a horrible adventure. As he was drying his face, he took off his helmet, and when he smelled the curds he turned to Sancho in great perturbation and accused him of having put them there, calling him a traitor and a scoundrel, and threatening to thrash him. But Sancho eyed his master innocently, and blamed it all on the devil or some enchanter, saying that his master might know that if he had had curds, he would have put them in his stomach and not in his master's helmet.

This was a convincing argument to the knight, who now busied himself with the cart, which had nearly reached them. He called out to the driver and a man on muleback, who were the only attendants: "Whither are you going, brothers? What cart is this? What have you got in it? What flags are those?"

The man on the mule answered that the cart was his, that he was transporting a pair of enormous lions as a present from the Governor of Oran to His Majesty the King; that the flags were those of the King, and that therefore the property was royal property. He added that the lions were hungry, since they had not eaten anything that day, and that he was in great haste to reach a place where he could feed them.

Here Don Quixote smiled a scornful, superior smile, and calmly told the keeper of the lions to open the cages and let out the beasts that they might learn who the courageous Don Quixote of La Mancha might be. When Sancho heard how mad his master was, he turned in sickly fear to the traveling gentleman and begged him for God's sake to keep his master from having a combat with the lions. The gentleman asked Sancho whether he thought his master would really be so foolish as to do such a thing; and Sancho's firm and emphatic reply made the gentleman hasten to the knight's side in an attempt to reason with him. He was promptly reprimanded by Don Quixote, however, who told him sharply to mind his own business, and then threatened to pin the keeper to the cart with his lance if he did not open the cages and chase out the lions at once.

There was an indescribable consternation and confusion. The driver pleaded with Don Quixote on his knees, and when they all saw that he was determined to meet with the lions in combat, they began to pick up their belongings and run away into safety. Sancho and the gentleman made still another attempt to bring him to his senses, but all their pleas were in vain. Sancho left his master with the tears falling down his cheeks, and Don Quixote ordered the gentleman to speed away on his flea-bitten mare as fast as he could, if he was afraid to be bitten by the lions.

Then Don Quixote decided it might be better to fight on foot, as he was afraid that his Rocinante might be frightened on seeing the beasts; so, sword in hand, he bravely advanced towards the cage. The keeper timidly opened the doors of the first cage, and a male lion of tremendous size, stretching himself leisurely, put his claws through the opening; then he yawned sleepily, and after some deliberation began to lick his eyes and face with his long, fierce tongue. Having thus washed his dirty face, he put his head out of the cage and stood gazing into space

with a ferocious look in his eyes, which resembled glowing
coals. Not even seeming surprised at the sight of the valiant knight, he then had the audacity to turn his back on
our hero, and calmly and proudly lay down, with his hindquarters under Don Quixote's very nose.

Such unheard-of scorn angered the knight, who commanded the keeper to take a stick and poke the beast out
of the cage; but here he met with unyielding obstinacy,
for this the man refused to do under any circumstances,
saying that the first one to be chewed to pieces, if he did
that, would be himself. Then he began to praise and flatter Don Quixote's courage which, he said, by this feat had
been unequaled in the world. His adversary the lion, he
said, had proven by his very action that he considered Don
Quixote a superior foe; and when the keeper promised to
give Don Quixote a certificate to the effect that the lion
had been challenged in true knight errant fashion and refused to give battle, Don Quixote was soothed, and bade
the keeper shut the doors to the cage and recall the fugi-
tives that they might hear from the keeper's lips the true
account of his remarkable achievement.

The first thing Don Quixote did when Sancho had
joined him was to order him to give two gold crowns to the
driver and the keeper for lost time; but before Sancho
carried out his master's command he was anxious to know
whether the lions were dead or alive. Whereupon the
keeper related how the valiant knight had single handed
dared the lions to come out of their cage, and how they
meekly and cowardly had refused at the sight of so bold
a warrior; and he embellished his story with numerous

[193]

little details—in anticipation of the gold crown—and added that when he returned to Madrid he would not fail to inform the King of his marvelous exploit.

When Don Quixote heard this, his heart beat faster, and he told the keeper that if the King should happen to ask who performed this great deed, to say it was the Knight of the Lions, since he had decided to adopt this name hereafter.

So the cart proceeded toward the capital, and Don Quixote, Sancho, and the traveling gentleman went their way. Don Diego bade them make haste that they might reach his village before nightfall, and he asked Don Quixote to spend the night at his house and rest after his exertions—an invitation that the knight accepted with profuse thanks.

CHAPTER XVIII

Of What Happened to Don Quixote in the Castle Or House of the Knight of the Green Coat, Together with Other Matters out of the Common

THE Knight of the Green Coat—which was the name Don Quixote had conferred on his host—reached his house in the afternoon, and he was welcomed home by his wife and son, who could not help staring in amazement at the strange figure Don Quixote presented. The latter advanced to the wife and kissed her virtuously on the hand, after having first asked her permission; and she received him courteously, as did the son also. Then he was escorted into the house, and Sancho helped him to remove his armor and to wash him clean of the curds, which had run down his face and his neck. This being done, Don Quixote joined father and son in another room.

It was not long before Don Lorenzo, the young son, was perplexed by the knight's behavior and conversation, and at his first opportunity he confided this perplexity to his father. Don Diego told him that he himself was at his wit's end, for he had heard him speak as sensibly as he ever heard any man speak; then again, he said, he had seen him perform the most unbelievable acts of madness. Don Lorenzo again engaged in conversation with Don Quixote, who told the young man that he had already learned from his father of his great talents as a poet. The youth modestly disclaimed being entitled to be called a great poet; and the absence of conceit in one of this calling pleased the knight greatly. And he went on, discoursing on matters pertaining to education, on universities, and degrees, and his opinions seemed to Don Lorenzo so authoritative and advanced that he was at a loss to know what to conclude, until Don Quixote suddenly began to talk about the science of knight-errantry, which he maintained surpassed all other sciences.

Don Lorenzo interrupted, of course, saying that he had never heard of any such science; he had read books of chivalry but had never believed that any knights had existed, he said. When Don Quixote heard the youth speak such blasphemy, he prayed that heaven should deliver him from his false illusions as to the existence of knight-errantry! Just then dinner was served.

While they were eating, Don Quixote asked Don Lorenzo to repeat some of his verses to him, and the youth read some of his glosses and sonnets. Don Quixote was extremely impressed with them, and he praised the youth's rare gift in eloquent language. This praise—although he knew it to come from a madman—so pleased Don Lorenzo's father that he begged Don Quixote to remain; and for four days the knight was entertained by Don Diego.

Then Don Quixote felt it his duty to break away from luxury and idleness in order to live up to the laws of knight-errantry, Sancho left with a sigh, and a tear in his eye, for never in his life had he lived so well. However, he saw to it that he was well provisioned before they departed. Don Quixote was anxious to see the poet turn knight-errant, he said, but since his parents no doubt would not permit him to give up his chosen work he thought it best not to attempt to sway them in their convictions. And so he and his squire took leave with many courtesies, while Don Diego and his family were pitying the poor demented knight in their hearts and still were wondering at his nonsense.

CHAPTER XIX

IN WHICH IS RELATED THE ADVENTURE OF THE ENAMORED SHEPHERD, TOGETHER WITH OTHER TRULY DROLL INCIDENTS

THEY had traveled but a short time when they met some students and peasants on muleback, and since they were going in the same direction Don Quixote offered them his protection if they would only make the pace of their young mules conform with that of his steed and Dapple. They agreed to do so, and it was not long ere the Knight of the Lions had introduced himself to his companions, and told them of his revival. The students were quick to perceive that he was demented; but not so the peasants, who could make neither head nor tail of what he said, and ascribed this to their own ignorance.

The students invited the knight to come with them to a wedding-feast, and immediately he asked which prince was to be married without his knowing it. The students informed him that it was not any prince's wedding, but that of a rich farmer by the name of Camacho, who was marrying the fair Quiteria, daughter of a rich man in their neighborhood. Quiteria, they said, was in love with one Basilio, a poor young shepherd, whom her father had sent away in anger from his house, forbidding him ever to see his daughter again. As a result of this banishment and his being separated from his love, he had now gone mad.

Don Quixote, having listened attentively to the students' story, began a discourse on love and marriage. Now and then Sancho interrupted him with strings of proverbs; this would infuriate his master by making him deviate from his subject. Finally Don Quixote retaliated by attacking and criticising Sancho's language, which he said was atrocious.

Soon their arguments were taken up by the students. One of them stood by Sancho; the other one took Don Quixote's point of view. Having once been involved, they argued first on one subject, then on another, until at last foils and the art of fencing became the subject. It so happened that one of them was carrying his foils with him, and he suggested that they settle their argument then and there. They did so under Don Quixote's chivalrous supervision, and when the engagement had come to an end, the one who had challenged was so worn and torn that Sancho felt sorry for him and went over to console him; at the same time he felt it his duty to advise him never again to fence, although he did not advise him against wrestling or throwing the bar, for he was strong enough for that, he thought. Whereupon the challenger rose and embraced his adversary, and after that they were better friends than ever.

They pursued their journey, and before long it grew dark. Soon afterwards they heard the musicians at the wedding, and saw the preparations that were being made for it. Here Don Quixote took leave of the students and the peasants, saying that being a knight-errant, he was obliged to give up the comfort of a bed, and would go to sleep in the woods or some lonely field. They did their best to persuade him to accept their hospitality—aided and abetted by the comfort-loving Sancho—but all remonstrances were in vain, much to Sancho's regret.

CHAPTER XX

WHEREIN AN ACCOUNT IS GIVEN OF THE WEDDING OF CAMACHO THE RICH, TOGETHER WITH THE INCIDENT OF BASILIO THE POOR

SANCHO was still snoring when his master was up and awake the next morning. After having soliloquized at length before the sleeping squire, he awoke him by ticking him with his lance. Sancho smelled the preparations for the wedding-feast, and at once was wide awake. His master asked him to hasten and come along, and they set off on their mounts and soon arrived at the place where the wedding was to be celebrated. They found there an arcade erected and through this they entered. There was being cooked and prepared enough food to feed every one in town, and when Sancho saw all the good things, his mouth began to water, and he could hardly control himself. As a matter of fact, he soon succumbed to his temptations and he did not have to beg twice, for the cooks told him that this was a day on which no one was to go hungry, that being the wish of the rich Camacho, and they even told him to keep the spoon. So Sancho skimmed all the pots to his heart's content.

Soon the musicians and dancers arrived, and these performed an allegorical dance and play, but nothing interested Sancho as much as the skimmings, to which he returned after having finished an argument with his master about the relative qualities of Camacho the Rich and the poor Basilio; Camacho being the better provider, Sancho was decidedly in favor of him.

CHAPTER XXI

IN WHICH CAMACHO'S WEDDING IS CONTINUED, WITH OTHER DELIGHTFUL INCIDENTS

SANCHO was still eating when suddenly loud exclamations and shouts were heard; and when he and Don Quixote looked to see what was the matter, they found that the bride and the bridegroom, accompanied by the priest and their relatives, were entering the arcade. They proceeded to a platform, on which they took places, and all noticed that the bride looked very pale. Scarcely had the bridal party seated themselves, when a voice was heard from behind them, calling out: "Wait a little, ye, as inconsiderate as ye are hasty!"

All turned and perceived Basilio, poorly clad, with a crown of cypress on his head, and carrying a staff in his hand. The staff had a sharp end, and this he buried deep in the ground; then, pale and trembling, he turned to the fair Quiteria and accused her of marrying Camacho because of his wealth, though she knew she loved no one but himself, Basilio, who was poor, and, therefore, helpless. As he nevertheless wished them happiness, he would now remove the last obstacle to this end.

So saying, Basilio pulled from the staff he carried and

THE INTERRUPTED WEDDING

which served as a sheath, a rapier, upon which in another instant he had thrown himself. There he lay on the ground, bleeding profusely, the point of the blade appearing through his back, when his many friends came running to give him aid. Don Quixote lifted up his head, and they found that he was still breathing. Some one suggested that they pull out the blade, but the priest warned them not to do that before the poor man had been given the sacrament, as the moment the rapier was removed, death would follow.

Just then Basilio was heard to say in a weak voice that if he could only he joined to his beloved one, he would die happy. The priest cautioned him to think of his soul rather than of his body in these last moments of his, but Basilio interrupted him stubbornly and said he would not confess until this had been done. When Don Quixote heard the dying man implore the priest to carry out his wish, he, too, besought him, and added that under the circumstances Señor Camacho could have nothing against marrying a widow of a man who had died so gallantly and honorably as Basilio. Camacho heard all this, and when Basilio's friends at the same time entreated him to think of the poor man's soul, he consented; and as Quiteria, too, was compassionate, the priest united them as man and wife, gave them his blessing with tears in his eyes, and hoped that Heaven would receive the soul of the wedded man.

But the instant the ceremony was at an end, the suicide jumped to his feet as lightly as a deer. Some began to shout that a miracle had been performed. But Basilio was honest and confessed that he had played a trick; and, indeed, it seemed as if the whole thing had been planned by the two lovers, for Quiteria said that if the marriage was not valid, she would now confirm it anew. Some of Camacho's friends became violent and threatened the life of Basilio, but the valiant Don Quixote did not abandon his new-found friend; he kept them all at a distance with his lance and his sword.

In the meantime Sancho was guarding a spot that to his mind was the most important one there, namely where the wine-jars were standing.

When Don Quixote had made himself respected by the followers of the rich Camacho, he addressed them on the subject of love and war, and held forth to them that all means to an end in these two games were justifiable, as long as no disgrace was brought on the object of one's love. Then he threatened to thrash any one who attempted to separate whom God now had joined; and they were all awed by his resolute language, not knowing who he was. Camacho showed that he was of good mettle, however, for he invited all to remain and have a merry time, and let the feast go on as if nothing had happened.

But Basilio was proud, and so were his friends, and they preferred to withdraw to Basilio's village. They were accompanied by Don Quixote, whom they had invited as a special guest of honor because of his stout defense of Basilio; and Sancho, of course, had to trail along, much to his disgust, for he had looked forward to stilling his hunger for days to come on the remnants of the rich man's wedding-feast. As he was rocking to and fro in his seat on his faithful Dapple, he was contemplating with a surly and melancholy countenance a glorious, but now past day.

CHAPTER XXII

WHEREIN IS RELATED THE GRAND ADVENTURE OF THE CAVE OF MONTESINOS IN THE HEART OF LA MANCHA, WHICH THE VALIANT DON QUIXOTE BROUGHT TO A HAPPY TERMINATION

DON QUIXOTE and Sancho remained at the home of the newly married couple for three days. Before the knight took leave of Basilio and Quiteria, he discoursed at length on love and matrimony: a discourse that Sancho seemed to take more to heart than they did, for when his master had finished he was heard muttering that he wished he had had such advice before marrying his wife.

"Is thy Teresa so bad then, Sancho?" asked Don Quixote.

"She is not very bad," replied the downtrodden squire, "but she is not very good; at least she is not as good as I could wish."

"Thou dost wrong, Sancho, to speak ill of thy wife," admonished his master; "for after all she is the mother of thy children."

And to this the squire answered: "We are quits, for she speaks ill of me whenever she takes it into her head, especially when she is jealous; and Satan himself could not put up with her then."

Having exchanged these thoughts with his squire, Don

Quixote decided it was time to take to the open again, and he begged one of the students who had invited him to the wedding to find him a guide to take him to the cave of Montesinos. The student provided him with a cousin of his own, a young scholar who was very much interested in tales of chivalry; and, followed by the earnest prayers of those they left behind, the three set out for the famous cave.

Don Quixote wanted the scholar to tell him all about himself, and when he learned, he had had books printed which were inscribed to princes, he wanted to know what kind of books they were. When he mentioned that he was writing one now that was to deal with the invention of customs and things, Sancho became interested and thrust this question at him, which he answered himself: "Tell me, Señor—and God give you luck in printing your books! —who was the first man that scratched his head? For to my thinking it must have been our father Adam."

Glad to have had his supposition corroborated by so great an authority as an author of books, Sancho was encouraged to ask numerous other questions of the same caliber; and this helped to make the time seem short. When night fell they had reached a little village, from where it was only a very short distance to the cave.

As Don Quixote was intent on discovering the cave's inmost secrets, he provided himself with a hundred fathoms of rope, and the following afternoon he was at the cavern, ready for the hazardous undertaking. Don Quixote was tied to the end of the rope, and all the while Sancho was admonishing him not to bury himself alive in the bottomless pit, telling him that he had no business being an explorer anyway. Before being lowered into the depths, Don Quixote commended himself to his Lady Dulcinea and sent up a prayer to Heaven on bended knees.

In order to enter the cave, he had to cut his way through the brush, and as he commenced to swing his sword, a whole city of crows and bats flew against him and knocked him to the ground. Sancho crossed himself and kept up his vigilance over his master to the last. Finally he saw him disappear in the coal-black depths, and then he called on all the saints he knew by name to protect the flower and cream of knight-errantry, the dare-devil of the earth, the heart of steel and the arm of brass.

At last Sancho and the scholar had given Don Quixote all the hundred fathoms of the rope, and then they got no more replies to their calls. They waited for half an hour, and then they were afraid that the knight was dead and decided to haul him up, Sancho weeping bitterly all the while. But when Sancho saw his master coming up, he could not restrain himself from being hopeful of a miracle, and he called out gleefully: "Welcome back, Señor, for we had begun to think you were going to stop there to found a family."

Don Quixote did not move, however, and they laid him on the ground and found he was fast asleep. When he came to, he was in an exalted state. He raised his eyes toward Heaven, and asked God to forgive them for having taken him away from such a glorious and spectacular pleasure. But Sancho was curious to know what he had seen down there in Hell, and he interrupted and asked the question.

"Hell!" cried Don Quixote. "Call it by no such name, for it does not deserve it."

Then he asked for something to eat, and Sancho put before him an abundance of food, since he said he was very hungry. When he had eaten, he asked them to sit still and listen to his story.

CHAPTER XXIII

OF THE WONDERFUL THINGS THE INCOMPARABLE DON QUIXOTE
SAID HE SAW IN THE PROFOUND CAVE OF MONTESINOS, THE
IMPOSSIBILITY AND MAGNITUDE OF WHICH
CAUSE THIS ADVENTURE TO BE
APOCRYPHAL

WHEN he was being hoisted down, Don Quixote said, he had suddenly landed on a precipice which led to a cave within the cave, large enough to hold a team of mules and a cart. There, he claimed, he fell asleep, only to wake and find himself in a beautiful field, from where he had gone on a regular sightseeing trip, visiting the most wonderful castles and palaces, and meeting with the most exalted personages. Among these was no other than the enchanted Montesinos himself. He had taken Don Quixote into his own palace, built of crystal and alabaster, and shown him the tomb of his friend Durandarte, who lay there in his enchantment, with his hairy hand over his heart. Don Quixote had asked whether it were indeed true that he, Montesinos, had cut out the heart of his dead friend, as

[206]

the story had told, and brought it to his Lady Belerma, and Montesinos had nodded in affirmation.

Suddenly they had heard the poor dead knight moan in the most heartrending way, and he had asked Montesinos again and again whether he had done as he had bade him and carried his heart to his Lady Belerma in France. Montesinos had fallen on his knees and had assured his cousin with tearful eyes that as soon as he had died he had cut out his heart with a poniard, dried it with a lace handkerchief as well as he could, and then departed to see his Lady. At the first village he had come to in France, he had stopped to sprinkle some salt on it to keep it fresh, and had given it to the Lady Belerma, who was now also enchanted in this cave.

Don Quixote continued his tale. The enchanter, the sage Merlin, so Montesinos had said, had prophesied that he, Don Quixote, reviver of knight-errantry, was to be the one to disenchant them all. He and Montesinos had almost come to blows, however, when the latter had inferred that during her enchantment the Lady Belerma had developed large circles under her eyes, and that if it had not been for these her beauty would have surpassed even that of the famous Lady Dulcinea of El Toboso. But Montesinos was courteous enough to apologize and acknowledge the truth of the proverb which says that comparisons are odious.

Sancho and the young author of books had some difficulty in persuading themselves that all these things had happened in so short a time, for Don Quixote had only been gone about an hour; but Don Quixote, hearing this, insisted that he had been absent three days and three nights. Then he proceeded to tell how he had felt no hunger whatever, that none down there ever ate, and that the enchanted never slept; he admitted, however, that their nails, hair, and beards grew.

When Sancho heard all this he asked to be forgiven by God for saying he thought his master was lying, but the next moment he had retracted it, and when his master asked what he really meant, he said he did not know.

There was one thing that had happened to our knight in the cave, which caused him infinite pain; he had met one of the enchanted ladies-in-waiting to his Lady Dulcinea, and she had told him in confidence that his beloved one wanted to borrow six reals on a petticoat which she had bought. He gave her all that he had, which amounted to only four reals, and she gave him in exchange her lady's blessing, saying that with it went many kisses. As she left him, he said, she had cut a caper and had sprung fully two yards into the air.

"O blessed God," cried Sancho, "is it possible that enchantments can have such power as to have changed my master's right senses into a craze so full of absurdity? O Señor, Señor, consider yourself! Have a care for your honor, and give no credit to this silly stuff that has left you scant and short of wits."

"Thou talkest in this way because thou lovest me, Sancho," said Don Quixote; and he ascribed his squire's incredulity to a lack of knowledge of the world and assured him that when the time came he would tell him even more

that took place in the cave, which would make him believe
what he now doubted.

CHAPTER XXIV

WHEREIN ARE RELATED SOME TRIFLING MATTERS, AS TRIVIAL AS THEY ARE NECESSARY TO THE RIGHT UNDERSTANDING OF THIS GREAT HISTORY

THE scholar was surprised that Don Quixote permitted his servant to talk to him in this way, but
ascribed his lenience to the good mood he was in. After
having whiled away still another hour talking pleasantly,
they proceeded to find a place where they might spend the
night. The scholar knew of a hermitage not very far off;
and on their way there they encountered a man with a mule
that was loaded with halberds and lances. Don Quixote
was curious to know where he was taking the weapons, but
the man answered that he was in great haste to reach the
inn beyond the hermitage. He would spend the night at
this inn, he said, and if they happened to be there too, he
would tell them some things that were both interesting
and curious. Don Quixote was so inquisitive that he decided to pass by the hermitage and go to the inn instead.

Just before coming to the inn, they met a happy looking
lad of eighteen or nineteen, who carried a sword over his
shoulder and a bundle on his back. Don Quixote stopped
him and asked where he was going; and the lad replied that

he was going to war for his king. He told the knight how
he had been in the service of office-seekers and adventurers in Madrid until he had tired of such a life; and this
pleased Don Quixote so much that he invited him to sit behind him on Rocinante and ride with him to the inn to
sup with him. But the page, seeing the leanness of the
knight's steed, said he preferred to walk, though he was
glad to accept the invitation for supper.

As soon as they had arrived at the inn, Don Quixote
asked the landlord for the man with the lances and halberds; and Sancho was happy to know that his master took
this inn for an inn and not for an enchanted castle.

CHAPTER XXV

WHEREIN IS SET DOWN THE BRAYING ADVENTURE, AND THE DROLL ONE OF THE PUPPET-SHOWMEN, TOGETHER WITH THE MEMORABLE DIVINATIONS OF THE DIVINING APE

DON QUIXOTE found the man with the arms feeding his mule in the stable, and he asked the knight to
accompany him to a quiet nook when he had finished this
duty to his beast. But Don Quixote's curiosity knew no
bounds, and he offered to help him sift the barley so that
he might begin his story at once. Being a good-natured
fellow, the man acquiesced. He related how a magistrate in his village, which was four leagues and a half
away, had lost a donkey through the carelessness of a serv-

ant. Some weeks later another magistrate of the same village was hunting in the woods, and when he returned he brought word to his fellow officer that he had come across the lost beast but that he was now so wild that no one could approach him. He suggested, however, that they go together in search for him; and they developed a plan whereby they thought they should surely be able to capture the animal. Both of them were expert in braying, and they decided to place themselves at different ends of the forest, each one braying at intervals. In this way they thought they should be able to round up the donkey, for they were certain that he would answer their calls.

But it so happened that both of them brayed at the same time, and when they ran to look, convinced that the donkey had turned up, they found not the ass but only each other, so naturally had they brayed. They tried the same scheme again and again, but every time with the same result; and at last they came in this way to a place in the woods where they found the dead donkey devoured by wolves.

The story of the two magistrates going about in the forest braying to each other like asses soon spread to the villages in the county; and in one village in particular the habit of braying whenever they observed any one from the village of the braying magistrates took such root that it was decided to teach them a lesson by taking arms against them. The arms he carried with him now, he said, were to be used against these scoffers, that they might never again behave like asses.

He had just finished his story when some one entered and cried out that the show of *The Release of Melisendra* and the divining ape were coming to the inn, and a minute later Master Pedro himself came into the yard, where he was greeted by the landlord and all the guests. Master Pedro's one eye was covered by a piece of green silk; Don Quixote judged by this that something had befallen him by accident. He asked the landlord to tell him all he knew of Master Pedro, and he learned that he traveled with his puppet-show from town to town, and was greatly renowned throughout the provinces as a showman. And the ape, the innkeeper said, was like a human being, so clever was he, and wise.

Soon the show was in readiness inside, and every one gathered around Master Pedro and his divining ape. Don Quixote and Sancho were eager to have their fortunes told, and both offered their reals at the same time; but Master Pedro refused to take any money until the ape had rendered satisfactory service.

The ape jumped up on his master's shoulder, and began to chatter his teeth as if he were saying something, all the while keeping his mouth close to Master Pedro's ear. When he had been chattering long enough to please himself, he jumped down just as quickly as he had jumped up. The next instant Don Quixote and Sancho were both frightened and awed by the showman's suddenly throwing himself before Don Quixote's feet and embracing his legs, while he exclaimed: "These legs do I embrace as I would embrace the two pillars of Hercules, O illustrious reviver of knight-errantry, O prop of the tottering, so long consigned to oblivion!" But not only were the knight and the squire aghast; the landlord and the guests were as startled as they were, for they had never seen Master Pedro act like that before.

But the showman had not finished, for in the next moment he lay at the feet of Sancho, to whom the divining ape brought cheer from his Teresa, saying that she was just soothing her feelings by indulging in wine from a pitcher which she was holding in her left hand and that had a broken spout.

Don Quixote was not very well pleased with this exhibition, for he thought it decidedly out of place that an ape should know more than he or any other human being; and he confided to Sancho that the ape was possessed by the devil. He brought Sancho to a dark corner in the stable where he was sure no one could overhear them, and told him there that he was convinced Master Pedro had made a bargain with the devil to get rich through the ape, and then sell him his soul, and he said it surprised him beyond words that the Holy Office had not already interfered with this dastardly scheme.

At this point Master Pedro came in search of Don Quixote, as the show was about to begin. Before entering the inn, however, Sancho entreated his master to ask the ape whether what he saw in the cave of Montesinos was true. Don Quixote did so, and the ape answered that some of it was true, some of it was not; and immediately Sancho scornfully broke in and said that he had told him so already. The ape intimated that by next Friday he should be able to tell more about the adventure; his mind was tired now.

They entered and found the stage set for the performance; the tapers of wax were lit, it was a bright and beautiful scene. Master Pedro disappeared and took his place behind the scenes, for he was the one who created the life in the puppets. A lad who acted as interpreter, calling out the scenes and describing the action of the play, placed himself outside the theater. Don Quixote, Sancho, the page, and the scholar seated themselves in the front row; and the show began.

CHAPTER XXVI

Wherein Is Continued the Droll Adventure of the Puppet-Showman, Together with Other Things in Truth Right Good

THE play, which depicted how Melisendra was released by her husband, Señor Don Gaiferos, from the hands of the Moors in the city of Sansueña, now called Saragossa, had only proceeded a short way when Don Quixote became impatient with the young man who was making the explanations to the audience. The knight thought he drifted into unnecessary and superfluous language, and was quick to reprimand him. The show was continued, and again Don Quixote broke in, criticising some of the stage effects: bells were never used by the Moors, only kettledrums, he said. But here Master Pedro begged him not to be so particular, pleading that the show was given for the sake of amusement.

Don Quixote acceded, and the show began again.

ADVENTURE OF THE PUPPET-SHOWMAN

But it was not long before a number of horsemen were galloping across the stage in pursuit of the two lovers. Their escape was accompanied by such blowing of horns and trumpets and beating of drums, that the noise and din of it all were too much for the poor knight's imagination which was now stirred to such a pitch that he believed himself in the midst of a real battle. He drew his sword and plunged against the Moorish horseman with such vehemence and force, cutting and slashing in all directions, that every one in the room was aghast at his madness, and ran to hide in safety. Master Pedro came within an inch of having his ear, not to say his whole head, cut off, and Don Quixote's fury was not at an end until he had decapitated all the Moorish pasteboard figures. Lucky it was that no blood could flow from them, or there would have been a plentiful stream of it. The ape took refuge on the roof, frightened out of his poor wits, and even Sancho Panza was more than ordinarily shaken with fear, for he admitted that he had never seen his master so wrought up.

When Don Quixote was certain of complete victory—in other words, destruction—he turned and addressed those who had dared to return after the storm: "I wish I had here before me now all those who do not or will not believe how useful knights errant are in the world. Just think, if I had not been here present, what would have become of the brave Don Gaiferos and the fair Melisendra!"

But Master Pedro was lamenting the loss of all his emperors and kings and knights and horses, and Sancho was so touched by what he said it would cost him to buy a new show, that he pleaded with his master to make restitution; and, although Don Quixote could not see that he had done any wrong, he generously ordered his squire to pay Master Pedro the sum of forty reals and three quarters, the landlord having duly functioned as arbiter and agreed that that was a fair price for the damage done to the figures. Besides this amount, Master Pedro was allotted two reals for his trouble in catching the ape.

While they were summing up, Don Quixote, however, had only one thought in his mind. He was wondering whether Melisendra and her husband had reached safety by this time: so possessed was he of his infernal imagination. Master Pedro promised him that as soon as he had caught his ape, he would put the question to him; and the showman began to worry about his African companion, hoping that he would soon be hungry, for then he would know whether he was still alive.

The rest of the evening was passed in peace, and drinking at Don Quixote's expense, and soon it was morning, and the man with the halberds took his departure. The scholar and the page left, too, and Don Quixote generously gave the page twelve reals. But the first one to depart was the showman: he was afraid that the knight might have another outbreak, and he had no desire to experience it twice, and perhaps lose his ape, which he had now caught.

The landlord was extremely pleased with Don Quixote's generosity, and was sorry to see him depart; but his madness he could make neither head nor tail of, for he had never seen any one thus afflicted.

MASTER PEDRO AND HIS APE

CHAPTER XXVII

Wherein It Is Shown Who Master Pedro and His Ape Were, Together with the Mishap Don Quixote Had in the Braying Adventure, Which He Did Not Conclude as He Would Have Liked or as He Had Expected

IT was no doubt a good thing for Master Pedro of the puppet-show that neither Sancho nor Don Quixote recognized in him the thief who stole the squire's donkey, when he was asleep; for he it was. None other than the galley-slave Gines de Pasamonte, or Don Ginesillo de Paropilla, as Don Quixote would have it. It was in the guise of a showman, with only one eye and a part of his face visible, that he found it an easy matter to evade being caught by the servants of the law, who had been hunting for him ever since he was liberated through the generosity and bravery of Don Quixote. The ape he had bought from some captives who had returned from Barbary; and he had soon taught him the tricks which made people think he was really divining things. Before entering a village the clever galley-slave would learn all he could about its inhabitants; and being blessed with a remarkable memory, he seldom had any difficulty in making the ape's feat seem impressive to the masses.

Now, when Don Quixote left the inn, it suddenly occurred to him that he ought to visit the banks of the Ebro

[217]

before steering towards Saragossa. So he kept on the road for two days, and on the third day as he was mounting a hill he was suddenly aroused by hearing a tremendous din of drums, mixed with the sound of trumpets and musket-shots. In as few instants as it took to make his charger ascend to the top of the hill, he was there; and he saw several hundred men, armed with weapons of every imaginable sort. There were flags, of various descriptions, and among them one in particular attracted his attention: it was a large standard in white, on which was painted a donkey, and also an inscription, reading thus:

> They did not bray in vain,
> Our alcaldes twain.

This made Don Quixote believe the warriors must be from the braying town, and he remarked to Sancho that the man to whom they had talked at the inn must have been misinformed, for evidently the two had not been magistrates but alcaldes, according to the sign. To this Sancho replied that having once been a magistrate should not exclude any one from becoming an alcalde; besides, somebody must have brayed, and whether it was an alcalde or a magistrate mattered little, he thought. Don Quixote, however, was in a quandary as to what to do that he might best live up to the laws of knight-errantry.

He finally went to the braying ones, and, having begged their leave to address them, he began a stirring discourse on war and peace that lasted a considerable time. He flayed those who would go into battle for trifling matters; but just when he seemed to be about to win the braying ones over to his way of thinking, he had to pause for breath.

Sancho thought it his duty to interrupt the silence and take up the broken thread here, so he continued in his own way, keeping more or less to the same subject. He started in by praising his master—the Knight of the Lions!—his bravery, his generosity, his knowledge of Latin (which Sancho unfortunately did not understand), and all his other virtues, and suddenly he bellowed out that they were fools to take offense at hearing some one bray. Then he became reminiscent and related how he as a boy used to like to go about braying, and told how envious every one in his village was because of his great gift in that direction. "Wait a bit and listen!" said he. "I'll show you!" And before his master had a chance to stop him, he had pinched his nose and brayed—had brayed such a bray that all the valleys and dales gave echo.

When some of the men heard the braying they thought he had come there to mock them, and they set upon him with such fury and force that Don Quixote, though he did his best to defend him, had to spur Rocinante into retreat, in order to save his own life. But Sancho was both stoned and pummeled into insensibility, and then he was put on his donkey and tied there; and when he came to, he had to put his trust in Dapple, who was forced to smell his way back to Rocinante.

The braying troops remained in the field until evening, but since no opposing army appeared, they returned to their village after dark.

CHAPTER XXVIII

OF MATTERS THAT BENENGELI SAYS HE WHO READS THEM WILL KNOW, IF HE READS THEM WITH ATTENTION

WHEN Dapple reached his faithful playmate, Rocinante, Sancho fell from his back and rolled at his master's feet. There he lay; but Don Quixote was angry and showed no compassion.

"In an evil hour didst thou take to braying, Sancho! Where hast thou learned that it is well done to mention the rope in the house of the man that has been hanged? To the music of brays what harmonies couldst thou expect to get but cudgels?"

Having thus reprimanded his squire, the good knight looked to his wounds, which Sancho complained of, but found him only discolored.

"I feel as if I was speaking through my shoulders," wailed Sancho; and then he begged his master to hasten away from such evil premises. Of course, he also had to say something scornful about Don Quixote's having abandoned him in the heat of battle; but the knight begged him to consider that there was a difference between flying and retiring.

Don Quixote succeeded in making Sancho mount and remain on the donkey's back, and then they set off toward a grove which they sighted in the distance. Sancho's back pained him fearfully, but he was much relieved when he learned from his master—who had seen the accident—that it was caused by his having been smitten by a man armed with a staff. The cause being removed as it were, Sancho was jubilant, although his heart and courage fell as soon as he, in the course of his usual chattering, touched upon the subject of knight-errantry. While bewailing his fate, he forgot his pain; therefore Don Quixote was generous and Christian enough to beg him to keep on talking to himself. Sancho suddenly was reminded of his island, and in turn reminded his master of his promise concerning it.

This impertinence was rewarded by the knight's demanding of him: "Well, how long is it, Sancho, since I promised thee an island?"

And Sancho retorted innocently: "If I remember rightly, it must be over twenty years, three days more or less."

Don Quixote then had to laugh, for it would have been ridiculous not to do so. His wrath was aroused, however, when Sancho again showed his covetousness—his one really great failing, Don Quixote thought—and he told him to keep all the money he had, and betake himself back to his Teresa.

Sancho was moved to tears by his master's wrath, and he confessed in a broken voice that if he had only had a tail he would have been a complete ass himself. But, he said, if his master should care to attach one to him, he would willingly wear one, and serve him all his life as an ass. Then he asked on bended knees to be forgiven, saying that if he talked much it was less from malice than from ignorance, and finished up his harangue with a proverb that had nothing whatever to do with the rest of his discourse.

So Don Quixote forgave his squire, and by that time they had reached the grove, and they spent the night there under the trees: Don Quixote in soliloquies and meditation, Sancho in pain and restlessness. In the morning they continued on their way to find the river Ebro.

CHAPTER XXIX

OF THE FAMOUS ADVENTURE OF THE ENCHANTED BARK

IT took them two days to reach the river. The very first thing that struck the knight's eye when he got there, was a boat without oars, tied to a tree. Immediately Don Quixote insisted that the boat had been sent by magic to fetch him to some great knight or other person in need of his help; and all Sancho's contradictions were fruitless.

Finally the proverb, "Do as thy master bids thee, and sit down to table with him," had its effect on Sancho, and, although certain he was about to give up his life, he tied the beasts to a tree on the bank, and seated himself in the boat, trembling like a leaf. Then the knight cut the rope, and they started to drift out into the stream, while Dapple was braying and Rocinante was trying to break away and plunge in after them. Seeing this, Sancho began to weep convulsively, but his master had no patience with him, and told him to control himself.

Soon they had reached midstream, and Don Quixote, much to Sancho's perplexity, began to talk about cosmography, the three hundred and sixty degrees of the globe, and the equinoctial line, which, the knight said, they were just then passing. A sure sign by which all seafaring Spaniards determined the passing of this latitude, Don Quixote went on, was that all lice died on everybody on board ship. So, in accordance with this custom, he asked his squire to take the test. Sancho let his hand creep stealthily into the hollow of his left knee, and he promptly told his master that either was the test not to be relied upon, or they had not passed the line that had just been mentioned by name.

"Why, how so?" asked Don Quixote; "hast thou come upon aught?"

"Ay, and aughts," replied Sancho, and in replying he let the stream wash his fingers.

Just then they came in view of some large floating mills, moored in midstream. At once Don Quixote became excited, crying to Sancho that there must be some fair princess or high-born lady in captivity in this castle.

Sancho did his best to make his master believe they were not castles but only mills that ground corn; but to no avail. Don Quixote insisted that either his squire or the mills were enchanted. They came closer and closer to them, and soon shouts were heard from some of the millers, who realized the danger of the boat's being upset by the suction of the water, and dragged into the mill wheels.

The men quickly got hold of some sticks and poles, and tried to stave off the boat, and when Don Quixote saw their white, flour-covered faces he turned to Sancho and begged him to take a good look at the monsters that had been sent to oppose him. The men were all the time crying out, unable to fathom such dare-deviltry or folly: "Devils of men, where are you going to? Are you mad? Do you want to drown yourselves, or dash yourselves to pieces among these wheels?"

In reply to these well-meant exclamations, Don Quixote stood up in the boat and began to swing his sword in a ferocious manner, calling them evil rabble, and demanding that they set free the princess who was imprisoned in the fortress; while Sancho said all the prayers he could think of, crawling on the bottom of the swaying boat, which was now close to the rushing water.

At last the millers caught the boat with their hooks, but in so doing Don Quixote and his squire both fell into the river. Don Quixote in his heavy armor made two trips to the bottom, but both he and Sancho were rescued, thanks to the devils in white. As soon as they had come ashore, Sancho sank upon his knees and thanked the Lord for having been saved from such a death as that from drinking too much water, and prayed that he should be delivered from all future temptations to risk his life in any more foolish causes.

As this moment the fishermen who owned the boat came running up, claiming damages for the wrecked craft, and after having failed to strike a bargain with this rabble for the delivery of the enchanted fair maiden in the castle, Don Quixote, wearied by their stupidity, paid them fifty reals for the boat, exclaiming: "God help us, this world is all machinations and schemes at cross purposes one with the other! I can do no more." Then, turning toward the water mills, he burst out into lamentations, confessing

to the imagined captive princess his inability to set her
free at this time; while the fishermen stood by, wondering
what it was all about.

Having ceased his lamentations, Don Quixote and Sancho joined their faithful beasts, and set out to find new adventures.

CHAPTER XXX

OF DON QUIXOTE'S ADVENTURE WITH A FAIR HUNTRESS

SANCHO left the river Ebro with no regrets, except for
the fifty reals just paid to the fishermen. He was
seriously considering in his own mind the foolishness of
remaining a squire to such a mad master as his. But late
the following afternoon they approached a field, and suddenly Don Quixote discovered in the distance a number
of people, and as they came closer they found it was a
hawking party.

Seeing in the party a lady with a hawk on her left hand,
and dressed so richly that Sancho said he had never seen
anything so fine in his life, Don Quixote decided that she
must be some lady of great distinction. Therefore he dispatched his squire with a message to her, asking her for
permission to kiss her hand in person. He instructed
Sancho to be particularly careful not to dispense any of
his proverbs to the lady; but Sancho said he could do without this warning, for had he not carried messages before

to the exalted Dulcinea, the highest lady of them all?

Soon Don Quixote saw his squire kneeling before the lady. Having given her his life's history and told her his name, Sancho proceeded with the message of his master, the valiant Knight of the Lions, formerly the Knight of the Rueful Countenance, explicitly explaining his master's modest desire. The lady, who was no other than a duchess, at once was interested, as she had read and laughed over the first volume of "The Ingenious Gentleman, Don Quixote of La Mancha"; and she immediately asked Sancho to return to his master and say that she would be delighted beyond words to have the worthy knight and his squire come and be her and the Duke's guests at a country place they had there.

Sancho was so flattered that the Duchess had recognized him from having read the book, and so pleased with the reception she had given him, as well as so taken by her great charm and beauty that he could not get back to his master quickly enough to tell him the good news. With his best manner and bearing Don Quixote, attended by his faithful one, rode into the presence of the august lady, and kissed her hand.

But while Sancho was on his way to his master with the Duchess' message, she had sent for the Duke, and they had arranged, both being gifted with a remarkable sense of humor, to receive and entertain the hero in true knight-errant fashion. Having read all the tales of chivalry, they knew exactly what to do.

Don Quixote was about to dismount, when he had kissed the Duchess' hand; and Sancho, as was his custom, wanted to get off Dapple in a hurry and hold his stirrup, as soon as he perceived his master's intention. But luck would have it that one of his legs caught in the trappings, and he fell head first towards the ground. There the poor squire hung, unable to get up or down, caught by the foot. Now, when Don Quixote, his eyes fixedly and courteously on the Duchess, thought that his squire was there with the stirrup, he pressed downward with all his weight, and knight and saddle both flew high in the air off Rocinante. When Don Quixote had reached earth, he lay there, writhing in pain and cursing and swearing at his stupid squire, who was still hanging by his foot.

The Duke and the Duchess, unable to constrain themselves at the amusing scene, finally were able through their laughter to order their huntsmen to their help; and, limping, the knight advanced to do homage to the Duke and his consort on his damaged knees. The Duke, however, nobly refused such honor, and instead, embraced the knight. He then regretted in a few well chosen words the knight's accident; but Don Quixote replied with an exalted speech, saying that if he had fallen to the depths of the bottomless pit, the glory of having seen such a noble and worthy pair would have lifted him up. Then, of course, he said something uncomplimentary about his squire, who did not know how to tighten the girths of a saddle, although he could not help giving him credit for having a loose tongue.

But when the knight began to praise the beauty of the Duchess, the Duke asked him courteously whether there were not others to praise, as, for instance, his own Lady Dulcinea. At this Don Quixote offered the Duchess his

services for a few days, together with those of his squire,
Sancho Panza, whom he now took pity on and praised as
being the drollest squire in the world. Whereupon the
Duchess flattered Sancho, saying that if he were droll, she
was sure he was shrewd as well; but Don Quixote broke
in and added that he was talkative. When the knight,
having heard himself addressed as the Knight of the Rueful Countenance, begged to correct it to the Knight of the
Lions, the Duke asked him to relate the episode that thus
changed his title. And then he invited all to come to the
castle to be present at a reception that he would give to
their great and distinguished guest.

With the Duchess in the middle, flanked by Don Quixote and the Duke, the whole company headed for the castle;
but it was not long before the Duchess found her desire
for conversation with the droll and amusing Sancho ir-
resistible. As soon as the Duchess' wish was made known
to him, the squire eagerly wedged his way between the
horses and chattered his way into the lady's good graces.

CHAPTER XXXI

WHICH TREATS OF MANY AND GREAT MATTERS

THE reception tendered Don Quixote was arranged
in true knight-errant fashion by the Duke, who had
ridden ahead and given full instructions to the servants.
So when Don Quixote arrived, he received a welcome that
surpassed anything he had ever read or dreamt of.

MANY AND GREAT MATTERS

The staircases and the galleries of the court were lined with servants, who greeted him with the exclamation: "Welcome, flower and cream of knight-errantry!" At the same time they cast pellets with scented water over him.

Sancho was taken aback at the sight of all this glory. He had followed the Duchess, but once in the castle, the absence of his Dapple made him feel worried. So he turned to one of the duennas, a dignified woman, named Doña Rodriguez de Grijalba, and asked her whether she would not favor him by going outside and seeing that his poor little Dapple was well taken care of. Doña Rodriguez was greatly incensed at his ordering a duenna of the ducal household to do things of that sort, and called him a garlic-stuffed scoundrel. Don Quixote, overhearing their conversation, reprimanded his misbehaving servant, and Sancho blamed it all on his love for his donkey.

After this, Don Quixote was escorted into a hall the walls of which were covered with cloth of gold and rich tapestries, and here he was stripped of his armor by six fair damsels. These maidens could scarcely control their laughter when they saw him stand there, thin, emaciated, tall and bony, dressed in his chamois doublet and tight-fitting breeches. They begged him to permit them to put a clean shirt on him, but that he refused with many assurances of his modesty, asking them instead to give it to Sancho. The two were taken to a room, where Don Quixote, alone with his squire, undressed and put on the shirt, while he gave Sancho admonitions galore, as to how to behave, begging him never again to have any quarrels with any duennas, for that only tended to lessen the respect for the master, who was always judged by his squire's behavior and actions.

Then Don Quixote returned to the hall, where he was attired in a rich baldric and a scarlet mantle, with a sword and a gorgeous montera of green satin. As he passed through the halls and chambers on his way to the state dining room, he was escorted by the seneschal and twelve pages; and the sides of each room, as well as the aisles, were lined with servants in pompous liveries.

Only four covers were laid. Besides Don Quixote and his noble hosts the confessor of the ducal household, a cold and austere churchman, occupied a seat at the heavily laden table, to which our knight was ushered ceremoniously by the Duke himself. But the dinner had not even begun when Sancho unloosened his tongue and began with his proverbs, much to the distress and mortification of his master, although to the great enjoyment of the Duchess. Sancho had been standing by Don Quixote, staring wide-eyed and open-mouthed at everything that was taking place, for he had never in his life seen anything so sumptuous and ceremonious. The exchange of courtesies between the Duke and our Knight, when the latter finally was induced to accept the seat of honor at the head of the table, impressed the squire considerably; and it was then he thought the time ripe for the introduction of a story about this matter of seats. The Duchess told him by all means to let them hear it, and he began, telling it in the most roundabout way, with twists and curves, and expeditions here and there to places and matters that had as much to do with the story as had the proverbs that he stuffed it with.

Don Quixote was beside himself, and the confessor interrupted the poor squire impatiently again and again; but on he went. All the while the Duchess was laughing so heartily that she could scarcely sit up straight in the chair. And while the Duke engaged himself with Don Quixote, she carried on a confidential conversation with Sancho, who told her how he had tricked his master into believing that his Lady Dulcinea was enchanted, saying she was as much enchanted as his father.

When the confessor heard the sacrilegeous conversation the Duchess was having with Sancho, discussing giants and enchantments, he severely reprimanded her and warned her that she would have to answer to God for whatever this man did and said. Then, addressing the Duke, whom he had forbidden to read the book about Don Quixote's adventures, he said: "This Don Simpleton, or whatever his name is, cannot be such a blockhead as your Excellency would have him, holding out encouragement to him to go on with his vagaries and follies." And then he turned to Don Quixote and told him to be on his way, and go home and bring up his children, if he had any; and he called him a numbskull, and other names, and a fool for believing that there were knights-errant in the world and Dulcineas and other such silly things.

Don Quixote sat still and never moved a muscle while the churchman was speaking, but as soon as he had said all he had to say, he sprang up from his seat, trembling in his whole body, his face contorted with rage.

CHAPTER XXXII

OF THE REPLY DON QUIXOTE GAVE HIS CENSURER, WITH OTHER INCIDENTS, GRAVE AND DROLL

HAD Don Quixote not been where he was and had the man who thus assailed him not been of the church, it is safe to say that Don Quixote would have made his defamer retract his words at the point of his sword. But instead he calmed himself, and began a long discourse on the virtues of knight-errantry, finishing it with an avowal of his intentions which, he swore, were to do good to all and evil to none. As for his deserving to be called a fool, he would leave that to the judgment of the Duke and the Duchess. But their worships never got a chance to utter a word before Sancho broke in with the most stupendous praise of his master's speech.

The churchman wanted to know whether he was the Sancho Panza of the book he had seen in print, to which Sancho replied that he most certainly was, and corroborated it with a string of proverbs, ending his long-winded reply to the confessor's question with a wish for long life for his master and himself, saying that neither one of them would be in any want of empires or islands to rule. Whereupon the Duke at once said he conferred upon Sancho this very moment the government of one of his islands; and hearing this Don Quixote whispered to Sancho—who

could not believe his own ears—to go down on his knees
and thank the Duke for his kindness.

The ecclesiastic could stand this impudence no longer,
and he rose from his seat and left the room in disgust and
ill-temper. The Duke wanted to call him back, but he
was in such hysterics from hearing Sancho's proverbial nonsense that he could not speak. After the churchman's departure Don Quixote again took to discoursing, and delivered a tirade on the subject of giving and taking offense,
comparing the confessor's rebuke to the offense of a woman,
whose only weapon was her tongue and who therefore
could not be punished by the sword. They marveled at
his knowledge and at the quality of his language, however
amusing he himself appeared; but it was Sancho who particularly took their fancy, for the ducal pair thought they
had never met any one quite so amusing and droll in all
their life. And when Don Quixote had ended his discourse, Sancho himself burst out regarding the priest: "By
my faith, I am certain if Reinaldos of Montalvan had heard
the little man's words, he would have given him such a
spank on the mouth that he would not have spoken for the
next three years."

The dinner was now over, and four maidens entered:
one carrying a silver basin, another one a jug, also of silver,
a third one towels, while the fourth had her sleeves rolled
up, and, approaching Don Quixote, began to soap his face
and beard. Don Quixote thought this must be a custom
after all ducal meals, so he submitted in amazement and
stretched out his legs comfortably, that he should not appear out of place in such surroundings. When his face

was all lathered, the barber maiden pretended there was no more water in the jug; and by this time the lather had worked its way into the knight's eyes, and he sat there making the most fierce and ludicrous faces until the water finally arrived.   Then the Duke, in order that Don Quixote should have no suspicions, ordered the maiden to wash his face and beard as well.   But the one who really was crying for and needing such a washing was Sancho.   He at last got up sufficient courage to ask the Duchess that he might share in the ceremony, and she promised him that if necessary the maidens would even put him in the bath-tub.   This kind offer Sancho declined—with many thanks, however—saying he would be just as grateful for having only his beard washed.

While Sancho went with the seneschal to have this attended to, Don Quixote lingered at the table with the Duke and the Duchess.   The latter was anxious to have the hero tell her something about his Lady Dulcinea; and Don Quixote became reminiscent and began to sigh, telling her in exalted and flowery language of his great platonic love for this lady, who was now enchanted by some evil sage.   When the Duchess asked Don Quixote if it were true that she was only an imaginary figure, he replied meekly that there was a good deal to be said on that point; still, he thought, one must not go to extreme lengths in' asking for proof.   They discussed many other things, not forgetting Sancho, whom his master praised for his drollery and criticised for being a booby.

Suddenly a great noise was heard and the next moment

Sancho burst into the room trembling with rage. He was followed by some of the servants in the kitchen. Round his neck was a straining cloth, and dirty lather was splashed in various places over his person. He presented an appearance that at once made the Duchess scream with laughter. He proceeded to tell how he had been set upon by the kitchen-boy, who had been appointed barber by the rest, and how the lad had attempted to lather his face with kitchen soap and dishwater, applied with a scrubbing-brush. Don Quixote thought it best here to make the servants understand that he would tolerate no such jokes on his squire, so he addressed them in severe fashion and then ordered them back to the kitchen, with the Duchess' kind consent.

When the servants had left Sancho thought it a duty to himself and his master—in order to uphold their mutual dignity and for the sake of freeing himself from any untoward suspicion—to speak on his own behalf: "Let them bring a comb here and curry this beard of mine, and if they get anything out of it that offends against cleanliness, let them clip me to the skin." And when the Duchess had acknowledged her faith in Sancho and his virtues, the poor squire's happiness knew no bounds. He offered to serve her for the rest of his life. He wished that he might soon be dubbed a knight that he might carry out his desire on that point. She thanked him for expressing such a friendly feeling for her, and told him that she could plainly judge by his courteous offer to her that he had been reared in no other school than that of the great knight Don Quixote of

La Mancha. And she assured him that the Duke would not forget the island he had promised him: she would see to that.

Don Quixote was now feeling the necessity for his mid-day nap, and begged to be permitted to retire. Sancho wanted to do the same, and remarked to the Duchess that he usually slept about four or five hours in the middle of a warm summer day; but upon her earnest request he promised her to try to wake up after an hour and come and visit with her and her duennas.

CHAPTER XXXIII

OF THE DELECTABLE DISCOURSE WHICH THE DUCHESS AND HER DAMSELS HELD WITH SANCHO PANZA, WELL WORTH READING AND NOTING

AS soon as Sancho had eaten his dinner, he decided to have no sleep that afternoon, but to hasten to the Duchess' chambers that he might talk to her the whole afternoon. The Duchess asked him innumerable questions about his master and the Lady Dulcinea, and about Teresa Panza and every one concerned in the book about Don Quixote; and Sancho managed to keep the Duchess and her duennas in an uncommonly good humor for the rest of the day. They soon drifted to Sancho's government, and the squire expressed the belief that perhaps after a fortnight he would be as well versed in the affairs of government as he was in the farm labor he had been doing all his life.

"Let them only put me into this government and they will see wonders," he said; "for one who has been a good squire will be a good governor."

And then he took leave of the high lady, who suggested that he go home and sleep for the rest of the afternoon. He promised that he would, and entreated her to see to it that good care was taken of his Dapple. When he had explained to the Duchess that Dapple was his faithful donkey, and told her of the incident with Doño Rodriguez, she assured him that Dapple would want for nothing in her stable. She suggested that when he had his government in hand, he ought to pension Dapple off and let him quit working; and Sancho thought that was by no means a bad idea, for, he said, he would not be the first ass to be so pensioned.

The Duchess, when he had left, hastened to tell the Duke of her amusing conversation with Sancho; and again they put their heads together, trying to invent new ways and plots whereby they might derive amusement from the presence of Don Quixote and his squire.

CHAPTER XXXIV

WHICH RELATES HOW THEY LEARNED THE WAY IN WHICH
THEY WERE TO DISENCHANT THE PEERLESS DULCINEA
DEL TOBOSO, WHICH IS ONE OF THE RAREST
ADVENTURES IN THIS BOOK

WHEN the Duke and the Duchess had hit upon a
plan they proceeded to make preparations for its
being carried out, and on the sixth day they invited Don
Quixote to go hunting with them. There was an array
of huntsmen and beaters, as great a retinue as the Duke
could possibly get together. Both Don Quixote and his
squire had been presented with splendid hunting suits; but
Don Quixote did not accept his, saying that he would soon
have to return to the hard pursuits of his calling, and that
it would only be a burden to carry it along.

Sancho did not know that his beautiful suit was destined
to be torn that very day. A wild boar came along, and
Sancho deserted his Dapple and climbed quickly up into
the tallest tree he could find; but fate would have it that
the branch gave way, and Sancho fell onto a branch below,
where he hung suspended by a great rent in his breeches,
screaming with all his might that he would be devoured
by the boar; but the boar fell in the next moment, pierced
by many spears, and Sancho was helped to the ground by
his master.

The boar was taken to some tents nearby, where dinner

soon was ready and being served for the hunters. Sancho
could not refrain then from showing the Duchess what had
befallen him in the tree-top, expressing to her his opinion
of hunts of that kind, involving so much risk. Much
better, he thought, it would be to hunt hares and other
little animals. And then he went on at a tremendous
speed, repeating proverb after proverb, one minute telling the Duchess how he would govern his island, and the
next minute talking about something in his home village.

Night fell as they were talking. It was a very dark
night, which helped to make the Duke's plan seem more
likely of success. They had all left the tents and gone into
the wood, when suddenly it seemed as if the whole space
was afire in one blazing red mass of flames; then there came
the sound of trumpets, numberless ones it seemed, and of
hoofs, as if hordes of horses had passed through the wood,
and of drums, and of battle-cries in Moorish. It was one
long, tremendous, indescribable confusion. The Duke
and the Duchess were seemingly taken aback; Don Quixote did not know what to think or do; and Sancho was absolutely panic-stricken. It was a din so overwhelming
that even those who had arranged it were aghast and afraid.

Then there came a sudden lull, and a messenger—dressed
like a demon and blowing a horn that sounded a weird and
sickly note—appeared before their eyes, apparently in
great haste. The Duke called to him and asked him where
he was going; and he replied in a coarse voice that he was
the Devil and was looking for Don Quixote of La Mancha. He pointed to the on-riding troops, and said that
they were enchanters who were bringing the famous Lady

Dulcinea del Toboso and the great Frenchman Montesinos on a triumphal car to seek their disenchantment through the only one who could accomplish it, the Knight of the Lions.

On hearing this, Don Quixote said: "If you are the Devil, you ought to know that I am Don Quixote!"

Whereupon the Devil exclaimed in surprise that he had not noticed the knight at all because he was so preoccupied with so many other things that he had almost forgotten what he was there for. Judging the Devil by his remark Sancho decided he was a very honest fellow and a good Christian; otherwise he would not have sworn—as Sancho did—by God and his conscience. After that the squire concluded that even hell had its quota of souls.

The Devil asked Don Quixote to communicate with Montesinos that he might receive instructions as to how to carry out the disenchantment of Lady Dulcinea; and then he turned around his horse and was gone. The whole thing had happened so suddenly that even Don Quixote was perplexed and seemed as if he did not know whether to believe what he had seen and heard. Sancho was dumbfounded and frightened out of his wits.

As Don Quixote made no move to follow the Devil's advice, the Duke turned to him and asked whether he intended to remain where he was. He answered that he would even if all the devils from hell should attack him. Scarcely had he vowed this when he had to gather all his courage in order not to give way to fear, for again there broke out a noise and din that surpassed anything that he had ever heard: shots of cannon and muskets, shouts and screams from all sides, and the terrific sound of all the trumpets, horns, drums, bugles and clarions; and then came the heavy creaking noise of carts, coming through the wood and all brightly lighted with rows of tapers.

It was too much for poor Sancho. He fell fainting on the Duchess' skirt. She ordered her servants to fan him and to throw water in his face, and he regained consciousness just as one of the carts was passing. It was drawn by four oxen, completely covered with black cloth, and attached to each horn was a lighted wax taper. Leading the oxen were two demons with such horrible, frightful faces that Sancho shut his eyes tightly after having got one glance of them. An old, worthy-looking man with a long, snow-white beard sat on a raised seat on the cart; and when he passed Don Quixote he said in a deep voice: "I am the sage Lirgandeo." And the cart continued. Then followed other carts, with other sages, and Sancho's face suddenly lighted up, for he heard sweet music in the distance, and he said to the Duchess: "Señora, where there is music, there can be no mischief."

But Don Quixote would not commit himself, for all he remarked was: "That remains to be seen."

CHAPTER XXXV

Wherein Is Continued the Instruction Given to Don
Quixote Touching the Disenchantment of
Dulcinea, Together with Other
Marvelous Incidents

AS the sound of the music came closer, they distinguished a triumphal car, several times larger than the other ones, and on it were seated two figures, surrounded by a great many penitents, robed in white, and with lighted wax tapers in their hands. One of the figures was a young maiden in the costume of a nymph. She was very beautiful. The other one was dressed in a robe of state and had her head covered with a black veil.

As the car reached the spot where the Duke and Duchess and Don Quixote were standing, the music suddenly ceased, and the figure in the long robe rose and removed both the robe and the veil. All were astonished to find themselves face to face with Death. Sancho was frightened; Don Quixote felt ill at ease; and even the Duke and the Duchess seemed uncomfortable.

Then Death began to declaim a long poem which ended with the announcement that the Lady Dulcinea was enchanted by himself, the sage Merlin, here in the guise of Death, and that she could be redeemed in but one way: by three thousand three hundred lashes administered on Don Quixote's squire Sancho.

When Sancho heard this ne exclaimed that he would

[242]

rather stab himself that take the lashes, for he failed to see what he had to do with the enchantment of the Lady Dulcinea. This talk infuriated Don Quixote, who threatened to tie him to a tree and lay on the lashes himself, if his faithful squire had so little respect for his beloved one that he would not sacrifice himself to such an extent. But Merlin said that would have no effect, for the worthy Sancho must do the sacrifice of his own free will, or the disenchantment could not be accomplished.

Sancho, however, was as stubborn as a mule, and it was not until the Duke himself took a hand in the matter and threatened him with the loss of his governorship that he gave in; and then a compromise was made whereby Sancho promised to inflict the three thousand three hundred lashes upon himself. Merlin assured him, however, that if he should make any mistake in counting them, it would soon be known; for the moment all the lashes had been dealt, the Lady Dulcinea would be released—neither one lash before, nor one lash after—and she would at once come to thank and reward him for his sacrifice.

As soon as Sancho had testified his willingness to serve his master and his master's lady, Don Quixote fell on his squire's neck and kissed him. The Duke and the Duchess praised him for his unselfishness. And the music played again. Then the car moved on, Lady Dulcinea bowed to Sancho and the ducal pair, and dawn appeared with its glowing smile. The muskets were again heard; and all was calm.

The Duke was pleased beyond measure with his idea, which had been so effectively carried out. The hunt was at an end, and all returned happy and content—all except Sancho, who could not help thinking of the pain he was to give himself. But the Duke was bent on hitting upon new schemes whereby he should be able to continue the gaiety that Sancho and his master caused.

CHAPTER XXXVI

WHEREIN IS RELATED THE STRANGE AND UNDREAMED-OF ADVENTURE OF THE DISTRESSED DUENNA, ALIAS THE COUNTESS TRIFALDI, TOGETHER WITH A LETTER WHICH SANCHO PANZA WROTE TO HIS WIFE, TERESA PANZA

THE Duke's majordomo had played the part of Merlin, and he it was who induced a page to appear as Dulcinea. This majordomo was a fellow full of pranks and good humor, and it was he who had written the verses he recited, too. To him the Duke now turned, and they contrived together another amusing scheme.

The next day Sancho was asked by the Duchess how many lashes he had given himself; and he replied meekly that he had commenced with five. After a moment's inquisition, however, the squire admitted that it had not been with lashes but slaps that he had done penance. The Duchess said she was certain that the sage Merlin would not tolerate any such false pretense. She suggested that he make a scourge with claws or knotted cords so that he would be sure to feel what he was doing to himself, and when the Duchess offered to bring him such a scourge in the morning, he had to promise to accept it. Then he told her that he had written a letter to his wife, Teresa Panza, in the governor style; and begged her to read it, which she did. The Duchess derived so much amusement from it that she hastened to show it to the Duke. And when Sancho was asked whether he had written the letter himself, he said that he only dictated it, since he could neither read nor write.

After dinner the Duke and the Duchess were sitting in the garden talking with Don Quixote and Sancho, when suddenly there was heard the sound of a deep doleful voice. They all turned quickly to see who was speaking, and there they saw approaching them a man with a snow-white beard that reached almost to the ground. He said he was Trifaldin, of the White Beard, squire to the Countess Trifaldi, otherwise called the Distressed Duenna, and that he had come in search of the valiant knight Don Quixote who he had heard was visiting at the castle. His mistress, he said, in order to find this knight had traveled all the way from the kingdom of Kandy without breaking her fast, and now he begged that Don Quixote would receive the lady, that she herself might tell him her misfortunes.

Don Quixote at once bade the squire go and fetch the Countess; at the same time he uttered a desire to the Duke that the confessor who did not believe in knights errant might have been present to see how appreciated and famed his achievements had become throughout the world.

CHAPTERS XXXVII—XXXIX

WHEREIN IS CONTINUED THE NOTABLE ADVENTURE OF THE
DISTRESSED DUENNA, INCLUDING HER
MARVELOUS AND MEMORABLE
TALE OF MISFORTUNE

THE Countess soon arrived, escorted by twelve duennas, who formed a lane through which she passed into
the Duke's presence.   On seeing so distinguished a guest,
he went to receive her with all the honors due to her rank.
When she had curtsied, she asked the Duke if it were
true that the famous Don Quixote of La Mancha was present in the company.   The import of her question was
heightened by the way she expresseed it, for these were
her words spoken in a deep and coarse voice: "Are there
present here that knight immaculatissimus, Don Quixote
de la Manchissima, and his squirissimus Panza?"

Before Don Quixote or any one else had had an opportunity to reply, Sancho opened his mouth and burst out:
"The Panza is here, and Don Quixottissimus too; and so,
most distressedest Duennissima, you may say what you
willissimus, for we are all readissimus to do you any servis-
simus."

Then Don Quixote stepped forward and begged the
duenna to give him an account of her distress that he might
know how to relieve it.   The duenna became emotional
almost beyond bounds.   She thrust herself before Don

[246]

Quixote and embraced his legs, imploring his and his squire's help, and then began to tell her story of misery.

All the while the Duke and the Duchess were in paroxysms of laughter, so well did the duenna act her part. And their enjoyment was further heightened by the remarks and questions that Sancho interspersed here and there, always at the wrong moment and much to his master's chagrin.

The weeping duenna went on to tell how she had been the ranking duenna at the court of the dowager-queen of Kandy; how she had been entrusted with the care and the bringing up of the Princess Antonomasia, the young heiress of the kingdom, and how she had permitted a young gentleman at the court, who was enamored of the Princess, to gain her favor in such a degree that marriage followed. The young Don had captivated both the Princess and the duenna with his accomplishments, for not only did he play the guitar and write poetry, and dance, but he could as well make bird-cages. But when the Queen learned of her daughter's marriage to one so much beneath her in rank, her heart broke in twain and she collapsed and was buried in three days, the duenna declared, tears streaming down her face all the while.

Sancho was curious at once, and wanted to have a doubt settled. "She died, no doubt?" he asked; and the duenna assured him that they did not bury the living in Kandy, only the dead. But Sancho thought it was a very stupid thing for the Old Queen to go and die thus; he said he could see no reason why she should have taken the whole thing so to heart, for the Princess might have married a page. That, in Sancho's opinion, might have been an excuse for dying; but the Don was such an accomplished man, and a gentleman at that, who could even make birdcages. Dying was too absurd!

Then the duenna resumed, and now came the worst of her story. She told how the two lovers, upon the Queen's death, had become enchanted by the giant Malambruno, the Queen's first cousin, who had sworn that they would not regain their right shapes until the famous and valiant knight of La Mancha had met him in single combat. Having sentenced them thus, he summoned all the duennas in the castle, charging them with the responsibility of the evil match, and saying that since he did not wish them to suffer death, he would punish them in some other way. Scarcely had the giant uttered these words before their faces began to sting, their pores opened, and when the duennas put their hands to their faces, they felt themselves punished in a most horrifying manner.

Here the thirteen duennas raised their veils, and the Duke and his company were amazed to see that all the women were bearded. The Distressed Duenna raised a wail, and assured those present that had it not been that she had cried so much that she had no tears left, she would now shed them copiously, and she exclaimed: "Where, I ask, can a duenna with a beard go? What father or mother will pity her? Who will help her? For, if even when she has a smooth skin and a face tortured by a thousand kinds of cosmetics, she can hardly get anybody to love her, what will she do when she shows a countenance turned into a thicket? O duennas! It was an unlucky moment when we were born and when our fathers begot us!"

As the unhappy duenna spoke these words, it seemed as if she were about to faint. With a deep and distressing moan, she covered her face with her hands.

CHAPTER XL

OF MATTERS RELATING AND BELONGING TO THIS ADVENTURE AND TO THIS MEMORABLE HISTORY

THE one who was most impressed by this sad story and enchantment was Sancho, who thought it a dastardly trick for any giant to do. Did not the enchanter know that it cost money to shave? In Sancho's opinion, it would have been infinitely better to have taken off a part of their noses, even if it would have given them an impediment of speech. The duennas replied that some of them had tried sticking-plaster in order to spare themselves the expense of shaving, but to jerk it off their faces, was a painful procedure, they said.

Don Quixote interrupted and declared that they would have to follow no such course, for he would rid them of their beards or he would pluck out his own in the land of the Moors. Such a noble declaration seemed to revive the Distressed Duenna. She came up to Don Quixote and told him that the giant Malambruno had been courteous enough to offer to send the famous wooden steed that the valiant Pierres used. Merlin had made it. This horse could go through the air with a speed that carried its rider to the ends of the world overnight. It was steered by a peg in his forehead, she said, and this peg also served as a bridle. Furthermore, there was room for two—one in the saddle, and one on the croup.

"I should like to see him," said Sancho; "but to fancy that I am going to mount him, either in the saddle or on the croup, is to ask pears of an elm-tree. Let each one shave himself as best he can; I am not going to be bruised to get rid of any one's beard."

But Countess Trifaldi insisted that Panza was indispensable to the shaving of the duennas; and when the Duchess had pleaded with him and he saw the Distressed Duenna's eyes fill with tears, he could hardly keep his own back. He bent to their will and resigned himself to his fate and the adventure of riding through the air on the croup of the mighty wooden steed.

CHAPTER XLI

THE END OF THIS PROTRACTED ADVENTURE

DON QUIXOTE was in a state of anxiety during the whole day for fear that Malambruno should not send the steed, but soon after nightfall there arrived in the garden four wild-men, clad in ivy, and carrying on their shoulders a large wooden horse. Don Quixote was summoned by the Distressed Duenna and he mounted the horse at once, not even putting on his spurs. By this time, however, Sancho had changed his mind and decided that he was not going to fly through the air like a witch. But upon the earnest and courteous solicitations of the Duke, Sancho at last consented to ride with his master.

Don Quixote begged Sancho to give himself five hundred lashes on behalf of his enchanted Dulcinea before they set off; but this request struck the squire as the absurdest one he had ever heard. How could his master expect him to sit on a hard wooden horse while he was all bruised and sore from the lashes? He did promise solemnly, however, that as soon as the duennas had been shaved he would turn to the fulfilling of the other debt.

The Distressed Duenna blindfolded them, saying that doing so would prevent them from getting dizzy when they rose to great heights; and Sancho, trembling and tearful, complained that the croup was too hard and begged for a cushion. But the duenna answered him that the magic steed permitted no trappings of any kind, and she suggested that he place himself sideways like a woman, for no doubt he would feel the hardness less in that position.

Sancho did so; and then he uncovered his eyes and looked in a tender fashion on those he was leaving behind, and began to cry piteously. Don Quixote told him sharply to cover his eyes again and not to act like a fool and a coward; and his squire did as he was bidden, after having commended himself to God and begged the duennas to pray all the paternosters and ave-marias they could for him. They in turn admonished him to stick tight to the croup and not to lose hold of it, warning him that if he fell, he would fall like a planet and be blinded by all the stars he would meet on his way down to Earth.

Sobbing, Sancho clung to his master, embracing him with his fat arms so tightly that Don Quixote came near being upset. The knight took a firm grip on the steering peg, and reprimanded his squire for squeezing him. He told him there was nothing to worry about, for it seemed to him he had never in his life ridden a steed that was so easy-going: one would hardly think they had budged from their original place, he said. When Sancho had calmed himself, he concurred in this opinion. He had never heard that there were people living in the air, and did he not hear voices quite close to his ears? Don Quixote then had to explain that affairs of this sort were not of the every-day kind, and that whenever one went on a trip like this, the voices from the Earth would reach thousands of leagues away.

Scarcely had Don Quixote said this, before a gust of wind came that threatened to unseat both the knight and his squire. (The fact was that it was the draught from a tremendous pair of bellows which the Duke had had un-earthed for the occasion.) Sancho was shaking in his seat, and Don Quixote warned him again to sit still, for they were in danger of having a runaway straight into the re-gions of air and thunder, and then into the region of fire. He feared he might not get the steed to turn before it was too late, he said; for it seemed as if the machinery of the peg were rather intricate, and did not work quickly.

Suddenly Sancho began to yell that they were already lost in the flames, and would be burned to death. (He felt his beard being singed by a torch. It was one of a great number that the majordomo had provided.) Don Quixote, too, felt his face warm up. But he would not permit Sancho to uncover his eyes; if he did, the knight said he would only be seized with giddiness and both of them would fall off their horse. Besides, he comforted Sancho with the thought that the journey would last only a few moments longer, and that they were now passing a final test before landing in the kingdom of Kandy. Don Quixote added that the distance they had traveled must have been tremendous, and Sancho replied: "All I know is that if the Señora Magallanes or Magalona was satisfied with this croup, she could not have been very tender of flesh."

At this moment came the culmination of their journey through the air. A torch was tied to the tail of the steed, which was stuffed with fire-crackers, and suddenly there was a tremendous noise and a flash, and in the next moment Don Quixote and Sancho Panza, both scorched, lay as if thunderstruck on the ground.

When the knight and his squire finally came to, and looked about, they were aghast at what they saw. The ground was strewn with bodies, but the bearded duennas were gone. Planted in the ground they saw a lance, attached to which they found a parchment which proclaimed that the enchantment of the duennas and of the Don and his royal bride was at an end, and that as soon as the squire Sancho Panza deigned to carry out the flogging he was to give himself, the peerless Dulcinea would appear in all her original beauty again.

[253]

Now the Duke and the Duchess, who were among the bodies lying on the ground, seemingly dead, lifted up their heads, as if just coming out of a long sleep; and Don Quixote hastened to tell them of the great miracle that had befallen him. They were both convulsed with laughter—which Don Quixote mistook for emotion—and when he had finished telling them about his marvelous adventure, they had all they could do to reply. The Duke finally gathered enough strength to embrace him and tell him that he was no doubt the greatest knight the world had ever known.

The Duchess was curious to know how Sancho had enjoyed the trip; and he confessed that in spite of his master's command he had peered from underneath the kerchief before his eyes, and had seen the earth below, and that the people seemed as little as hazelnuts and the earth itself looked like a grain of mustard-seed; and when he passed through the region of fire he had seen the goats of heaven, he said.

CHAPTER XLII

Of the Counsels Which Don Quixote Gave Sancho Panza Before He Set Out to Govern the Island, Together with Other Well-Considered Matters

THE heaven-riding adventure had been such a success that the Duke and the Duchess could not rest until they had seen Sancho installed as governor of his island; for they felt certain they should derive a great fund of amusement from such an experiment. So Sancho was told to prepare himself.

But Sancho, having seen heaven, seemed less keen to be governor now, since he felt how small humanity really was, particularly in comparison with the goats of the sky which he claimed he had seen, and he replied that he would much rather have a bit of heaven than any island on earth. The Duke, however, told Sancho that, not being the ruler there, it was for God to dispose of such domains. So Sancho promised to come down to earth and be governor, and to attire himself in the regalia befitting the office.

This being done, Don Quixote and Sancho withdrew to the knight's room, and there Don Quixote gave his squire advice about governing. He admonished him to be a champion of virtue always, to strive to know himself and not to puff himself up like a peacock, whose feathers, he bade him remember, were fine, but who had ugly feet. And the advice and instructions that master gave servant were such that no one would have thought it was a madman speaking.

CHAPTER XLIII

Of the Second Set of Counsels Don Quixote Gave Sancho Panza

DON QUIXOTE then told his squire to forget neither to cut his nails nor to supply his servants with livery. The latter, he said, must be neat and never showy. If he could do with three servants instead of six, he advised him to clothe three poor men: thus he would have pages for heaven as well as for earth. He must never eat garlic or onions, the knight said, and he begged him to leave out all affectations. When it came to drinking, he asked him always to bear in mind that too much wine kept neither secrets nor promises. Another thing he must not do was to flatter people; Don Quixote considered this a very odious practice. Last, but not least, said Don Quixote, he must remember not to use such quantities of proverbs as he had been wont to.

Here Sancho felt he had to break in and say a word, and he retorted: "God alone can cure that, for I have more proverbs in me than a book, and when I speak they fall to fighting among themselves to get out; that's why my tongue lets fly the first that comes, though it may not be pat to the purpose." And here Sancho in the very face of his master's admonitions, let go a string of proverbs so long that Don Quixote was almost in despair.

"My mother beats me, and I go on with my tricks," said Don Quixote. "I am bidding thee avoid proverbs, and here in a second thou hast shot out a whole litany of them. Those proverbs will bring thee to the gallows some day, I promise thee."

SANCHO TAKES LEAVE OF HIS MASTER

CHAPTER XLIV

How Sancho Panza Was Conducted to His Government;
and of the Strange Adventure That Befell Don
Quixote in the Castle

BEFORE Sancho departed for his island—which was
in reality a village belonging to his new master's
duchy, and surrounded by land on all sides—Don Quixote
wrote out carefully the advice he had given him in the
morning of the same day. To escort the new governor to
the village the Duke had chosen the majordomo, who had
played the part of the Countess Trifaldi; and the moment
Sancho saw his face and heard him speak, he confided to
to his master the resemblance in voice and appearance.

Always suspicious of enchanters, Don Quixote bade his
late squire to keep a sharp eye on the man, and to be sure
to inform him whether anything happened that confirmed
his suspicion.

Then Sancho was dressed in the garb of a lawyer and
mounted on a mule. Dapple followed behind with new
trappings, and Sancho was so pleased with the appearance of Dapple that he could not help turning around
from time to time to look at him. Don Quixote wept
when it came to the leave-taking, and Sancho kissed de-
votedly the hands of the Duchess and the Duke.

But as soon as Sancho had left, Don Quixote felt a
great loneliness in his heart; and that night, after having
supped with the ducal pair, he begged to be excused early

[257]

and retired to his room, saying he wanted no servant to wait on him.

He undressed at once, and went to bed, leaving the window overlooking the garden open. Soon he heard the voices of two young maidens, and he was surprised to hear that they were speaking of him. One of them he recognized as the fair Altisidora, and, persuaded by the other voice, she commenced to serenade the knight, to whom in her song she bared her aching heart, and the passion that burned there for him.

But the knight could not be moved. His was a love for no one but his Dulcinea. To indicate to the young maiden that he was aware of her intentions and could not be swayed, he rose from his bed, and went to the window and feigned a sneeze. When that was of no avail and neither produced reticence in the maidens nor drove them away from his window, he sighed: "O what an unlucky knight I am that no damsel can set eyes on me but falls in love with me!" And he went on to bewail his fate, crying out in the night that all the empresses in the world were jealous of the love he bore in his heart for the sweet Dulcinea, and saying that he must and would remain hers, pure, courteous, and chaste, in spite of all the magic-working powers on earth.

Then the worthy knight shut his window with a bang, and thrust himself on his bed, entirely out of patience with the enticing and sinful young maidens.

SANCHO PANZA BECOMES GOVERNOR

CHAPTER XLV

OF HOW THE GREAT SANCHO PANZA TOOK POSSESSION OF HIS ISLAND; AND OF HOW HE MADE A BEGINNING IN GOVERNING

WHEN Sancho arrived in his village he learned that his island was called Barataria. He was greeted with great demonstrations: the whole community had turned out to meet him, and all the churchbells were ringing. He was first taken to the church, where he gave thanks to God; then he was presented with the keys of the town. From the church he was taken to the judgment seat outside, and there he was told to answer numerous questions which the majordomo put to him, saying that that was an ancient custom on taking office.

The questions were cases of quarrels between the villagers, and Sancho answered each one of them so sagely that every one gaped in wonder, for, judging by his appearance and the way he talked, they had thought their governor a fool. Instead of thinking thus, they now began to admire him and to consider themselves lucky and blessed by having him in their midst.

CHAPTER XLVI

OF THE TERRIBLE BELL AND CAT FRIGHT THAT DON QUIXOTE
GOT IN THE COURSE OF THE ENAMORED ALTISIDORA'S
WOOING

THE thought of Altisidora's love bothered Don Quixote so that he could not go to sleep. He had torn
his green stockings, while undressing, and having neither
needle nor thread he could not mend them, and this increased his annoyance. Soon it was morning, and to put
an end to his agony, he rose and dressed himself. But on
his way to the ante-chamber, where the Duke and Duchess
would receive him, he passed through a gallery, where he
was surprised to find the fair Altisidora and her friend
who had been with her outside his window the night before.

When Altisidora laid eyes on the knight errant, she fell
in a dead faint, but was caught in the arms of her friend,
who began to unlace her dress. Don Quixote remained
cold and untouched, mumbling all the while to himself
that he knew perfectly well why she had fainted. Her
friend retorted with venom in her voice that she wished
he would disappear from the castle, for if he remained
there much longer Altisidora would be wasting away into
nothingness—even if she were the healthiest and most
buxom maiden there at the moment—and die from a broken
heart. This seemed to touch Don Quixote, for he replied
that if she would see to it that a lute was put in his room

THE TERRIBLE BELL AND CAT FRIGHT

that night, he would sing to her and try to comfort her in the night while she stood outside his window.

The damsels went at once to tell the Duchess what had happened, and she was pleased beyond words; and together they hit upon a new joke which would bring them fresh merriment.

Just before midnight Don Quixote came to his chamber and found there a guitar; and, having tuned it as best he could, he began to let out his rusty voice into the notes of a ballad that he himself had composed that day. While he stood there on his balcony singing, there suddenly broke out a tremendous din; and from above was let down a cord to which hundreds of bells were attached, making the most deafening sound. At the same time a bag of cats, each with a bell tied to its tail, came shooting down upon the unfortunate knight, who was frightened beyond words by the meowing and squalling and screaming of the cats and by the jingling of the bells.

Don Quixote stood paralyzed, with the guitar clutched in his hand, when suddenly it struck him that his room must have been invaded by jumping devils—for the cats had knocked the candles down on the floor, extinguishing them as they did so, and the room was now in pitch darkness. He suddenly flung his guitar away and drew his sword, charging the enchanters with all the fervor and energy that he possessed.

All the cats flew toward the balcony, from where they escaped into the garden—all except one, which Don Quixote had cornered, and was making violent stabs at, without hitting anything but the air, the wall and the floor.

This little beast, fighting for its life, like one beset, jumped at the knight, put its teeth and claws into his nose, and remained there, holding on infuriated, while Don Quixote gave out the most terrible screams and howls.

When the Duke and the Duchess heard what was going on, they became afraid that some harm might be done the knight errant; so they ran to his chamber with all haste. The Duke rushed to the rescue of Don Quixote's nose; but in spite of the horrible pain he must have been in, the knight was brave enough to decline all aid, shouting aloud that he wished to fight the malignant enchanter alone. At last, however, the Duke could see the poor fellow suffer no longer, and he managed to separate the cat from Don Quixote's nose.

The fair Altisidora was given the task to cover the damaged parts of the knight's face with ointment, and she did this with a loving and caressing hand, although she could not resist telling him that he would not have been in this predicament if he had listened to her the night before. She jealously hoped, too, that his squire Sancho would forget all about the whippings so that Dulcinea would remain enchanted forever. But Don Quixote was insensible to anything she said; he only sighed and sighed. And then he thanked the Duke and the Duchess for all their kindness; and they really felt sorry in their hearts for the end the joke had taken. They bade him good-night; he stretched himself on his bed; and there he remained for five days.

CHAPTER XLVII

WHEREIN IS CONTINUED THE ACCOUNT OF HOW SANCHO PANZA
CONDUCTED HIMSELF IN HIS GOVERNMENT

HAVING held court, Sancho was escorted to a magnificent palace, where dinner had been laid in a large and gorgeous chamber. There were numerous ceremonies that he had to pass through as he entered; but he went through them all undisturbed and with phlegmatic dignity. He was seated at the head of the table, his own guest of honor as it were, for he found he was the only one present there, excepting a number of pages who surrounded him. But then he discovered behind himself a gentleman who turned out to be a physician, and who soon aroused Sancho's ire. For every time a dish was passed to Sancho, it had first to be passed upon by the physician; and this dignitary seemed to have made up his mind that governors were not meant to live, for every dish was sent back to the kitchen, and Sancho found that a governor's meal consisted in starvation.

This finally enraged the new governor so that he ordered the doctor out of his sight, threatening to break a chair over his head if he did not disappear quickly enough; but just at that moment there arrived a messenger with a letter for the Governor from the Duke, and Sancho became so excited that he forgot about his physician's expulsion for the moment. The majordomo read the letter, which

[263]

was addressed to the Governor of the Island of Baratària. In it the Duke warned Sancho that attacks would be made upon the island some night in the near future by enemies of the Duke, and also, the Duke said, he had learned that four men had entered the town in disguise, and that they would make an attempt upon the Governor's life. He therefore cautioned Sancho to eat nothing that was offered to him.

At once Sancho decided that the worst conspirator against his life was the physician, who wanted to kill him by the slow death of hunger. He said he thought it best to have him thrust into a dungeon. And then he asked for a piece of bread and four pounds of grapes, feeling sure that no poison would be in them, announcing at the same time as his maxim that if he were going to be able to combat enemies he would have to be well fed.

He then turned to the messenger and bade him say to the Duke that his wishes would be obeyed; at the same time he sent a request to the Duchess that she should not forget to have the letter he had written to his Teresa Panza delivered, together with the bundle, by a messenger. Last but not least, he asked to be remembered to his beloved master Don Quixote by a kiss of the hand.

SANCHO GOVERNS WISELY,

CHAPTERS XLVIII—XLIX

Of What Happened to Sancho in Making the Round of His Island

A T last the physician felt it to his advantage to consent to prescribe a good supper for the Governor that
evening. The day had been taken up with all sorts of
applicants, who, it seemed to Sancho, would always arrive at the wrong time, either when he was about to eat
or wanted to sleep.

The supper hour, which Sancho had been longing for all
that day arrived at last, and he was delighted with the beef,
salad, onions, and calves' feet that were put before him.
He told the doctor that for the future he ought never to
trouble himself about giving him dainty dishes and choice
food to eat, for it would only unhinge his stomach. Then
to the head-carver he said: "What you had best do is to
serve me with what they call *ollas podridas*—and the rot-
tener they are the better they smell!" The others he addressed proverbially thus: "But let nobody play pranks on
me, for either we are or we are not. Let us live and eat in
peace and good fellowship, for when God sends the dawn,
he sends it for all. I mean to govern this island without
giving up a right or taking a bribe. Let every one keep his
eye open, and look out for the arrow; for I can tell them
'the devil is in Cantillana,' and if they drive me to it they

shall see something that will astonish them. Nay, make yourself honey and the flies will eat you."

In reply to this the head-carver took it upon himself to speak for the rest of the inhabitants on the island, assuring Sancho that every one was greatly pleased with his mild government, and that he already stood high in their affections.

This brought forth a declaration from Sancho that if the people were not pleased with his government, they would be fools; and then he went on to state that he intended to see to it himself that the island was purged of everything unclean and of all idlers and vagabonds. The latter he compared to the drones in a hive, that eat up the honey the industrious bees make. Furthermore, he emphasized that he would encourage and reward the virtuous, and protect the church and its ministers.

The majordomo was genuinely filled with admiration for all the excellent ideas and remarks of the new governor, particularly when he considered that he was a man without either education or culture; and he could not help admitting to himself that even a joke could sometimes become a reality, and that those who had played a joke on some one might live to find themselves the victims of the very same joke.

That night the Governor as usual made his rounds, accompanied by the majordomo and his whole staff, including the chronicler, who was to record the deeds of Governor Don Sancho Panza; and before the night was over he had given fresh proof of his wisdom, for he settled a quarrel between two gamblers and decided to break up gambling on his island. He kept a youth out of jail. And he restored a young girl, who wanted to see the world as a boy, to her father.

CHAPTER L

WHEREIN IS SET FORTH HOW GOVERNOR SANCHO PANZA'S WIFE RECEIVED A MESSAGE AND A GIFT FROM THE DUCHESS; AND ALSO WHAT BEFELL THE PAGE WHO CARRIED THE LETTER TO TERESA PANZA

THE Duchess did not forget her promise, and she sent the page who had played the part of Dulcinea when the Devil entered a plea for her disenchantment, with Governor Sancho's letter and bundle to his wife. At the same time the Duchess entrusted him with a string of coral beads as a gift from herself to Teresa Panza, with which gift went a letter as well.

When the page reached the village of La Mancha he saw, on entering it, some women washing clothes in a brook; and he found that one of them was no other than the Governor's young daughter. She eagerly ran to the good-looking young man, and, breathless with excitement at the thought of his having news from her father, she skipped along in front of him until they had reached their little house.

Teresa Panza was spinning, and she came out in a gray petticoat, vigorous, sunburnt and healthy, and wanted to

[267]

know what all the excitement was about. The page quickly jumped from his horse, thrust himself on his knees before her, and exclaimed to the bewildered woman: "Let me kiss your hand, Señora Doña Panza, as the lawful and only wife of Señor Don Sancho Panza, rightful governor of the island of Barataria."

But by this time the poor woman had got over her first surprise, and she bade him rise, saying that he should not do things like that, and that she was only a poor country woman, and the wife of a squire errant, not a governor. However, when the page had given her the letters and the gifts, her doubts were crushed, and she decided that Sancho's master must have given her husband the government he had promised him, the one that Sancho had been talking about all the time. And then she asked the page to read the letters to her, since she herself had not learned that art, although she could spin, she said.

When the page had finished reading the Duchess' letter, poor Teresa Panza was overcome with gratitude to the gracious lady who had made her husband, a poor illiterate booby, governor—and a good one besides—and who had deigned to ask her, humble woman that she was, for a couple of dozen or so of acorns.

"Ah, what a good, plain, lowly lady!" she exclaimed. "May I be buried with ladies of that sort, and not with the gentlewomen we have in this town, that fancy, because they are gentlewomen, the wind must not touch them, and go to church with as much airs as if they were queens, no less, and who seem to think they are disgraced if they look at a farmer's wife! And see here how this good lady, for all she is a Duchess, calls me her friend, and treats me as if I were her equal!"

Then she told her Sanchica to make ready a meal, with plenty of eggs and bacon, for the lad who had brought them such good news, while she herself ran out and told the neighbors of their great luck. Soon Samson Carrasco and the curate came to the house, having heard the news, and wanted to know what madness had taken possession of Sancho's wife. But when they had read the letters and had seen the presents, they themselves were perplexed, and did not know what to make of it; and when they had met the page and he had confirmed everything that was said in the letters, they were convinced, although they were at a loss to understand how it all had come to happen.

The Duchess' asking for a few acorns, they could not quite comprehend, but even this was soon explained, for the page assured them that his lady, the Duchess, was so plain and unassuming that she had even been known to have borrowed a comb from a peasant-woman neighbor on one occasion; and he added that the ladies of Aragon were not nearly as stiff and arrogant as those of Castile.

Sanchica's greatest concern centered around her father's legs. She was anxious to learn how he covered them, now that he had become governor. She was hoping that he would wear trunk-hose, for she had always had a secret longing, she said, to see her father in tights; "What a sight he must be in them!" she added.

The page replied that he had not observed her father's legs or how they were dressed; but the joking way in which he gave his answer furnished the curate and the bachelor

[269]

with a fresh doubt as to the reality of the governorship and Sancho's position. Yet they could not forget the coral beads and the fine hunting-suit that the page had brought, and which pointed to some truth in the matter.

Sanchica was anxious to make the trip to her father's island at once with the messenger, who told them he had to leave that evening; and Teresa Panza wanted to know whether the curate had heard of any one in the village going to Madrid or Toledo, for she thought that she at least ought to provide herself with a hooped petticoat, now that she was the wife of a distinguished governor and no doubt destined to be made a countess.

And while mother and daughter were contemplating and worrying about their new position in life, they interspersed their sentences with so many proverbs that the curate felt obliged to remark that he thought that all the Panzas were born with a sackful of proverbs in their insides. The page told them here that the Governor uttered them most frequently and spontaneously, much to the amusement of the Duke and the Duchess; and then he reminded the Governor's lady of his hunger. But the curate softly took him by the arm and whispered to him that poor Teresa Panza had more will to serve than she had means, and invited him to sup at his own house.

In order not to lose weight or starve, the page consented; and the curate was glad to have an opportunity to talk with him alone.

Sanchica again expressed her desire to travel with the page; and the page tried to persuade her not to come along, for, he said, the daughters of governors must travel in a

coach and in style, with many attendants. The girl
thought that was nonsense, however, and it was not until
her mother hushed her up with her proverbial logic that
she ceased arguing. Said mother Teresa Panza to her
daughter: "As the time so the behavior: when it was Sancho it was Sanchica, when it is governor it is señorita."
And that settled it.

The bachelor offered to write letters for Teresa Panza
to her husband and the Duchess; but, somehow, she did
not seem to trust him, for she refused his offer. Instead
she induced a young acolyte to write the epistles for her,
paying him with the eggs which she was to have used for
the page's supper.

CHAPTER LI

OF THE PROGRESS OF SANCHO'S GOVERNMENT; AND OTHER SUCH ENTERTAINING MATTERS

THE thing that troubled Sancho most was not his
manifold duties nor his judgments, but his appetite. It was as keen as ever, yet he got next to nothing to
eat. The morning after he had made his round, they gave
him only some water and a little conserve for breakfast, the
doctor advising him that light food was the most nourish-
ing for the wits, and especially to be recommended to
people who were placed in responsible positions—such as
governors, for instance. Thus poor Sancho was persuaded
to submit to a process of starvation which was gradually

making him regret, and finally curse, his ever having become governor.

He sat in judgment that day but a short time, and made a decision in an intricate case with so much good sense and wit that the majordomo was overwhelmed with admiration, and could not refrain from taking pity on the governor's stomach. So he stood up and announced, knowing it would have the Governor's immediate and unqualified sanction, that the session had come to an end for the morning; then turning to Sancho, he promised to give him a dinner that day that would please him.

Sancho was grateful in advance, and felt moved to thank him. "That is all I ask for," he declared: "fair play! Give me my dinner, and then let it rain cases and questions on me, and I shall despatch them in a twinkling." And since it had been arranged by the conspirators in the joke that this was to be the last day of Sancho Panza's reign as governor, the majordomo gave him the best dinner that he could.

Just as the Governor was finishing his repast a courier arrived with a letter from Don Quixote. The secretary read it aloud to him, and he listened attentively and respectfully to the wisdom and good and sound advice that his beloved Don Quixote gave him in the letter. All who heard it read were agreed that they had seldom had the fortune to hear such a well-worded and thoroughly sensible epistle; and Sancho was proud of the praise that was being bestowed on his former master, to whom he still was as devoted as ever.

The Governor withdrew with his secretary into his own

room, and there he dictated at once his reply to Don Quixote's letter. In this he confided to him all that had happened on his island, the reforms he had undertaken, and
the judgments he had handed down. He finished by asking the knight to kiss the hand of the sweet Duchess for
him and tell her that she had not thrown it into a sack
with a hole in it, as she would see in the end: meaning
by this that he would show her how grateful he was as
soon as he had an opportunity.

The courier returned to the ducal palace with the Governor's message; and Sancho spent the afternoon in making
provisions for all sorts of beneficial improvements in his
government, reducing prices on a number of necessaries,
and confirming laws that tended to help the poor and
needy, while they would incriminate those who were im-
postors, good-for-nothings, and vagabonds. Even to this
day some of these laws are in existence there, and are
called *The constitutions of the great governor, Sancho
Panza.*

CHAPTER LII

WHEREIN THREE DELECTABLE EPISTLES ARE READ BY THE DUCHESS

DON QUIXOTE had now been healed of his scratches,
and he began to long for the road; for the life was
too easy, he thought, for one who had dedicated himself
to knight-errantry and valorous deeds. But the day he

had decided to break the news to the Duke and the Duchess, the messenger that the Duchess had sent to Sancho's wife returned, bringing with him two letters, one addressed to "The Duchess So-and-so, of I don't know where," and the other one to "The Governor, Sancho Panza of the Island of Barataria, whom God prosper longer than me!"

The Duchess was so eager to read her letter that she opened it at once; and having read it to herself, she felt she ought to give amusement to the others too, so she read it aloud to all who were there. She was dying to see what the letter to the Governor contained, so she asked Don Quixote whether he thought it would be a breach of etiquette to read it; and Don Quixote took it upon himself, as Sancho's late master and guardian, to open it. Then he read it to the Duke and the Duchess, who laughed to their heart's content at the many drolleries with which Teresa Panza had stuffed her epistle.

Just as the merriment was at its peak, the courier with Sancho Panza's reply to Don Quixote arrived, and that communication too was read aloud; and the Duke could not omit remarking that it was a most excellent and sane letter. The Duchess, however, was anxious to question the page about his visit with Teresa Panza, so she excused herself, and withdrew with the page and her presents; for, besides the acorns, the Governor's wife had sent her a cheese, much to the gratification of the Duchess.

END OF SANCHO PANZA'S GOVERNMENT

CHAPTER LIII

Of the Troublous End and Termination of Sancho Panza's Government

THE seventh day of Sancho's government was approaching its end. The Governor lay in his bed, resting after all the judgments and proclamations he had made that day upon a fasting stomach. Suddenly he rose in his bed, for he heard the most deafening noise, intermingled with the ringing of churchbells. To this sound was added that of trumpets and drums, and the combination made a din that frightened Sancho almost out of his wits. He flew out of bed, put on a pair of slippers, and rushed into the street, dressed in nothing but his night shirt. He was startled to see the streets crowded with men, carrying torches, and crying: "To arms, Señor Governor, to arms! The enemy is here, and we are lost, unless you come to the rescue with your sword!"

Sancho was lost; he did not know what to do, for swordsmanship was not among his accomplishments. And so he simply asked them whether the enemy could not wait until he had a chance to summon his master Don Quixote of La Mancha, who, he said, knew all about arms.

Just then one of the inhabitants came along, carrying two shields, and without any ceremony he told Sancho in plain language that it was his duty as their governor to lead them into battle. Then he covered him—without

[275]

giving him a chance to put on anything besides his night-shirt—with the two shields, one in front and the other one behind; pressing them together as tightly as he and another man could manage, they laced them with rope, so that Sancho could neither move a muscle, nor bend a leg. Then they put a lance in his hand and told him to lead them into battle against the enemy, for now they were no longer a-fraid of the outcome, they said.

"How am I to march, unlucky being that I am," asked Sancho, "when I cannot stir my knee-caps for these boards that are bound so tightly to my body! What you must do is to carry me in your arms, and lay me across or set me up-right in some postern, and I shall hold it either with this lance or with my body."

When the men heard the Governor speak thus, one of them was bold enough to suggest that he could not move because he was too frightened; and this angered poor San-cho into a frantic attempt to take a step in the direction of the invading army. But this step was a fatal one, for the Governor fell in his undignified stiffness flat on his back with such a crash that he thought he had broken every bone in his body.

The men now quickly extinguished their torches, and began to step on his shield, slashing their swords over his head, shouting and yelling, and making all the noise they could. Had Sancho not pulled in his head like a tortoise in his shell, he might have fared ill. One man boldly placed himself on Sancho's roof, calling in a mighty voice, now and then filled with an agonized grunt, such direc-tions as these: "Hold the breach there! Shut the gate!

END OF SANCHO PANZA'S GOVERNMENT

Barricade those ladders! Block the streets with feather-beds! Here with your stink-pots of pitch and resin, and kettles of boiling oil!"

All these exclamations put fear in the already hard-pressed and squeezed heart of Sancho Panza, who was wishing where he lay that he had never seen the sight of an island. He was in such an agony that he began to pray to the Lord in Heaven to have mercy on him and let him die, or else let this terrible strife and warfare come to an end.

Heaven must have heard Sancho's prayer, for suddenly he heard cries of: "Victory! Victory! The enemy retreats!" Then some one jerked him by the arm, and told him to stand up and enjoy the victory; and finally some of the bystanders took pity on him, and lifted him up from his vertical position. But Sancho refused to enjoy any victory. All he asked for, he said, was that some one wipe the perspiration from his body, and give him some wine for his parched throat. When they had fulfilled this desire of his, they carried him to his chamber, were they put him to bed. Hardly had they got him to bed before he fainted away, overcome with excitement and governments.

The attendants sprinkled some water in the Governor's face, and he soon came back to life. The first thing he asked was what time it was. They replied it was early morning. He rose without saying a word, dressed himself in haste, and then went out to the stable, where they found him hanging round his Dapple's neck, kissing and embracing him, while tears were streaming down his face. Having swallowed the first flood of tears, the late squire addressed his faithful donkey in the tenderest and most

[277]

heartrending terms, telling him that he should have stuck by him all the time, and not let himself be carried away by ambitions to become governor of islands.

Sancho then put the pack-saddle on Dapple's back, and mounted—a process of much pain—and from his dear confederate's back he addressed the majordomo and those of his staff who had followed him to the stable. "Make way," he said, "and let me go back to my old freedom; let me go look for my past life, and raise myself up from this present death. I was not born to be a governor or to protect islands or cities from the enemies that choose to attack them. Ploughing and digging, vine-dressing and pruning, are more in my way than defending provinces or kingdoms. Saint Peter is very well in Rome: I mean, each of us is best following the trade he was born to. I would rather have my fill of the simplest pot-luck than be subject to the misery of a meddling doctor who kills me with hunger; and I would rather lie in summer under the shade of an oak, and in winter wrap myself in a double sheepskin jacket in freedom, than to go to bed between Holland sheets and dress in sables under the restraint of a government. God be with your Worships! Tell my lord, the Duke, that naked was I born, naked I find myself, I neither lose nor gain: I mean that without a farthing I came into this government, and without a farthing I go out of it—very different from the way governors commonly leave other islands. Stand aside and let me go. I have to plaster myself, for I believe every one of my ribs is crushed, thanks to the enemies that have been trampling over me to-night."

Here the doctor offered to give the retiring governor a

draught that would cure him of all pain. He also promised Sancho if he would stay he would behave better in the future, and give him as much to eat as he desired. But Sancho was not at a loss for an answer this time.

"You spoke late," said he. "I should as soon turn Turk as stay any longer. Those jokes will not pass a second time. By the Lord, I should as soon remain in this government, or take another one, even if it was offered me between two plates, as fly to heaven without wings. I am of the breed of Panzas, and they are every one of them obstinate, and if they once say odds, odds it must be, no matter if it is evens, in spite of all the world. Here in this stable I leave the ant's wings that lifted me up into the air for the swifts and other birds to eat them, and let us take to the level ground and our feet once more; and if they are not shod in pinked shoes of cordovan, they shall not want for rough sandals of hemp. Every ewe to her like and let no one stretch his leg beyond the length of the sheet. And now let me pass, for it is growing late with me."

After this meditation, strung with proverbs, the major-domo turned to Sancho and said that before he departed it was necessary that he render an account for the ten days that he had governed the island. But this was not Sancho's idea, and he quickly replied that he would seek out the Duke and give an accounting to him, for he was the only one to whom he was responsible. He added that as he would come to him naked, that would be the best proof that he had governed like an angel.

So they all agreed to let him proceed, for they were certain that the Duke would be delighted to see him. They offered him anything that he might need for the journey; but all Sancho asked for was some barley for his Dapple, and some bread and cheese for himself. Then they all bade him godspeed and embraced him; and Sancho, with tears in his eyes, took leave of them. The majordomo and the rest of Sancho's staff could not help thinking that he had displayed more sense than most men might have under the same circumstances; for when Sancho left his government he had earned their admiration for many and good reasons.

CHAPTERS LIV—LV

OF WHAT BEFELL SANCHO ON THE ROAD; AND OTHER THINGS THAT CANNOT BE SURPASSED

SANCHO had almost reached the Duke's castle, when night suddenly fell and it grew so dark that he considered it best to stop where he was and remain there overnight. Accordingly he took Dapple off the road, and they went in search for some comfortable place where they could rest. Presently Sancho found himself among some old ruins, and as he was stumbling along he suddenly felt himself and Dapple falling deep into the earth. He thought it was going to be an endless journey, but when he struck bottom he discovered that nothing had happened to him or to his faithful donkey, for there he was, still mounted even.

Of course he was somewhat shaken by this sudden plunge into the lower regions, and taken aback; but as soon as he realized that he was unhurt he began to praise the Lord and to give thanks to him on behalf of himself and Dapple, who had burst into lamentations upon finding himself separated from meadow and green grass. Then Sancho began to look about for a way out, but he searched in vain, and it became plain to him that here he was buried alive. He thought of his master's descent into the cave of Montesinos, and was envious of Don Quixote's imagination which could conjure up so easily soft beds to sleep in and good food to eat. He could already see himself as a skeleton, and he shed a tear when he thought of having no one to close his or Dapple's eyes, when they had breathed their last breath.

All that night they sat there in somber reflection on the strange fates of man and beast; and when dawn came Sancho found that he was in a cave that had no outlet but which seemed to extend for miles underneath the ground. He crawled with Dapple from one cavern or compartment to another one; one dungeon was dark, the next one had a bit of flickering light; and as he proceeded he kept calling aloud, "God Almighty, help me!" at every step he took, fearing that he would be plunged still deeper into the insides of the earth, into still darker abysses. And then he wished that it had been his master instead of himself who had landed in this spot, for he was sure that Don Quixote would have welcomed such an adventure.

It so happened that Don Quixote was riding along the countryside that day on Rocinante, and suddenly his steed's hoof grazed against a hole in the earth. Rocinante might have fallen into the hole had not Don Quixote swiftly pulled in the reins and held him back. As the knight was passing, and about to continue on his journey, he turned in his seat to observe the spot well, and then he was startled by a cry that seemed to come from the depths of the earth and found an outlet through this pit. Still more startled he was, when he recognized the voice of his own squire Sancho! These were the words he heard: "Ho, above there! Is there any Christian that hears me, or any charitable gentleman that will take pity on a sinner buried alive, or an unfortunate, disgoverned governor?"

Of course it never entered our valiant knight's mind, devout Catholic that he was, that it was the voice of any Sancho Panza in the flesh. He thought that his devoted squire had suddenly met with death, and that his soul was now in Purgatory, and that it was from there that these sounds emanated. So he answered that he would do all in his power to have Sancho released from his pains.

This brought forth an emphatic and tearful denial from below. Sancho swore that he had never died in his life. As if to corroborate that his master was not a liar, Dapple at this moment brayed most tellingly, and Don Quixote believed everything that Dapple told him in that short space of time, for Don Quixote knew Dapple's braying as well as if he had been his father. The knight errant assured Sancho that he would get him out of his prison in a very short time, though he thought it best to return to the castle first and get some men to help him in the task. Sancho begged his master to hurry, for he was afraid unto death, and could not stand the thought of being buried there much longer.

SANCHO VISITS THE LOWER REGIONS

As soon as the Duke heard what had happened to his governor, he was extremely surprised, for he had had no news from the island of Barataria about Sancho's departure. He sent men with ropes and tackle, and after much trouble they finally succeeded in hoisting Sancho and his beloved donkey out of the cave.

Surrounded by a crowd of children and others, they arrived at the castle, where the Duke was awaiting them; but Sancho would not present himself before him until he had seen that Dapple was being taken good care of in the stable. Then he went before the Duke, and as soon as the Duke had greeted him, Sancho commenced a speech that seemed to last forever, stuffed with proverbs galore. In it he related to the Duke everything that happened during the time he was governor, ending it thus: "I have come by the knowledge that I should not give anything to be a governor, not to say of an island, but of the whole world; and that point being settled, kissing your Worship's feet, and imitating the game of the boys when they say, 'Leap thou, and give me one,' I take a leap out of the government and pass into the service of my master Don Quixote. For after all, though in it I eat my bread in fear and trembling, at any rate I take my fill; and, for my part, so long as I am full, it is alike to me whether it is with carrots or with partridges."

When Sancho had finished his discourse Don Quixote was grateful, for he was constantly worried that his squire might say something that would cover both of them with discredit, and Sancho made no great blunders in his speech this time.

[283]

The Duke and the Duchess both embraced Sancho with warmth, and he was greatly touched when they told him that they would try to find him another position, less responsible but more profitable, on their estate; and they gave orders that he was to be well taken care of and his wounds and bruises properly and carefully bandaged.

CHAPTERS LVI—LVII

WHICH TREATS OF HOW DON QUIXOTE AGAIN FELT THE CALLING OF KNIGHT-ERRANTRY AND HOW HE TOOK LEAVE OF THE DUKE, AND OF WHAT FOLLOWED WITH THE WITTY AND IMPUDENT ALTISIDORA, ONE OF THE DUCHESS' DAMSELS

AGAIN the feeling came over Don Quixote that he was wasting his life while he was staying at the castle in luxury and ease as the Duke's guest. Out yonder was the great, wide world in which adventures were calling to him all the time. So it finally came about that after much hesitation he requested of the Duke and his consort that they grant him his release. They gave it to him, although they were sorry to see him go, they said.

Early the following morning Sancho was soliloquizing in the courtyard of the castle, when suddenly Don Quixote appeared, in full regalia, ready to take to the road again for new adventures. The Duke and all in the castle were observing the departure from the corridors. Unobserved by Don Quixote, the majordomo gave Sancho a purse, in which he counted no less than two hundred gold crowns.

When knight and squire had mounted, the fair Altisidora declaimed with touching voice some verses of poetry which she had written in the night, and in which she bewailed her cruel fate that had thrust her in the path of the valorous Don Quixote. Each verse ended with a denunciation of his coldness toward her, and a curse upon him and his Dulcinea. Then the daring maiden had inserted lines in which she accused the innocent knight of having taken possession of three kerchiefs and a pair of garters belonging to her. Don Quixote blushed with perplexity, but his squire came to the rescue and said that he had the kerchiefs, but knew nothing about the garters. The Duke, who was well initiated in the joke, now rose and announced that it was beginning to seem like a serious matter; and if the knight had the garters and did not wish to part with them, he, the Duke, would have to defend the fair maiden's honor and challenge him to single combat.

Now Don Quixote was beside himself. Surely, he said, it would never occur to him, who had enjoyed such unbounded, superlative hospitality at the hands of one so illustrious as the Duke, to let such things come to pass as to bear arms against him; and he swore again by everything he could think of that he was innocent of what the maiden had inferred. Here the damsel gave a little shriek, and announced in a giggling voice that she had found the garters. Don Quixote was much relieved, and so seemed the Duke (though in reality both he and the Duchess were just about to burst from the pain that their own joke had inflicted upon them).

Now the knight errant could depart without any smudge or stain on his honor, and quickly and resolutely he gave Rocinante the spur, and his steed gathered all the strength he had and turned around. Gallantly saluting the Duke and the whole assembly with a sweep of his lance, Don Quixote set off on the road to Saragossa, followed by the retired governor, who sat on his Dapple's back as phlegmatically as if the two were grown together.

CHAPTER LVIII

Which Tells How Adventures Came Crowding on Don Quixote in Such Numbers That They Gave One Another No Breathing-Time

OUT on the open road Don Quixote was himself again, and he turned to Sancho and began to discourse on freedom, telling his squire that it was more precious than anything else in the world. And he ended by saying: "Happy he to whom Heaven has given a piece of bread for which he is not bound to give thanks to any but Heaven itself!"

Here Sancho broke his silence, for he felt that, in spite of what his master had just said, a good deal of thanks was due to the majordomo for the purse with the two hundred crowns, which he was carrying like a plaster next to his heart.

While they were conversing thus, they suddenly came to a spot from where they could see a great many men, dressed like laborers, lying on the grass of a meadow, and partaking of their noonday meal. Here and there on the grass were scattered some objects or figures covered with white cloth, and as soon as Don Quixote observed them he could constrain himself no longer but had to learn what they were. So he politely approached the men and asked them what was hidden underneath the white coverings, and was told that they were images of saints that they were transporting to their village church; and in order not to soil them, they had covered them thus.

The man took great pride in showing our knight the figures—there were Saint George, Saint Martin, Saint James the Moorslayer, and Saint Paul. Don Quixote spoke learnedly on each one of them. When he had seen them all, he bade the men cover the images with the cloths again. Then he declared that he considered it a happy omen to have come upon the images; for, said he, they were knights like himself. There was this difference, however, that while he fought with human weapons, poor sinner that he was, they used divine ones. And he added that if only his Dulcinea could be saved from her sufferings, perhaps his own mind might be restored to its proper function, and a desire for a milder and better life than he was leading now be the result. At this Sancho reverently chirped: "May God hear and sin be deaf!"

The men, having finished their repast, took leave of

Don Quixote and Sancho and continued the journey to
their village. They were not out of sight before Sancho
broke loose with praise for his master, who knew everything under the sun, it seemed. Then he added: "In
truth, master, if what has happened to us to-day is to be
called an adventure, it has been one of the sweetest and
pleasantest that has befallen us in the whole course of our
travels; we have come out of it without having drawn
sword, nor have we been left famishing. Blessed be God
that he has let me see such a thing with my own eyes!"

The conversation now turned to other things, and soon
love became the topic. Sancho could not understand why
his master, as ugly as he was, should have turned the head
of the fair Altisidora; and why his master had not fallen
head over heels in love with her was entirely beyond Sancho's comprehension. Had he himself had the same opportunity he should not have foregone it, he could have promised his master. Here Don Quixote tried to explain to
Sancho that there were different kinds of love: love of the
mind, and of the body; but this explanation seemed to
remain a puzzle to the squire.

While they had been talking in this manner, they had
come into a wood, and suddenly Don Quixote rode into a
green net which entangled him so completely that he began
to shout that he had been enchanted again. He made
ready to cut and slash with his sword, when two beautiful
girls dressed as shepherdesses came from amidst the trees
and began to plead with him not to tear the nets, which
they had spread in the woods that they might snare the
little birds. There was a holiday in the neighborhood,

and they were to give a pageant and a play, they said, and they wanted the birds to be actors in the play with them. Then they courteously begged Don Quixote to be their guest and remain with them; but Don Quixote in return told them that the urgency of his calling made it necessary for him to refuse, whereupon he made them aware of who he was. As soon as the girls heard that they had Don Quixote of La Mancha in their midst, they became still more eager that he should remain, for they had all read and heard of their illustrious guest, they said, through the book that the whole of Spain and all the world was devouring just then.

A gay youth, who was the brother of the young maidens, came up at this moment and joined his sisters in their persuasions, and at last Don Quixote gave in and consented to stay. The youth, who was attired as a shepherd, brought Don Quixote to their tents, and after a morning of gaiety a repast was served, at which the knight was given the place of honor.

When the meal was over, Don Quixote rose and addressed the gathering in his usual dignified manner. He chose for his topic gratitude, and said that there was but one way in which he could show his full appreciation of the hospitality he had enjoyed that day at their hands: namely, to maintain in the middle of the highway leading to Saragossa, for a period of two days, that these two damsels were—with the exception of his lady Dulcinea—the most adorable and beautiful maidens in the world.

Don Quixote had got so far in the course of his speech, when the faithful Sancho could restrain his admiration for his master no longer. Brimming over with enthusiasm, he burst out: "Is it possible there is any one in the world who will dare to say and swear that this master of mine is a madman? Tell me, gentlemen shepherds, is there a village priest, be he ever so wise or learned, who could say what my master has said; or is there a knight errant, whatever renown he may have as a man of valor, who could offer what my master has offered now?" This outburst of his squire's infuriated Don Quixote. He began to foam at the mouth, and after having scolded the meek and meddlesome Sancho, he told him abruptly to go at once and saddle Rocinante. His hosts were astounded at his remarkable behavior and proposal, and did all they could to stay him from carrying it out, but he was not to be swayed. So they all followed at a distance to see what would happen to the knight, who in his anger had not been slow to mount and disappear with Sancho trailing behind on Dapple at his usual gait.

As soon as Don Quixote had posted himself in the middle of the road, he shouted out his challenge. But no one who passed seemed to pay any attention to what he said, much less were they inclined to take up the challenge, if they heard it. Suddenly, however, the knight sighted a troop of men on horseback, all armed with lances. They were coming closer at a fast pace, and as soon as the shepherds and shepherdesses saw them they withdrew in great haste. Sancho, overcome with some innate foreboding of disaster, took refuge in the shade of Rocinante's hindquarters; but Don Quixote stood resolute and held his ground.

Ahead of the oncoming troop rode a man, who, observing Don Quixote's position, began to make violent signs to him to get away from the road; and when he saw that he was not being understood or obeyed, he yelled out with fierceness: "Get out of the way, you son of the devil, or these bulls will knock you to pieces!"

But all Don Quixote was concerned about was his challenge, and permitting no evasions, he retorted heroically: "Rabble! I care nothing for bulls! Confess at once, scoundrels, that what I have declared is true; else ye have to deal with me in combat."

Hardly had he spoken these words before the drove of bulls was on him and Sancho, trampling them both to the ground as if they had been figures of pasteboard; for they were no common bulls, they were fierce animals that were being taken to a nearby village for a bull-fight on the following day. Yet when they had passed, and the valiant knight came to, he had lost none of his intrepidity, for as soon as he could stand up he kept shouting at them to return and he would fight them all alone.

The knight was so enraged and so humiliated to have been stepped on in such an unromantic fashion, that he sat down and buried his head in his hands; and Sancho could not persuade him to return to their hosts to bid them farewell. And so he decided instead to be on his way to Saragossa, and master and squire mounted again and continued their journey dejectedly.

CHAPTER LIX

Wherein Is Related the Strange Thing, Which May Be Regarded as an Adventure, That Happened to Don Quixote

DON QUIXOTE was extremely weighed down and oppressed by the disaster of the morning. When they had ridden but a short way they came to a place where there was a spring, and they dismounted to refresh their dusty throats and to wash themselves. The knight was wearied, and Sancho suggested that he lie down and rest for a while. The suggestion pleased his master, who said he would do so if his squire would give himself three or four hundred lashes with Rocinante's reins in the meantime, as a help toward his Dulcinea's disenchantment. But after some arguing, Sancho wiggled himself out of the business for the moment, having pleaded an ill-nourished body—in spite of his constant eating. He said it was, besides, no easy matter to flog oneself in cold blood, but promised to make good some time, unexpectedly. Then they both ate a little, and soon afterward they fell asleep beside their faithful beasts. They awoke, refreshed, and made off to reach an inn—and Sancho gave thanks to Heaven that Don Quixote took it for an inn—that they had sighted in the distance before they went to sleep.

When they arrived at the inn Sancho at once took the beasts to the stable and fed them, while Don Quixote re-

tired to his room. When supper time came the landlord
brought in a stewpan which contained cow-heels that tasted,
he swore, like calves' feet; and the knight and his squire
gathered gluttonously around the meal. They had scarcely
began eating, however, when Don Quixote heard his name
mentioned next door, and, surprised, he listened and heard
some one say: "What displeases me most in this Second
Part of 'Don Quixote of La Mancha' is that it represents
Don Quixote as now cured of his love for Dulcinea del
Toboso."

Like a flash the knight was on his feet, shouting to
the adjoining room: "Whoever he may be who says that
Don Quixote of La Mancha has forgotten Dulcinea del
Toboso, I will teach him with equal arms that what he says
is very far from true; for his motto is constancy, and his
profession is to maintain the same with his life and never
wrong it."

Immediately voices from the other room wished to know
who was speaking; and Sancho shouted back that it was
his master, and that his master was none other than Don
Quixote of La Mancha himself. In the next instant two
gentlemen entered the room, and as soon as they perceived
Don Quixote, they fell on his neck and embraced him, saying that they were pleased and proud beyond measure to
meet so distinguished and illustrious a personage, their
own morning star of knight-errantry. One of the gentlemen, Don Jeronimo, assured him that there was no doubt in
his mind that he was the real Don Quixote of the First Part,
and not the counterfeit one of the Aragonese Second Part.
With these words he put his copy of the Second Part, which

he had just been reading, into Don Quixote's hands and begged him to read it. Don Quixote took it and glanced it through, and after having read a few pages, he returned it to the gentleman, with the remark that he had already discovered three things in the book that ought to be censured; and he said that when an author could make such a colossal mistake as to speak of Sancho's wife as Mari Guiterrez, one would be likely to doubt the veracity of every other statement of his in the book.

When Sancho heard of this audacious libel, he became red in the face with indignation. "A nice sort of historian, indeed!" he burst out. "He must know a deal about our affairs when he calls my wife, Teresa Panza, Mari Guiterrez! Take the book again, señor, and see whether I am in it and whether he has changed my name!"

The gentleman looked at Sancho in an expectant manner, and said: "From your talk, friend, no doubt you are Sancho Panza, Señor Don Quixote's squire."

When Sancho affirmed this, saying he was proud of it, it was Don Jeronimo's turn to become indignant; for it seemed to him nothing short of blasphemy to take all the drollery out of the Sancho, whom he saw before him here, he said, and who had furnished him with so many enjoyable moments through his amusing talk, while he was reading the First Part. The Sancho of the Second Part was a stupid character, a fool with no sense of humor whatever, he declared; and his declaration promptly brought forth a proverb from Sancho's lips, which summed up his contempt for the new author. "Let him who knows how ring the bells," he exclaimed.

DON QUIXOTE'S IRE IS ROUSED

The two gentlemen now invited the knight errant to join them at supper, as they knew, they said, that the inn could afford nothing that was befitting a warrior as illustrious as he. Always courteous, Don Quixote acquiesced, and they withdrew to the adjoining room, leaving Sancho and the landlord to sup by themselves. At supper Don Quixote related to the two gentlemen his many strange adventures, and they listened with the utmost interest; they could not help admiring his elegant and finished speech, and at the same time were astounded at the strange mixture of good sense and wit and absurd nonsense that flowed from his lips.

.When Sancho had finished his cow-heels, he betook himself to the room where his master and the gentleman were supping; and as he entered he asked Don Jeronimo: "If this author calls me glutton, as your Worships say, I trust he does not call me drunkard too."

Don Jeronimo said that the author had been impertinent enough to do so, although he assured Sancho that he could see by his face that the author had lied. "Believe me," declared the squire, "the Sancho and the Don Quixote of this history must be different persons from those that appear in the one Cid Hamet Benengeli wrote, who are ourselves—my master, valiant, wise, and true in love, and I, simple, droll, and neither glutton nor drunkard."

The other gentleman, Don Juan, was of Sancho's opinion, and he added that he thought no one but Cid Hamet, the original author, should be permitted to write the history of Don Quixote's achievements—just as Alexander issued an order that no one but Apelles should presume to paint his portrait.

They carried on a conversation in this manner until quite late in the night. Don Juan offered the Second Part to our hero to read, but Don Quixote declined it, saying that it would only be flattering and encouraging to the author if he should, by chance, learn that he had read his book. Then they asked him where he would be bound for when he left the inn; and when he told them Saragossa, they mentioned that the author had given a description in the book of a tilting at the ring in that city, in which he who was called Don Quixote had participated.

That made the knight change his intentions at once. Now he was determined not to set foot in Saragossa: thus he would make the author commit perjury, trap him as a complete liar, and hold him up to ridicule before the whole world. The gentlemen thought this a most ingenious way to treat the blaspheming author, and made a suggestion that there were to be other jousts at Barcelona, to which he would be welcomed; and Don Quixote announced that he would go there instead. Then he begged leave in his usual courteous manner to retire, and withdrew to his room.

Early on the following morning the knight rose, and bade good-by to his two new friends by knocking at the partition that separated their rooms, while Sancho paid the landlord for the lodging and the cow-heels.

ON THE WAY TO BARCELONA

CHAPTER LX

Of What Happened to Don Quixote on His Way to Barcelona

FOR six days Don Quixote and Sancho traveled without anything happening to them worth recording. At the end of the sixth day they came to a grove of oak and cork trees, where they dismounted and settled themselves for the night. Sancho, who had been nourished plentifully that day, at once fell asleep, but Don Quixote's mind wandered hither and thither into strange regions and imaginary places; and he thought of the sad plight of his beloved one. The more he considered the cruelty of his squire, the more enraged he became; and at last he decided that the only thing for him to do was to strip Sancho and administer the beating himself. With this intention he began to undo the squire's garments.

Sancho, being awakened and realizing his master's foul play, now had lost all desire for sleep. He reminded his master that the whipping would have no effect toward Dulcinea's disenchantment, unless it was applied voluntarily and by his own hand. But Don Quixote insisted that there must be an end to this nonsense, for he had no desire to let his peerless Dulcinea suffer because of his squire's uncharitable disposition. And then he proceeded, with Rocinante's reins in his hand, to give his squire, as he said, two

[297]

thousand lashes on account of the three thousand three hundred. But Sancho was on his feet in an instant, and began to grapple with his master, and he crushed his emaciated body almost to flatness in his firm grip. Then he suddenly let him loose and despatched him with a kick to no mean distance, and, still pursuing his victim, he there sat upon him. Don Quixote managed at last to gather all the breath that had not been squeezed out of him by the combat, and supported by that he ejaculated in a hoarse whisper:

"How now, traitor! Dost thou revolt against thy master and natural lord? Dost thou rise against him who gives thee his bread?"

"I neither put down king, nor set up king," replied Sancho, himself somewhat out of breath. And then he proceeded to dictate the peace terms, and he extracted a promise from his natural lord never to try to whip him again, neither awake nor asleep.

Then the victor disappeared in the grove and went to lie down against a tree: but just as he had placed himself comfortably, he was frightened almost to death by seeing two feet, with shoes and stockings, dangling in the air above his head. He ran to another tree, thinking he had been dreaming, and there he found a like apparition haunting him. He began to scream aloud, calling upon his master for help, and ran to search for him. Don Quixote asked him what had frightened him, and the squire replied that all the trees were full of feet and legs. Don Quixote calmly looked at the dead bodies in the trees and told his squire that no doubt they were outlaws that had been hanged by the authorities; and he took them to be a sign that they were now close to Barcelona. They then lay down to rest for the night.

When they awoke at dawn, they found themselves surrounded by a band of men who turned out to be highwaymen. The band stripped them of all they possessed, and were just about to search Sancho further for money, when a swarthy-looking man in his thirties appeared, mounted on a splendid horse and armed with many pistols. It was their captain, and none other than the notorious Roque Guinart, a man who had taken to the life of banditry and hold-ups because of having been wronged by the authorities.

When the bandit captain observed what his men were about to do to Sancho, he commanded them to stop, and to return everything they had taken away from the knight and his squire. He asked Don Quixote why he looked so dejected, and the knight responded that he was grieved that he had been taken unaware, saying that had he been armed with his lance and shield and mounted on his Rocinante when he found himself surrounded by these men, he would have defended himself to the last drop of his blood, in accordance with all the rules of knight-errantry. And then he told Roque that he was the Don Quixote of La Mancha who had filled the whole world with the wonder of his achievements; and he thanked him for his great courtesy and mercifulness.

Just then they heard the violent sound of hoofs clattering against the hard road, and as they turned they beheld a youth, extremely pleasing in appearance, who was coming their way in a wild gallop. As he reached them, he flung himself from his horse and addressed Roque, who then perceived that it was not a lad but a maiden. She said she was the daughter of his friend Simon Forte, and named Claudia Jeronima, and that she, unbeknown to her father, had fallen in love with and become engaged to the son of her father's arch enemy, Clauquel Torrellas, whose son was named Vicente. Yesterday, she went on, she had learned that he had promised to marry another one, and full of jealousy she had stolen upon him this morning in the guise that he now saw her in and shot him in the presence of his servants near his house. She had left him at once, and she now wanted Roque to procure for her a safe-conduct that she might take refuge in France where she had relatives. She also wanted to extract a promise from him to protect her father from the wrath and revenge of the Torrellas.

Roque was evidently much taken with the girl, for he gave her a glance full of admiration; nor had she failed to make an impression on Don Quixote and Sancho. Don Quixote wanted at once to go in quest of the knight and make him keep his troth, and Sancho added that his master was an admirable match-maker. But Roque hastily took leave of them, and accompanied only by the fair Claudia, he had soon come to the spot where she had left Don Vicente. This young gentleman was surrounded by some servants who had been attempting to carry him to his home, but he had begged them to take him no further, for the pain was too great, he said and he felt that he was dying. All were astounded at the sight of the feared Roque, who dismounted with Claudia.

The fair maiden approached her lover, and clasping his hand, she said: "Hadst thou given me this according to our compact thou hadst never come to this pass." And then the young lady told Don Vicente what she had heard; but he disavowed to her any intention to marry any one else but herself. Hearing this she broke down completely, flung herself upon his breast, and sobbed convulsively; and then she fainted.

When she came to, she found that her beloved one had passed away, and her grief then knew no bounds. Again and again she would be overcome by her feelings, and swoon so that they had to sprinkle water on her face. Roque was moved to tears, and so were the servants, and Claudia said that she would go into cloister for the rest of her life to atone for her sin. Roque approved of her decision, and offered to conduct her wherever she wished to go, but she declined his company, with many thanks, and bade him farewell in tears. Roque then directed the servants to take the body of Don Vicente to the dead man's father, and returned to his band.

He found Don Quixote addressing his men on lawlessness, but they seemed to be little impressed with his sermon. Soon afterward a sentinel came up to his captain, and reported that people were coming along on the road to Barcelona, and Roque, having made certain that they were not armed troops out to enforce the law and in search of bandits, gave order to capture the travelers and have them brought before him.

Here the outlaw revealed himself again to Don Quixote as a naturally kindly and tender-hearted man, for though the travelers possessed a good deal of money, he assessed them but one hundred and forty crowns. Of this money he gave the men of his band two crowns each; that left twenty crowns over, and this he divided between some pilgrims who were on their way to Rome and our worthy Sancho. The travelers were two captains of Spanish infantry, and some titled ladies; and the women felt so grateful to Roque for his generosity, and his unusual behavior and courtesy touched them so, that they wanted to kiss his hand, considering him in the light of a hero rather than a robber. Roque did not forget to give them a safe-conduct to the leaders of his bands, for there were many of them, operating all through that region.

One of Roque's men seemed dissatisfied with such leniency as he had seen displayed, and voiced his opinion rather too loudly, for the leader of the band heard it, and the offender's head was nearly cleft open in the next second. The captain turned to Don Quixote and remarked that that was the way he punished impudence; then he calmly sat down and wrote a letter to a friend of his in Barcelona, telling him of the early arrival there of the famous Don Quixote of La Mancha, of whose exploits in knight-errantry the whole world knew; and, to be exact, he fixed Saint John the Baptist's day as the very day on which our knight would make his first appearance in the very midst of the city of Barcelona under the auspices of him to whom he addressed this letter, and who would be grateful for the infinite joy Don Quixote and his droll squire Sancho

Panza would afford him and the city. He sent the letter by one of his trusted followers, who, disguised as a peasant, made his way into Barcelona and delivered the letter to the right person.

CHAPTER LXI

Of What Happened to Don Quixote on Entering Barcelona, Together With Other Matters That Partake of the True Rather Than the Ingenious

DON QUIXOTE remained with Roque for three days, and they were hectic days for our knight. Roque always slept apart from his men, for the viceroy of Barcelona had placed a great price on his head, and Roque was in constant fear that some one in his band would be tempted to deliver him up. On the fourth day he and Don Quixote, accompanied by Sancho and six of the band, made their way toward Barcelona; and on the night of St. John's Eve they reached the city. There Roque took farewell of the knight and his squire, and returned to his haunts in the woods.

Throughout the night Don Quixote·kept guard over the city; and there he was still sitting on Rocinante when dawn appeared on the horizon, and Don Quixote and Sancho Panza for the first time in their lives beheld the sea. It seemed to them it was ever so much greater than any of the lakes they had seen in La Mancha. As the sun rose it was suddenly greeted with the ringing of bells, the din of drums, the sound of clarions, and the trampling and clatter of feet on the streets; and from the galleys along the beach a mass of streamers in varied colors waved its welcome, to the music and the noise of bugles, clarions and trumpets from shipboard. Then cannons on ship and shore began to thunder, and a constant fire was kept up from the walls and fortress of the city. It was a noise and a spectacle that might have over-awed any one, even a less simple-minded person than Sancho, who stared open-mouthed at the wonders he beheld. He gasped when he saw the galleys rowed about by their oarsmen on the water, and he told his master he had never seen so many feet in his life. A troop of horsemen in extravagant liveries rode past them, where they were standing, and suddenly Don Quixote was startled by hearing some one call out in a loud voice: "Welcome to our city, mirror, beacon, star and cynosure of all knight-errantry in its widest extent! Welcome, I say, valiant Don Quixote of La Mancha! Not the false, the fictitious, the apocryphal one, but the true, the legitimate, the real one that Cid Hamet Benengeli, flower of historians, has described to us!"

Don Quixote felt flattered by the attention he suddenly attracted, for all eyes had turned to gaze upon his lean and queer person; although it may be said here, in confidence, that the man who had recognized the hero was no other than the one to whom the rogue Roque had written. The cavalier divulged his identity to Don Quixote, and begged him politely to accept his services while in Barcelona; and Don Quixote replied with as much courtesy that he would follow him wherever he pleased and be entirely at his disposal. Then the horsemen closed in around him and they set out for the center of the city, to the music of a gay tune played by the clarions and drums.

The Devil, however, was not asleep. He put temptation into the hearts of some street urchins, who stole their way into the close proximity of Rocinante's and Dapple's hindquarters, and there deposited a bunch of furze under their tails, with the fatal result that their riders were flung headlong into the crowd. Our proud hero, covered with dust and shame, pulled himself together and went to pick the flowers from the tail of his hack, while Sancho extracted the cause of Dapple's capers from his own mount. Then they mounted again, the music continued to play, and soon they found themselves at a large and impressive house, which they learned was occupied by the cavalier, who was a friend of Roque's.

CHAPTER LXII

Which Deals with the Adventure of the Enchanted Head, Together with Other Trivial Matters Which Cannot Be Left Untold

THE cavalier turned out to be one Don Antonio Moreno, a gentleman with a great sense of humor, well read and rich. As soon as Don Quixote had entered the house, Don Antonio persuaded him to discard the suit of armor; then he took him out on the balcony, where he at once attracted all the boys in the street and crowds of people, who gazed at him as if he had been a monkey. The cavaliers passed in review before the balcony, and the knight was given the impression that it was in his special honor they were bedecked as they were, for he did not realize that it was a holiday. Sancho was delighted beyond description. He was treated royally by the servants, who thought that they had never met any one quite as amusing as he. Don Antonio's friends were all instructed to pay homage to Don Quixote and at all times to address him as if he were a knight errant.

The flattery and honors were too much for the poor knight: they turned his head completely, and he became puffed up with his own importance. Sancho, too, amused Don Antonio and his guests exceedingly, and they enjoyed particularly hearing about his escapades as governor.

After dinner that day, the host took Don Quixote into a distant room, which contained no furniture except a table, on which was a pedestal supporting a head made of what seemed to be bronze. After having acted in the most mysterious manner, and having carefully ascertained that all the doors to the room were shut and no one listening, Don Quixote swore the knight to secrecy. Then he proceeded to tell Don Quixote that the head he saw there before him had been made by a Polish magician, and possessed the magic faculty of being able to answer any question whispered into its ear. Only on certain days, however, did its magic assert itself, and the following day, which was the day after Friday—it had been astrologically worked out—would again witness the miracle. Don

THE ENCHANTED HEAD

Antonio asked the knight whether there was anything he should especially like to ask the head; if so, he could put the question to it on the morrow. Don Quixote seemed sceptical, but made no comment, and they returned to the other guests.

In the afternoon the knight errant was placed on a tall mule, bedecked with beautiful trimmings, and himself encased in a heavy and uncomfortably warm garb of yellow cloth; then, unbeknown to him, they pinned on his back a parchment with this inscription in large letters: THIS IS DON QUIXOTE OF LA MANCHA.

As they were parading through the streets the knight's vanity swelled more and more, for from every nook and corner there came great shouts of recognition. Soon he was unable to restrain his vainglorious nature, and he turned to his host and remarked to him with much satisfaction: "Great are the privileges knight-errantry involves, for it makes him who professes it known and famous in every region of the earth. See, Don Antonio, even the very boys of this city know me without ever having seen me." Finally the crowds increased so that Don Antonio was obliged to remove the parchment, and soon they had to take refuge in his house.

In the evening Don Antonio's wife gave a dance, and it was amusing to see the tall and lank hero move about on the ballroom floor; the men gave him the opportunity to dance every dance, for they themselves enjoyed watching him better than dancing. At last Don Quixote was so exhausted both by the dancing and by the lovemaking that

THE STORY OF DON QUIXOTE

the ladies had imposed on him—and how they delighted in hearing him avow his great love for Dulcinea—that Sancho had to take him to his room and put him to bed.

The next day Don Antonio took his wife, Don Quixote, and a few intimate friends into the secret chamber, and after many mysterious preliminaries, the questioning of the head began. All seemed particularly interested in what Don Quixote would have to ask, and felt rewarded when his turn came, for this is what he demanded: "Tell me, thou that answerest, was that which happened to me in the cave of Montesinos the truth or a dream? Will my squire Sancho's whipping be accomplished without fail? Will the disenchantment of Dulcinea be brought about?"

In a mysterious voice that seemed to come from a great distance, the head returned these answers: "As to the question of the cave, there is much to be said; there is something of both in it. Sancho's whipping will proceed leisurely. The disenchantment of Dulcinea will attain its due consummation."

Don Quixote heaved a sigh and declared that if only his peerless one were disenchanted, it would be all the good fortune he could wish for. Then Sancho tried his luck; but at the conclusion of Sancho's audience with the head, he did not seem properly awed, and his master became displeased with his pretentious expectations and reprimanded him severely in the presence of the whole company.

All the while Sancho's incessant talking and his master's exalted behavior kept every one in an uproarious humor. The joke that Don Antonio had arranged consisted in having a student, a young nephew of Don Antonio's, placed in

[308]

a chamber underneath the one in which the head was, to receive the questions and speak the replies through a tube that lead from the inside of the head to the room below. Soon after this form of amusement had taken place, it was agreed upon by the gentlemen of the city to arrange for a tilting at the ring, for they were convinced that such an exhibition would afford greater opportunities for mirth and laughter than anything else they might think of.

One day Don Quixote and Sancho, accompanied by two of Don Antonio's servants, were walking on foot through the city, when they suddenly passed a printing shop; and, never having seen one, the knight entered with Sancho and the servants. He was as curious as usual, and asked the printer innumerable questions about the books that he was printing. He saw some of the printers reading the proofs of a book, and he turned to them and inquired what the title of the book was. They told him it was the Second Part of "The Ingenious Gentleman Don Quixote of La Mancha," adding that is was written by a certain person of Tordesillas. Upon hearing this, Don Quixote grew quite cold in his demeanor, and having moralized that fiction resembling truth is always greater than absurdly untruthful stories, he uttered a hope that the book would be burned to ashes. And then he turned his back on the astonished men and left the shop in great haste.

CHAPTER LXIII

The Mishap That Befell Sancho Panza Through the Visit to the Galleys

THE afternoon of that same day Don Antonio took Don Quixote and Sancho on board one of the galleys, amid all the honors that accompany the visits of great and famous personages. There were fanfares, and cheers, and the firing of guns, and all the high-ranking officers of the army and navy who were in the city had been appealed to by Don Antonio Moreno and turned out to pay him their respects.

Don Quixote was delighted. He could scarcely find words to express his appreciation of such a magnificent and royal reception; and Sancho was almost carried away by the honors that were being paid his master. But when he saw all the men at the oars—stripped to the skin by the captain's command—he became afraid, for they seemed to him like so many devils.

When Don Quixote and Sancho Panza had been presented to all the dignitaries, the captain escorted them to a platform on which he begged them to take their seats beside him. Sancho sat at the edge of the platform, next to one of the rowing devils (who had been instructed in advance by the captain what to do) and suddenly he felt himself lifted in the air by a pair of strong, muscular arms. The next instant he was in the clutches of another devil;

and passing from hand to hand, he went the rounds of the crew with such swiftness that the poor superstitious Sancho did not know whether he was dead, dreaming, or alive. Sancho's aërial expedition did not come to an end until he had been most unceremoniously deposited on the poop, where he landed in a strangely unbalanced condition—to the tremendous amusement of the crew and the onlookers. He was so dazed that it is doubtful whether he would have known his name, if he had been asked.

Seeing what had happened to his squire, Don Quixote thought it best to forestall himself from being put through any such ceremony; so he stood up, his hand on the hilt of his sword, and announced with fire in his eyes that any one who dared to attempt such a thing to him would suffer by having his head cut off. He had hardly finished his sentence before a noise was heard that frightened Sancho almost into insensibility. He thought that Heaven was coming off its hinges and about to fall on his sinful head. And even Don Quixote trembled with something closely akin to fear, and grew (if that were possible) pale under his yellow hue.

What the crew had done was to strike the awning and lower the yard and then hoist it up again with as much clatter and speed as they could produce, yet without uttering any human sound. This being done, the boatswain gave orders to weigh anchor, and as he went about on deck signaling with a whistle, he continually lashed and beat the backs of the naked oarsmen with a whip he had in his hand.

When Sancho saw all the red oars moving, he took them to be the feet of enchanted beings, and he thought to himself: "It is these that are the real enchanted things, and not the ones my master talks of. What can those wretches have done to be whipped in that way; and how does that one man who goes along there whistling dare to whip so many? I declare this is Hell, or at least Purgatory!"

But when Don Quixote noticed his squire's interest in the naked creatures at the oars, he turned and said to him softly: "Ah, Sancho my friend, how quickly and cheaply you might finish off the disenchantment of Dulcinea, if you would strip to the waist and take your place among those gentlemen! Amid the pain and sufferings of so many you would not feel your own much; and, moreover, perhaps the sage Merlin would allow each of these lashes, being laid on with a good hand, to count for ten of those which you must give yourself at last."

But Sancho was not to be persuaded, and the general of the fortress, who was eager to know why Sancho was urged to lash himself, could not wait for a reply to his question, for there loomed up on the horizon a ship which attracted his attention, and he immediately gave orders to the captain to steer down upon it.

After an adventure on the seas, the first they had ever experienced, Don Quixote and Sancho came back to Barcelona that afternoon, and returned to the house of their host, escorted by the Viceroy, the General and the other high dignitaries.

CHAPTER LXIV

TREATING OF THE ADVENTURE WHICH GAVE DON QUIXOTE MORE UNHAPPINESS THAN ALL THAT HAD HITHERTO BEFALLEN HIM

A FEW days after Don Quixote had visited the galley, he was riding along the beach one morning on Rocinante dressed in his armor, when suddenly he observed coming toward him a knight, also in full regalia, with a shining moon painted on his shield. As he came close to Don Quixote, he held in his horse, and spoke to our knight thus: "Illustrious knight, and never sufficiently extolled Don Quixote of La Mancha, I am the Knight of the White Moon, whose unheard-of achievements will perhaps recall him to thy memory. I come to do battle with thee and prove the might of thy arm, to the end that I make thee acknowledge and confess that my lady, let her be who she may, is incomparably fairer than thy Dulcinea del Toboso."

And then the Knight of the White Moon went on to say that should he conquer Don Quixote, the Knight of the Lions must retire to his native village for a period of one year, and live there in peace and quiet, away from all knightly endeavors and deeds. Should, however, Don Quixote turn out to be the victor, he, the challenger, would gladly forfeit his head, as well as the renown of his many deeds and conquests, his arms and horse to him. He bade

[313]

THE STORY OF DON QUIXOTE

Don Quixote consider the challenge and give a speedy answer, for he had but that day at his disposal for the combat.

Don Quixote was taken aback at the audacity and arrogance with which the knight had stated his demands, particularly when he took into consideration that he had never in his whole life heard him even spoken of, much less had he heard of the deeds and victorious combats he had named. But he accepted the challenge with calm pride on the conditions the Knight of the White Moon had given, barring the one which involved transferring his renown to Don Quixote's shoulders in case of his being vanquished. To our knight that seemed like taking too great chances, since he had no idea what the nature of the challenger's deeds might be, and since he was thoroughly satisfied with his own achievements.

It so happened that the Viceroy had observed the Knight of the White Moon in conversation with Don Quixote, and thinking that some one had planned another joke on him, he hastened to Don Antonio's house, and got him to accompany him to the beach, where they found the two knights just taking their distance, and about to commence the combat. Don Antonio was as startled when he saw the other knight as the Viceroy had been, and neither one could make up his mind whether the whole thing was a joke, or not, for no one there seemed to know who the Knight of the White Moon was. However, the two gentlemen at last decided it could be nothing but a prank, planned by some gentleman for his own amusement. The Viceroy then turned to the knight and, learning that the

[314]

combat was being fought to decide a question of precedence of beauty, bade them set to if both of them still remained unshaken and inflexible in their convictions. The two combatants, having thanked the Viceroy for his permission, separated and again took up the necessary distance. Their horses wheeled around and the knights came against each other with all the speed their mounts were capable of. But the Knight of the White Moon was mounted on a steed that completely outshone the poor Rocinante, for when they clashed, the poor hack fell from the mere force of the contact, and Don Quixote leaped over his head onto earth. At once the unknown knight held his lance over his visor and threatened him with death unless he confessed to being vanquished and acknowledged that he would abide by the conditions of the combat.

In a feeble voice Don Quixote answered him that in spite of his defeat Dulcinea still was the most beautiful woman in the world, but that now that his honor had been taken away from him, he might as well die; and he begged the knight to drive home the blow of his lance. But the Knight of the White Moon was a generous gentleman. He said he would not have our hero deny the beauty of his Dulcinea in deference to his own lady; all that he asked was that Don Quixote return to his village of La Mancha and give up knight-errantry as he had promised. Don Quixote rose in a sorry and battered condition and swore that he would keep his word like a true knight errant; and in the next instant the mysterious Knight of the White Moon set off toward the city at a quick canter.

As soon as the unknown knight had left, the Viceroy, Don Antonio and Sancho hastened to Don Quixote's side. They found him covered with perspiration and stiff in all his limbs. Rocinante had not yet stirred, for he, too, was in a deplorable condition. Sancho for once had lost his speech, and all that had happened to his master in so short a time seemed to him proof that the enchanters were still pursuing him. Now that his master for some time to come was to be confined to their own village, there would be no chance for him to redeem the promise he had made to his squire. Altogether it seemed to Sancho a sad state of affairs.

Don Quixote was in such a dilapidated condition that he had to be carried into the city in a hand-chair which the Viceroy had sent for, and they all escorted him to the house of Don Antonio.

CHAPTER LXV

WHEREIN IS MADE KNOWN WHO THE KNIGHT OF THE WHITE MOON WAS; LIKEWISE OTHER EVENTS

IN the city the Viceroy and Don Antonio tried to locate the Knight of the White Moon, and when they had found the hostel at which he was staying Don Antonio went to call on him and learned that he was the bachelor Samson Carrasco, from the very same village as Don Quixote. The bachelor, having explained his aims regarding the knight, packed his arms in a knapsack, took leave as soon as he had told his story, and set off at once for La Man-cha, mounted on a mule.

A few days later, much to the sorrow of Sancho—who had never been so well fed in his life—Don Quixote and he took a fond farewell of their estimable and generous host who had heaped so many honors on them and who had enjoyed himself so tremendously at their expense. This time it was a sad and lonely journey on which they started. Don Quixote was mounted on Rocinante, who had some-what recovered from his shock, but Sancho had to tread the trail on foot, for his Dapple had to serve as a carrier for the discarded armor of our late and lamented valiant Knight of the Lions.

CHAPTERS LXVI—LXVII

OF THE RESOLUTION WHICH DON QUIXOTE FORMED TO TURN SHEPHERD AND TAKE TO A LIFE IN THE FIELDS WHILE THE YEAR FOR WHICH HE HAD GIVEN HIS WORD WAS RUNNING ITS COURSE; WITH OTHER EVENTS TRULY DELECTABLE AND HAPPY

TOWARD the end of the fifth day Don Quixote was resting in the shade of some trees, and as always happened when he lay down to rest, his thoughts turned to the disenchantment of his Dulcinea and a feeling of im-patience with his selfish and uncharitable squire rose up within him. He pleaded with Sancho and implored him to go through with the ordeal bravely; but Sancho was un-flinching in his stubborness and insisted he could see no

reason why he should be coupled with the disenchantment
of the peerless fair one. Thus Don Quixote could only
pray that his squire might be moved by compassion to perform some day the deed that would liberate his lady.

While discussing this subject so close to his heart Don
Quixote had decided to pursue his journey, and while they
were traveling along on the road to their village they again
engaged in conversation. Suddenly they found themselves passing the spot where they had been trampled on
by the bulls, but Don Quixote, not wishing to have his
thoughts return to anything so bitter, turned to Sancho
and remarked that this was where they had encountered
the gay shepherds and shepherdesses. And the next instant he had decided to emulate their example and turn
shepherd himself, now that his calling of knight errant had
come to an end; he would buy some ewes, he said, and together they would retire to some quiet pastoral nook where
the woods and the fields met, and where pure crystal water
sprang from the ledge of a rock and the fragrance of flowers was in the air. And there he would sing to Dulcinea,
his platonic and only love. The thought of a life so calm
and so far away from danger and knightly adventures
pleased Sancho so greatly and made his enthusiasm run
so high that he could not restrain a row of proverbs from
falling from his lips. It was a flow so incessant that Don
Quixote at last felt obliged to ask for a truce.

Night had now fallen, and Don Quixote thought it best
to withdraw from the roadway and take refuge for the
night some distance away from it. Having supped, Sancho at once fell asleep, but his master sat up all that night,

thinking of Dulcinea and making up rhymes to the sweetness of her memory.

CHAPTER LXVIII

OF THE BRISTLY ADVENTURE THAT BEFELL DON QUIXOTE

DON QUIXOTE could not bear to see his squire sleep so restfully while he was being weighted down by all the cares of the world. So he woke Sancho, whose stolid unconcern about Dulcinea again was brought home to him, and almost went on his knees in order to induce him to scourge himself. He nearly wept in his efforts to have Sancho inflict the meager amount of three or four hundred lashes upon himself; but as ever the cruel squire remained unmoved. Don Quixote did everything in his power to entice him to do this beautiful deed of sacrifice. He held forth to him what a blessed night it would be for them, if he would only comply with his master's request, for then, Don Quixote suggested, they could spend the remainder of it singing, thus making this the beginning of the pastoral life to which they were about to devote themselves. But Sancho said he was no monk; and the idea of getting up in the middle of the night to perform such rituals did not appeal to him, he frankly avowed. The bewailings of his master, both in Castilian and in Latin, made no impression upon the hard-hearted Sancho, who remained as firm as the rock of Gibraltar, as far as the disenchantment was concerned.

[319]

THE STORY OF DON QUIXOTE

Don Quixote had just made up his mind that it was a useless task to try to prevail upon Sancho at that hour to do his duty, when suddenly there was heard a tremendous and terrifying noise, which increased as it seemed to come closer. Sancho was so frightened that he at once took refuge behind Dapple, entrenching himself between the pack-saddle and his master's discarded armor; and Don Quixote got palpitation of the heart, and began to shiver. As Sancho peeped from behind his entrenchments and Don Quixote took courage to look, the grunting drove of six hundred pigs—for that is what it was—was so close upon them that in the next moment they found themselves knocked to the ground; but it was some time before all of the snorting, disrespectful animals had passed their dirty feet over the prostrate bodies of the knight, his squire and their beasts and provisions.

Sancho rose first, smeared with dirt, and having been stirred to unusual depths by the condition in which he found himself, he begged his master to let him take his sword, saying he felt he had to kill some of the pigs in order to be soothed. The exceedingly bad manners they had displayed and especially the fact that they had crushed all the provisions into nothingness, had produced an ire in Sancho that seemed wellnigh irrepressible.

But Don Quixote calmed his squire with these words, spoken with a melancholy air: "Let them be, my friend. This insult is the penalty of my sin, and it is the righteous chastisement of Heaven that jackals should devour a vanquished knight, and wasps sting him and pigs trample him under foot."

THE ADVENTURE OF THE PIGS

To this Sancho Panza retorted pensively: "I suppose it is the chastisement of Heaven, too, that flies should prick the squires of vanquished knights, and lice eat them, and hunger assail them. If we squires were the sons of the knights we serve, or their very near relations, it would be no wonder if the penalty of their misdeeds descended upon us, even to the fourth generation. But what have the Panzas to do with the Quixotes? Well, let us lie down again and sleep out what little of the night there is left, and God will send us dawn and we shall be all right."

Sancho lay down and slept, but his master sat up and commenced his emulation of the life of a shepherd by singing the song he had composed to his great love, accompanying it with his own sighs, and many wet tears. At last daylight came, and the sun awakened them both. Sancho began to rub his eyes, and they both got up and made ready to journey further. But before leaving Sancho again cursed the pigs for having ruined his stores.

He and his master had traveled the whole day, when they encountered a number of men on horseback, and four or five men on foot, all heavily armed. Don Quixote's heart ached, for he could not forget his promise to the Knight of the White Moon. The men who were mounted approached our hero and Sancho, and surrounded them without speaking a word. Don Quixote attempted to ask a question, but one of them warned him to be silent by putting a finger to his lips, while another one pointed his lance against the knight's breast. Still another one took Rocinante by the bridle; while Sancho was being treated in the same manner by some of the others. Both

THE STORY OF DON QUIXOTE

Don Quixote and Sancho began to be worried as to the outcome of this adventure, for the whole proceeding seemed to them utterly mysterious.

They rode all that day, unable to make out where they were being taken, or who their mysterious captors were, and at last night came. All the while the men were calling them all kinds of names, such as "bloodthirsty lions," "cannibals," "murderous Polyphemes." etc.; and Sancho was scared out of his wits, while Don Quixote was at his wits ends. Both were convinced that some terrible misfortune was in store for them, and they could only pray that they would get out of it as easily as possible.

Before they knew it, it was midnight, and soon after that Don Quixote recognized a castle, which he saw in the distance, as that of the Duke. He was amazed when he found that the men were taking him there, and he said to himself: "God bless me! What does this mean? It is all courtesy and politeness in this house; but with the vanquished, good turns into evil, and evil into worse." They entered the court, and found it arrayed in such a manner that they could not help being amazed and speechless, and they felt fear creeping into their hearts.

CHAPTER LXIX

OF THE STRANGEST AND MOST EXTRAORDINARY ADVENTURE THAT BEFELL DON QUIXOTE IN THE WHOLE COURSE OF THIS GREAT HISTORY

AS soon as the horsemen had dismounted, they and the men on foot carried Don Quixote and Sancho bodily into the center of the court, which was illuminated with hundreds of torches and lamps placed all around it. In the very center there was a catafalque, elevated to a height of several yards above the ground and covered by a huge canopy of black velvet. To the catafalque steps led from all around, and on the steps were hundreds of wax tapers burning in silver candlesticks. On the catafalque lay the dead body of a beautiful maiden. On one side of the stage there was a large platform on which sat two figures, with scepters in their hands and crowns on their heads: judging by this, Don Quixote thought they must be royal personages. On the side of this platform were two empty chairs, to which Don Quixote and Sancho were led. And when they had seated themselves and turned around to observe what was going to happen, they were suddenly startled by seeing their friends, the Duke and the Duchess, mount the platform and seat themselves next to the royalty.

Don Quixote and Sancho both paid them homage by rising and bowing profoundly, and the ducal pair returned their compliment with a slight bow of the head. Following them came a long row of attendants. Then suddenly Don Quixote came to realize that the corpse was none other than that of the fair Altisidora, whose love he had scorned, and that shocked him greatly.

Some one connected with the ceremonies passed at that moment and threw a robe of black buckram covered with painted red flames of fire over Sancho and, removing his cap, put on his head a miter of the kind that those who were undergoing the sentence of the Holy Office wore. At the same time he whispered in Sancho's ear that if he opened his lips, his life would not be safe.

At first Sancho, seeing all the flames that seemed to be licking his body, got frightened, but when he found that no heat ensued and nothing else happened, his worries ceased. In the next moment his and his master's attention was attracted by low, sweet sounds of music and singing that seemed to vibrate from underneath the catafalque; and then there appeared a youth with a harp, and he sang a song that dealt with the cruelty of Don Quixote toward the fair Altisidora, who now was dead from a broken heart.

When he had sung of her charms, one of the two who seemed like kings rose from his seat and spoke. He, Minos, who sat in judgment with Rhadamanthus, now begged the latter to stand up and announce what must be done in order to affect the resuscitation and restoration of the damsel Altisidora. As soon as he had declaimed all he had to say, he sat down, and in the next moment Rhadamanthus rose and decreed that all the officials gather quickly and attach the person of Sancho Panza, as through him alone Altisidora's restoration could be effected, he said, by his receiving twenty-four smacks in the face, twelve pinches and six pin-thrusts in the back and arms.

Nobody but Sancho objected to the King's proclamation; but Sancho was emphatic enough for a multitude. "Body of me!" he replied unhesitatingly. "What has mauling my face got to with the resurrection of this damsel? The old woman takes kindly to my persecution; they enchant Dulcinea, and whip me in order to disenchant her. Altisidora dies of ailments God was pleased to send her, and to bring her to life they must give me four-and-twenty smacks, and prick holes in my body with pins, and raise weals on my arms with pinches! Try those jokes on a brother-in-law; I am an old dog, and its no use with me."

But Rhadamanthus was bent in carrying out his threat. He gave a sign to one of the attendants, and in the next moment a procession of duennas started toward Sancho with raised hands. Sancho saw them coming against him, he grew frantic, and began to bellow like a bull, crying out: "I might let myself be handled by all the world; but allow duennas to touch me? Not a bit of it! Scratch my face, as my master was served in this very castle; run me through the body with burnished daggers; pinch my arms with red-hot pincers; I shall bear all in patience to serve these gentlefolk; but I will not let duennas touch me, though the devil himself should carry me off!"

Here Don Quixote thought it was time for him to add his plea to that of the King, and he began to reason with Sancho. At last he subdued him somewhat, and by that time the duennas had reached the spot where Don Quixote and Sancho were seated, and one of them came up, curt-sied, and gave the poor squire a smack on the face that nearly unseated him, and that made him exclaim: "Less politeness and less paint, Señora Duenna. By God, your hands smell of vinegar-wash!"

No sooner had Sancho uttered these words than he was smacked and pinched by nearly all the rest of them, until at last he lost his temper and seized a lighted torch, with which he pursued the flying duennas in an uncontrollable rage, crying: "Begone, ye ministers of Hell! I am not made of brass not to feel such out-of-the-way tortures."

But just then Altisidora—who probably was tired of lying on her back such a long time—moved, and in the next moment exclamations were heard from all in the court: "Altisidora is alive! Altisidora lives!"

Now that the great miracle had been attained, Rhada-manthus turned to Sancho and bade him still his anger; and Don Quixote again entreated Sancho, since he so nobly had proven that virtue now was ripe in him, to go to work and disenchant his Dulcinea in the same breath. To this Sancho replied:

"That is trick upon trick, I think, and not honey upon pancakes. A nice thing it would be for a whipping to come now, on the top of pinches, smacks, and pin-prod-dings! You had better take a big stone and tie it round my neck, and pitch me into a well; I should not mind it much, if I am to be always made the cow of the wedding for the cure of other people's ailments. Leave me alone; or else by the Lord I shall fling the whole thing to the dogs, come what may!"

THE STRANGEST ADVENTURE OF ALL

By this time Altisidora had entirely recovered from her death and was now sitting up on the catafalque. The music was again heard, the voices sang, and all came forward to help the young maiden down from her elevated position.

Altisidora acted as if she were just coming out of a long, long sleep; and when she saw the Kings and the Duke and the Duchess she bowed her head to them in respect. Then she asked the Lord to forgive Don Quixote for his cruelty, while she praised and thanked Sancho Panza for his sacrifice, and offered to give him six smocks of hers to make into shirts for himself, adding that if they were not quite whole, they were at least all clean. On hearing this, Sancho fell on his knees and kissed her hands; and then one of the attendants approached him, at the order of the Duke, and asked him to return the red robe and the miter, Sancho, however, wanted to keep them to show to his villagers as a remembrance of his marvelous experience; and when the Duchess heard of his desire she commanded that they be given to her friend as a token of her everlasting esteem.

Soon everybody had left the court and retired to their quarters, and the Duke had Don Quixote and Sancho shown to their old chambers.

CHAPTER LXX

Which Follows Chapter Sixty-Nine and Deals with Matters Indispensable for the Clear Comprehension of This History

SANCHO slept that night in the same chamber with Don Quixote. It was some time before he went asleep, however, for the pain of the pinching and smacking was quite evident. Don Quixote was inclined to talk, but Sancho begged him to let him sleep in peace for the remainder of the night, and at last both master and servant fell into slumber.

In the meantime it might be told how it came about that Don Quixote came to visit the ducal castle again. The bachelor Samson Carrasco, having learned as much as he could from the page that carried the letter to Teresa Panza of the whereabouts of the hero, decided that the time had come for another combat with him. Thus he procured a new suit of armor and a fresh horse and set out to find the Duke's castle. Having reached it, he had a long conversation with the Duke, wherein he told him it was his great desire to bring Don Quixote back to his village and his friends, hoping that if he could defeat him in battle Don Quixote could be made to return of his own free will and in time be cured of his strange affliction. He then followed him to Saragossa, for which city he had set out when he left the Duke's castle, but finally traced him to Barcelona, where the bachelor encountered him with the result that he promised to return to his village and give up knight-errantry for a year.

On his way home, the bachelor, at the Duke's request, had stopped at the castle to inform him of the outcome of the combat, and it was then that the Duke decided to play the knight and his squire another joke. The Duke had his men stationed everywhere on the road that led from Barcelona, and it was thus that they were able to bring in Don Quixote in the manner and at the hour that they did.

When daylight arrived the morning after Altisidora's coming to life, Don Quixote awoke and found her in his presence; and the instant he saw her he showed his modesty and his confusion by pulling the sheet over his head. But while Don Quixote was not inclined to converse with a maiden so early in the morning, Sancho showed no aversion to it whatever, for he bombarded Altisidora with all kinds of impertinent questions as to what was going on in Hell when she was there. Of course Altisidora denied having any intimate knowledge of this place, for in spite of her immodesty she had only got as far as the gates, she said.

Don Quixote now entered into the conversation and asked why the fair Altisidora had been so persistent in her love, when she knew that he would never change or give up his beloved Dulcinea, to whom he maintained he was born to belong. When she heard Don Quixote talk in this manner, Altisidora grew very angry with him, and exclaimed: "God's life! Don Stockfish, soul of a mortar, stone of a date, more obstinate and obdurate than a clown asked a favor when he has his mind made up! If I fall upon you I shall tear your eyes out! Do you fancy, then, Don Vanquished, Don Cudgeled, that I died for *your* sake? All that you have seen to-night has been make believe; I am not the woman to let the black of my nail suffer for such a camel, much less die!''

Sancho interrupted her here and said he could well believe that; then he added: "All that about lovers pining to death is absurd. They may talk of it, but as far as doing it—Judas may believe that!''

Now the Duke and the Duchess entered, and after an animated conversation during which Sancho's amusing sayings as usual captivated his distinguished friends, Don Quixote begged leave to be on his way to his village. They granted him his request, and then they asked him whether he had forgiven Altisidora for having tried to capture his love. He replied saying that this lady's lack of virtue had its root in her idleness, and he recommended that the Duchess see to it that Altisidora was put to making lace or given some other employment. Sancho approved of his master's advice, and remarked sagely that he never had seen any lacemaker die for love; and he further illustrated the truth of Don Quixote's remark by his own experience on that score: when he was digging, he vowed, he never bothered with the thought of his old woman. The testimony of two such staunch friends of hers as Don Quixote and Sancho made the Duchess promise that hereafter she would keep the fair Altisidora employed so that no foolish thoughts might take her away from the path of virtue. As soon as the fair maiden heard her mistress speak thus, however, she assured her that there was no longer any need of her being worked to death in order to divert her thought from the person of our knight errant, for his cruelty to her had been such that the very thought of that had now blotted him out of her memory forever. And, pretending to wipe a tear from her eye, she made a curtsy to the Duchess and left the chamber.

It was now time for dinner, and soon afterward Don Quixote, having dined with the Duke and the Duchess, made his departure from the castle with Sancho, and started again for his home.

CHAPTER LXXI

Of What Passed Between Don Quixote and His Squire Sancho on the Way to Their Village

DON QUIXOTE and Sancho traveled along, both in a state of depression. Don Quixote was sad because he had been forced to give up the glories of knight-errantry and chivalry; Sancho because Altisidora had not kept her word when she promised to give him the smocks. To Sancho it seemed a terrible injustice that physicians should be paid even if their patients died, and here he had brought back a human being from the dead, and was being rewarded in this ungrateful manner!

But Don Quixote's sadness was suddenly brightened by a hope that he might at last be able to prevail upon Sancho to bring about the disenchantment of Dulcinea. Knowing Sancho's covetousness, he offered him money as a bribe.

Now Sancho became interested, and consented, for the love of his wife and children, to whip himself at a price of a quarter-real a lash, generously throwing the five lashes he had already given himself into the bargain.

"O blessed Sancho! O dear Sancho!" exclaimed Don Quixote. "How we shall be bound to serve thee, Dulcinea and I, all the days of our lives that Heaven may grant us! But look here, Sancho: when wilt thou begin the scourging? For if thou wilt make short work of it, I will give thee a hundred reals over and above."

Sancho swore that he would begin the scourging that very night, and begged his master that he arrange it so that they spend the night in the open.

Night came at last, and when they had supped, Sancho proceeded to make a sturdy whip out of Dapple's halter. When he had finished this task he made off for a distant part of the woods. He left his master with such a determined look in his eyes that Don Quixote thought it best to warn him not to go too fast but to take a breathing-space between lashes so that he would not cut his body to pieces. He was afraid also, he said, that Sancho might become so enthusiastic over what he was doing, or so anxious to come to the end of the lashes that he might overtax his strength, collapse and die; and he begged Sancho particularly not to do that, for then he would have gone through all his suffering in vain. When Sancho had stripped himself to the waist, Don Quixote placed himself where he could hear the sound of the lashes, and counted them on his rosary that Sancho would make neither too much nor too little effort to disenchant Dulcinea.

SANCHOS' SACRIFICE

After half a dozen lashes, Sancho felt that he had inflicted a sufficient measure of pain upon himself already, and demanded a higher price for his service. Don Quixote told Sancho that he would pay him twice the amount promised; and the squire began again. But this time he did not whip himself but let the lashes fall on a tree; and with each lash he gave out the most heartrending cries, and uttered such groans that his master began to feel the pain of his squire's torture in his own heart. When he had counted a thousand lashes or thereabout, he was quite worried about Sancho and begged him to stop for the present, but Sancho told his master he might as well brave the remainder of the ordeal now.

Seeing his squire in such a sacrificing mood, Don Quixote retired at his request, and Sancho continued with the lashing, which he administered to a perfectly innocent tree with such brutality and ferocity that the bark flew in all directions. All the while he gave vent to his pain by fierce shrieks, and then there came one long agonizing cry, which nearly rent Don Quixote's heart, and Sancho exclaimed piteously: "Here dies Sancho, and all with him!" Don Quixote hastened to his squire's side, and insisted for the sake of his unsupported wife and children that he go no further, but to wait until some other time with the rest. Sancho retorted with a request that his master cover his shoulders with his cloak, as the exertion had been too great and had made him perspire freely, and he did not wish to run the risk of catching cold. Don Quixote did as he was asked and begged Sancho to lie down; then he covered him with the cloak.

At dawn they resumed their journey, and when they had traveled three leagues, they came to an inn. Don Quixote did not take it for a castle this time; as a matter of fact, ever since he had found himself vanquished, he had begun to talk of and see things in a more rational way. They entered, and when Sancho saw the painted pictures on the wall he remarked to his master that not long from now there would be paintings picturing their deeds in every tavern and inn in the country. Don Quixote then turned to his squire and asked him whether he would like to finish the whipping business that day, and Sancho said it made no difference to him when he did it; he only made a suggestion that he thought he would prefer to do it among the trees as they seemed to help him bear the pain miraculously. But on second consideration Don Quixote deemed it advisable to put it off till a later time, when they were closer to their village, in case Sancho should have a breakdown as a result of his flogging himself. Their conversation came to an end when Sancho began to shoot proverbs at his master out of the corner of his mouth at such a speed that Don Quixote was overwhelmed and tore his hair in desperation.

CHAPTERS LXXII—LXXIII

OF THE OMENS DON QUIXOTE HAD AS HE ENTERED HIS OWN VILLAGE; AND OTHER INCIDENTS THAT EMBELLISH AND GIVE A COLOR TO THIS GREAT HISTORY

WHEN they had left the inn that day Don Quixote and his squire traveled all through the night, and the following morning they arrived at their own village,

"WITH EACH LASH HE GAVE OUT THE MOST HEARTRENDING CRIES."

—*Page 333*

from which they had been absent so long. Among the
first to meet them were the curate and Samson Carrasco,
who had discovered at a distance the red robe the Duchess
had given to Sancho as a memento of their friendship.
Sancho had thrown it over his donkey and the discarded
armor, and it shone in the morning sun as brightly as a
fiery sunset. Dapple was also adorned with the miter,
which proudly crowned the beast's head.

When Don Quixote saw his old friends, he dismounted
and embraced them; and all the little boys in town came
running to see the sight of Dapple and the returning re-
vivers of knight-errantry. They called out to their play-
mates: "Come here, fellows, and see how Sancho Panza's
donkey is rigged out; and take a look at Don Quixote's
horse: he is leaner than ever!"

As they walked through the village, it was a whole parade that followed them; and at Don Quixote's house they
were received by the niece and the housekeeper, who had
already heard of the return.

Teresa Panza, too, had been given the news, but she was
sorely disappointed when she ran out with her two dirty
children to welcome the returning Governor. She scolded
him soundly for coming home dressed like a vagabond.
But Sancho told her to put a clamp on her tongue, for he
did bring her money, at any rate, he said. Then his
daughter fell on his neck and kissed him, and in the next
instant the whole family had dragged him inside their
little cottage.

Don Quixote shut himself in with the curate and the
bachelor, as soon as he had entered his house, and related

to them the sad story of his defeat, and the promise he had made to the Knight of the White Moon; and then he broached his new idea, that of turning shepherd. He told his friends he had chosen new names for them, for he hoped that they would share his new life with him; and they at once praised his scheme and promised that as shepherds they would accompany him in his pursuit of happiness. Samson added that he would be an especially valuable member of the pastoral colony, for he knew how to write poetry, and would devote his time to singing the praises of their simple life. Of course, there must be shepherdesses, too, Don Quixote ruled, and they could be represented by such modest and virtuous women as Dulcinea and Teresa Panza.

When they had conversed in this pleasant manner for some time, the curate and the bachelor left, begging Don Quixote to take good care of himself and to eat plentifully. As soon as they had departed, the niece and the housekeeper, who had overheard the three men, entered the late knight's room and begged him not to turn shepherd saying that his health was not such as to allow him to dwell in the open in the damp night air; sooner or later he would succumb, they said, and take ill and die. They were both agreed that the foolishness of knight-errantry was much better than this craze. They entreated him to remain at home, to go to confession often, and to indulge in doing good deeds and being kind to the poor, instead. But Don Quixote would have none of their advice. He told them he knew where his duty lay. Then he implored them to put him to bed, saying that they ought to know he had always their interest at heart, no matter what happened.

The two women began to weep, and then they helped Don Quixote to bed, and there they did all they could to make him comfortable, and gave him something to eat.

CHAPTER LXXIV

Of How Don Quixote Fell Sick, and of the Will He Made; and How He Died

THE following day Don Quixote did not rise from his bed, and he was taken with a fever which kept him in bed for six days. All this time his faithful Sancho remained at his bedside; and his friends, the curate, the barber and the bachelor, visited him frequently. They all did what they could, for they seemed to sense that the sickness was brought on by the sad thought of his having been forced to give up his great hope of reviving knight-errantry.

When the doctor was sent for, he said frankly that it was time for Don Quixote to turn his thoughts to his soul; and when the niece and the devoted housekeeper heard this, they began to weep bitterly. The physician was of the same opinion as the curate and Don Quixote's other friends: that melancholy and unhappiness were the cause of the present state of his health.

Soon Don Quixote asked to be left alone, and then he fell into a long sleep, which lasted over six hours. It provoked the anxiety of the two women, who were afraid he would never wake up again. At last he awoke, and as he opened his eyes he exclaimed in a voice of exaltation and joy: "Blessed be the Lord Almighty, who has shown me such goodness! In truth his mercies are boundless, and the sins of men can neither limit them nor keep them back!"

The niece was struck by the unusual saneness of these words. She asked Don Quixote gently what he meant, and what sins of men he was speaking of. He replied in a voice full of calmness and serenity that God had just freed his reason, for he realized now how ignorance in believing in the absurdities of the books of chivalry had distorted his mind and vision so sadly. He regretted, he said, that he saw the light so late in life that there was no time for him to show his repentance by reading other books, which might have helped his soul. Then he begged his niece to send for the curate, the bachelor Carrasco, and the barber, as he wished to confess his sins and make his will before he departed from this earth.

The moment the three friends stepped over the threshold to his chamber, he called out happily: "Good news for you, good sirs, that I am no longer Don Quixote of La Mancha, but Alonso Quixano, whose way of life won for him the name of the Good." And he went on to say how he now loathed all books of chivalry which had brought him to the state he was in, and how happy he was in the thought that God had made him see his folly. The three men could only think that this was some new craze of their friend's and tried to persuade him not to talk thus, now that they had just got news of his peerless Dulcinea and were all of them about to become shepherds in order to keep him company; and they begged him to be rational and talk no more nonsense. But soon they realized that Don Quixote was not jesting, for he begged them to send for a notary, and while the bachelor went to fetch him, the barber went to soothe the women; and the curate alone remained with Don Quixote to confess him.

When the good curate came out after the confession, the women gathered about him and when he told them that Don Quixote was indeed dying, they broke into sobs, for they loved him genuinely and dearly. The notary then came, and Don Quixote made his will. The first person he thought of was his faithful and beloved companion, Sancho Panza, whose simplicity and affection he rewarded by leaving him all the money of his own that was now in Sancho's possession. Had he had a kingdom to give him, he said, it would scarcely have been sufficient reward for all that Sancho had done for him. Then turning to Sancho, who stood at his bedside with tears in his eyes, he said to him: "Forgive me, my friend, that I led thee to seem as mad as myself, making thee fall into the same error I myself fell into, that there were and still are knights errant in the world."

"Ah," said Sancho, in a voice that was choked with tears, "do not die, master, but take my advice and live many years; for the foolishest thing a man can do in this life is to let himself die without rhyme or reason, without anybody killing him, or any hands but melancholy's making an end of him. Come, do not be lazy, but get up from your bed and let us take to the fields in a shepherd's trim as we agreed! Perhaps behind some bush we shall find the Lady Dulcinea disenchanted, as fine as fine can be. If it be that you are dying of vexation at having been vanquished, lay the blame on me, and say you were thrown because I girthed Rocinante badly."

But although Samson Carrasco tried to persuade the dying knight that Sancho had reasoned rightly, they at last came to the conclusion that Don Quixote really was in his right senses, and that God had worked a miracle.

They now let the notary proceed and one of the stipulations in the will was that if his niece, Antonia Quixana, ever married a man who had read books of chivalry, she should by so doing forfeit all that he had left to her, and instead it would go to charity. Another clause contained a request to the executors to offer his humble apologies to the author of the Second Part of "The Achievements of Don Quixote of La Mancha" for his having committed so many absurdities that had been a provocation to the author to write this book.

When he had dictated the last words of his will, a sudden faintness came over Don Quixote, and for three days after that he was in a state between life and death. At last the end came, and he passed away so calmly that the notary felt compelled to confess that he never had read of any knight errant in the whole wide world who had breathed his last breath so peacefully.

The bachelor, Samson Carrasco, wrote an epitaph for his tomb; and there is written on a tombstone in a little village of La Mancha the praise that those who knew and loved the valiant and doughty, yet gentle Don Quixote of La Mancha felt in their hearts for him, whose last wish was that he might die as Alonso Quixano the Good.

THE END